Birds of
Malheur
National
Wildlife
Refuge,
Oregon

Carroll D. Littlefield

Illustrated by Susan Lindstedt

Oregon State University Press

This book is dedicated to
Gaylin Dawn Beckley
and
Robert Gene Holloway

This third printing was made possible in part
by a contribution by
Paul L. King
The Oregon State University Press
is grateful for this support

The paper in this book meets the guidelines for permanence and durability of the Committee on Production Guidelines for Book Longevity of the Council on Library Resources and the minimum requirements of the American National Standard for Permanence of Paper for Printed Library Materials Z39.48-1984.

Library of Congress Cataloging-in-Publication Data

Littlefield, Carroll D.
The birds of Malheur National Wildlife Refuge / Carroll D. Littlefield.
  p. cm.
Includes bibliographical references.
ISBN 0-87071-360-4 (alk. paper)—ISBN 0-87071-361-2 (pbk. alk. paper)
1. Birds—Oregon—Malheur National Wildlife Refuge. 2. Malheur National Wildlife Refuge (Or.). I. Title.
QL684.O6L57 1990
598.29795'95—dc 20   89-77930
                                                      CIP

Foreword

Back before The High Desert Museum was founded, I was lucky enough to teach and work for several years in southeast Oregon on Malheur National Wildlife Refuge. The landscape took a strong hold on me, and part of the reason was because Carroll "C.D." Littlefield was there. He seemed as much a part of that landscape as the willow thickets, the burreed wetlands, the dunes, and the rim-rocks.

C.D. was the singular point of contact for anyone interested in birds of the area. Like a small-town switch-board operator of long ago, he knew intimately what was going on among the birds across several hundred thou-sand acres. He knew just where and when—and usually why—to look for any given member of the tremendously diverse avian community. C.D. had a constant, intense, and contagious interest in the movements and welfare of North American birds, and was well known among birdwatchers and ornithologists throughout the country. He seemed to me to have a sixth sense for what the birds were doing along the Pacific Flyway. His keen, inquiring nature and the breadth and depth of his knowledge and research directly inspired many of the students at Malheur Field Station to pursue careers in field ornithology and conservation.

But the main reason he was at Malheur was because the "king of birds," as he called them, nested and gathered there—the Greater Sandhill Cranes, the objects of his life-long work.

As a boy of five, he had moved with his family to an isolated farm near Muleshoe National Wildlife Refuge in west Texas. Wave after wave of dabbler ducks would fly out of the western sky, like a fast-motion thunderhead forming overhead. So for play, he would line up and organize not toy soldiers or plastic cowboys, but hun-dreds of rocks, each kind a different species of bird. He chose sandstone pebbles for mallards, gypsum chunks for wigeon, green marbles for green-winged teal, lumps of coal for coots. He performed feeding flights with boards that were arranged in perfect V-formations. When the family packed for a new house, his exasperated father had to load C.D.'s dozen boxes of carefully sorted "birds."

Eventually he switched them all to sandhill cranes. His imagination had been captured by the gangly gray birds that landed beyond the barn to feed in the surrounding milo fields. In flocks and family groups, they called to each other in strange staccato voices which he later referred to as "the sound of the Pleistocene," after the antiquity of the taxon.

Littlefield has been keeping track of the real cranes since the mid 1960s, working first to document and then to slow the decline of the Central Valley population of Greater Sandhill Crane throughout its range, on nesting and wintering grounds in Oregon, California, and Nevada. Because the refuge harbored the largest segment of nesting cranes, and because crane production was deteriorating, he conducted much of his research at Malheur.

Carroll worked on an early draft of *The Birds of Malheur National Wildlife Refuge* in the 1970s, with involvement and encouragement from several of us. When I left the refuge in 1977 to help establish The High Desert Museum, I thought perhaps we could help publish the book. But it turned out to be a big job to plan and build and expand the museum. Meanwhile, C.D. moved his home base to Texas and OSU Press published this guide.

The museum now operates a diverse program of classes and field excursions, including trips to Malheur. The book is an invaluable reference for me and other leaders, the first to be packed into our field library box. It is indeed a labor of love for me to write of the context that hatched and fledged this guide. I am delighted it will continue to be available to and treasured by birders across the country.

Caryn Talbot Throop
The High Desert Museum
March 1994

Preface

It has now been 50 years since the publication of Gabrielson and Jewett's *Birds of Oregon*. Before this classic was published in 1940, both authors had spent considerable time in the Malheur-Harney Lakes Basin. Several of the state's earliest arrival and latest departure dates which they listed for birds found in this region are still valid today, though many of their records have now been surpassed. In an effort to update this information, I decided in the mid-1970s to present a report on arrival and departure dates for bird species found on Malheur National Wildlife Refuge (NWR). As years went by, additional dates and records continued to accumulate, and finally in the mid-1980s it was decided to summarize this information and place it in a single report entitled *Birds of Malheur National Wildlife Refuge, Oregon*.

A major objective of this report is to present the data which have been collected on Malheur NWR since the refuge was established in 1908. In addition to this information from refuge files, historical documents dating back to the 1870s are available. From 1874 to 1878, Captain Charles Bendire was stationed at Camp Harney (about 10 miles north of Malheur Lake). During and after this tour of duty, Captain Bendire published several reports on the birds of the Malheur-Harney Lakes Basin. Therefore, bird records for this remote region of the west are available from 1874 through 1988, a period of 112 years.

To my knowledge, this is the first book to be published on the birds of a national wildlife refuge in the United States, though several are presently available for national parks. It is my hope that publication of this book will provide a stimulus for Fish and Wildlife Service personnel at other refuges to summarize and publish information which has been accumulating in the files for decades but which does not benefit anyone as long as it remains in basement filing cabinets.

Numerous people have been involved in this project. Among these were the birders who provided their records, as well as researchers who have spent time on Malheur NWR collecting data which were used in this report. Of the researchers, Dr. Steve Herman, Evergreen State College, has been most instrumental. Dr. Denzel Ferguson and his wife Nancy and Caryn Talbot provided encouragement to proceed with an earlier draft of the manuscript, while Lucile and Ann Marie Hausley provided support and encouragement during later phases. Roland Wauer's 1973 publication *Birds of Big Bend National Park and Vicinity* was used as a guide for format and style in this report. But most importantly, I would like to express my appreciation and thanks to several staff members of Oregon State University. In particular, Dr. Joseph Beatty was instrumental in the publication of this report. Not only was he the first to suggest publication by Oregon State University Press, but he was also involved with all phases from coordination to word-processing. In addition, I am most grateful to Debra Bumgarner, Ann Marshall, and Monica McClellan who have spent many hours word-processing during the past year, and to Dr. Robert Storm and Dr. Fred Ramsey for proof-reading the manuscript. If it were not for these individuals this report would not have been possible.

Carroll Littlefield
February 17, 1990
Muleshoe, Texas

Contents

Introduction	1
The Area	2
Malheur-Harney Lakes Basin	2
Migration Routes	4
Climate	5
Malheur National Wildlife Refuge	6
Double O	6
The Lake Regions	8
Blitzen Valley	12
Vegetation and Bird Habitat	14
Bird Finding	26
Spring Migration	27
Summer Birds	33
Autumn Migration	35
Winter Season	38
Species Accounts	41
Order: Gaviiformes	43
Family: Gaviidae	43
Order: Podicipediformes	44
Family: Podicipedidae	44
Order: Pelecaniformes	49
Family: Pelecanidae	49
Family: Phalacrocoracidae	50
Order: Ciconiiformes	52
Family: Ardeidae	52
Family: Threskiornithidae	60

Order: Anseriformes 61
    Family: Anatidae 61
Order: Falconiformes 90
    Family: Cathartidae 90
    Family: Accipitridae 91
    Family: Falconidae 101
Order: Galliformes 104
    Family: Phasianidae 104
Order: Gruiformes 108
    Family: Gruidae 108
    Family: Rallidae 110
Order: Charadriiformes 114
    Family: Charadriidae 114
    Family: Scolopacidae 118
    Family: Recurvirostridae 132
    Family: Laridae 134
Order: Columbiformes 143
    Family: Columbidae 143
Order: Cuculiformes 146
    Family: Cuculidae 146
Order: Strigiformes 146
    Family: Tytonidae 146
    Family: Strigidae 147
Order: Caprimulgiformes 155
    Family: Caprimulgidae 155
Order: Apodiformes 157
    Family: Apodidae 157
    Family: Trochilidae 159
Order: Coraciiformes 161
    Family: Alcedinidae 161
Order: Piciformes 162
    Family: Picidae 162
Order: Passeriformes 168
    Family: Tyrannidae 168
    Family: Alaudidae 176
    Family: Hirundinidae 177
    Family: Corvidae 184
    Family: Paridae 189

Family: Aegithalidae   190
Family: Sittidae   191
Family: Certhiidae   193
Family: Cinclidae   194
Family: Troglodytidae   194
Family: Mimidae   199
Family: Muscicapidae   202
Family: Motacillidae   211
Family: Bombycillidae   212
Family: Ptilogonatidae   214
Family: Laniidae   214
Family: Sturnidae   216
Family: Vireonidae   217
Family: Emberizidae   220
Family: Fringillidae   271
Family: Passeridae   278
Literature Cited   281
Appendix: List of Common and Scientific
   Names of Plants, Mammals, Fish, and Reptiles   285
Index of Common Names of Birds   289

List of Maps
Malheur National Wildlife Refuge
   and Vicinity   *facing page* 1
Malheur NWR   7
Malheur NWR: Units I (Double O) and II (Harney Lake)   9
Malheur NWR: Unit III (Malheur Lake)   11
Malheur NWR: Unit IV (North Blitzen Valley)   13
Malheur NWR: Unit V (South Blitzen Valley)   15
Spring Migration Tour   31
Autumn Migration Tour   34

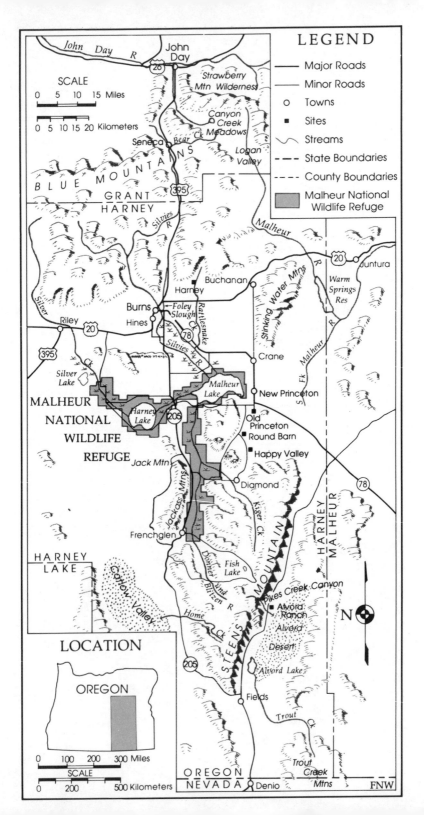

Introduction

In the desert regions of southeastern Oregon, a traveller's impression is one of endless miles of wasteland and very little water. Speeding along the three major highways which traverse the region, the motorist mostly sees great expanses of desert shrubs, broken only by rimrocks, occasional stands of junipers, and widely scattered, isolated ranches. Most people do not realize that about 20 miles south of Burns, in Harney County, is one of the largest wetland complexes in North America.

The largest freshwater marsh in the western United States—Malheur Lake—is located in the central portion of Harney County. Beginning in 1982 and continuing through 1986, this marsh became Oregon's largest lake as a result of an abundance of precipitation coupled with low evaporation rates. Surrounding this marsh, or lake, are thousands of acres of meadows, ponds, alkali flats, shrub uplands, and rimrocks, providing habitat for a multitude of bird species. Especially vital to many wildlife species are the native meadows. During spring migration over 250,000 ducks, 125,000 geese, and 6,000 Lesser Sandhill Cranes may use this habitat simultaneously. In addition, nearly 25,000 duck pairs, 2,000 Canada Goose pairs, 1,500 Long-billed Curlews, and hundreds of other shorebirds, marshbirds, and songbirds remain through the summer to nest. In the deeper marshes, gulls, terns, ibises, herons, egrets, and cormorants usually find ideal nesting habitat. Although much of this area is privately owned, the federally owned Malheur National Wildlife Refuge (NWR) is the regional center for species diversity and abundance.

The purpose of this report is to summarize bird data which have been accumulating on Malheur NWR, or what was to become the refuge, for over 110 years. Bird descriptions and distributions are not included here as this information is readily available in numerous recently published field guides.

Included in this report are the time periods when species have been present on the refuge and, for most forms, locations and habitat where they have been recorded in the past. However, because birds are highly mobile organisms, individuals of any species can be seen almost anywhere on the refuge. Dates presented here are certainly not carved in stone, as each year three or four species establish new arrival or departure records. Also, usually one or two species new to the refuge are added annually. Therefore, by the time this report becomes available, some species will have likely established new arrival or departure dates. Information contained in this report is through December 31, 1988.

The Area

Malheur-Harney Lakes Basin

The Malheur-Harney Lakes Basin (also called Oregon Closed Basin) is at the northern extremity of the Great Basin. There is no outlet to the sea, and the only way for water to escape is by evapotranspiration. Three major water systems empty into the basin. The Silvies River has its headwaters in the Blue Mountains to the north, and drains about 1,350 square miles, entering Malheur Lake from the north. In years with below normal precipitation, most water is diverted onto privately owned meadows south and east of Burns and little water reaches Malheur NWR. The Donner und Blitzen River (Thunder and Lightning River, referred to in the rest of this book simply as the Blitzen River) heads on Steens Mountain (southeast of the refuge), and drains 1,000 square miles. This system flows north from the west base of Steens Mountain through the Blitzen Valley, draining into Malheur Lake near refuge headquarters from the south. Silver Creek flows southeast from the Blue Mountains (northwest of the refuge) and empties into northwest Harney Lake after draining a 900-square-mile region. Harney Lake is a natural sump and is at the lowest point in the basin (4080 ft.). In high-precipitation years, Malheur Lake overflows westward into Mud Lake and eventually into Harney Lake; in the early 1980s all three lakes filled and joined to become Oregon's largest body of inland water.

The northern portion of the Malheur-Harney Lakes Basin is mountainous and covered with coniferous forest. Western juniper and ponderosa pine are the dominant trees at lower elevations, while Douglas-fir, western larch, white fir, and lodgepole pine are important dominants at higher elevations. Quaking aspen clones are scattered throughout this region, especially on moist soils. Elsewhere in the basin, low hills and rimrocks covered primarily with sagebrush predominate. Big sagebrush finds ideal growing conditions on deep relatively moist soils, while black sagebrush is the characteristic shrub in shallow rocky soils at higher elevations. Dense western juniper stands occur in some regions, particularly on steep slopes and in rocky soils.

Steens Mountain rises to an elevation of over 9,700 feet in the basin's southeast region. Dense juniper stands occur on the lower slopes, while aspen clones dominate at higher elevations. No trees survive near the summit. Several glaciated U-shaped gorges of Pleistocene origin occur on the western slope of the mountain. Moisture-laden air from the Pacific Ocean, uplifted against Steens Mountain during the winter months, generally results in deep snowpacks. This snowpack is the life line for the Blitzen Valley, supplying water to the wetlands from Page Springs to Malheur Lake.

The basin lowlands consists of alluvial soils deposited primarily in a pluvial lake which covered more than 900 square miles to 70 ft. depths during the late Pleistocene

(Houghton 1976). Malheur and Harney lakes are the remnants of this lake, which was the third largest of the once numerous Great Basin lakes. A number of alkali playas are found in the basin. The larger playas are generally devoid of vegetation though fringed with greasewood, while the smaller less alkali playas may support dense silver sagebrush stands, particularly where the water table is near the surface.

Migration Routes

The Malheur-Harney Lakes Basin is an important spring "refueling" point for migrant birds heading for their northern nesting grounds. Three migration routes converge at Malheur NWR, and from there many birds move north to the meadows south and east of Burns. The major migration route is from the California Central Valley; geese, ducks, shorebirds, and marshbirds use this corridor. In California, migrants fly to the Lower Klamath-Tule Lakes region, turn east-northeast to Summer and Abert lakes in Oregon, and enter the basin at the refuge's Double O unit. Many birds fly northeast directly to the meadows near Burns, while others move east to Malheur Lake before heading north to these meadows. This is the principal route used by Snow, Ross', and Greater White-fronted geese, Northern Pintails, American Wigeons, Long-billed Curlews, and Willets.

The second migration corridor begins in the California Central Valley, extends through Warner Valley, Oregon, and enters the refuge along a broad front from Frenchglen to Double O. Tundra Swans, Northern Pintails, Canvasbacks, Lesser Sandhill Cranes, among others, use this route. Most Tundra Swans congregate in the eastern section of Malheur Lake. Lesser Sandhill Cranes move directly to the meadows near Burns; about 23,000 normally migrate through the basin in spring.

A minor flyway through the desert regions of eastern California and western Nevada leaves Salton Sea, California, and enters the refuge near Frenchglen. Herons, egrets, Northern

Pintails, and American Wigeons use this corridor. All three routes converge at Malheur Lake, making it one of the most important resting and feeding locations on the Pacific Flyway. It is difficult to determine the exact number of waterfowl, marshbirds, and shorebirds migrating through the basin because of continuous arrivals and departures in March, April, and May. Bellrose (1976) indicates that Northern Pintails number between 1 and 1.7 million, Snow Geese 250,000 to 900,000, American Wigeons 400,000 to 650,000, Green-winged Teals 66,000 to 150,000, Northern Shovelers 115,000 to 200,000, and Canvasbacks 21,000 to 50,000. More than one-third of the Pacific Coast Tundra Swan population has been seen on Malheur Lake at one time. No number estimates are available for shorebirds, marshbirds, and other species which migrate through the basin, but their numbers must be immense.

Climate

The climate of the Malheur-Harney Lakes Basin is arid to semi-arid, as is typical of the Intermountain West. Maritime air moving eastward from the Pacific Ocean is greatly modified by the Coastal and Cascade Mountain ranges, resulting in a high proportion of sunny days in southeast Oregon. Precipitation occurs primarily during two periods: November through January and April through June. Annual precipitation varies from 9 inches at Malheur NWR headquarters to over 70 inches in the surrounding mountains. About one-third falls as snow, but snow depths rarely exceed 6 inches on the refuge. Exceptional snow accumulations occurred in 1951–52 and 1955–56, with winter totals of 88.1 and 96.7 inches, respectively. Thunderstorms occasionally produce hail in the summer months, but such storms rarely cause damage (NOAA, Burns, Oregon). Storms from late July through mid-September usually have little precipitation, but do produce lightning strikes which often cause spectacular range fires and reduced visibility.

Temperatures are cold in winter, and usually warm in summer. The average maximum January temperature in Burns is 35.7 °F, with an average minimum of 16.3 °F. Average maximum and minimum temperatures in July are 86.2 °F and 52.1 °F, respectively. Extreme temperatures have ranged from − 40 °F to 109 °F.

Malheur National Wildlife Refuge

Malheur NWR is one of the largest of the four hundred or so national wildlife refuges in the United States, containing more than 184,000 acres. Within its boundaries are freshwater marshes and meadows, alkali playas, two large lakes, and shrub uplands. Three distinct geographical units are recognized: the Double O; the lake regions; and the Blitzen Valley.

Double O

The 19,700-acre Double O unit (see map of Unit I) west of Harney Lake contains alkaline soils and numerous small to medium-sized ponds and lakes. The 300-acre Stinking Lake is the largest water body in the unit. Greasewood and saltgrass are the plant dominants surrounding the wetlands, but south of Derrick and Stinking lakes extensive big sagebrush stands cover the uplands.

Silver Creek is the only water source in the unit's northern portion, and in years of below-normal precipitation little or no water reaches this area. Water for Stinking Lake is provided by a large spring, while two other large freshwater springs (Double O and Hughett) supply an abundance of water for Warbler Pond, Derrick Lake, and the meadows and marshes west of Harney Lake. This is the only refuge area which is not dependent on mountain snowpacks for water.

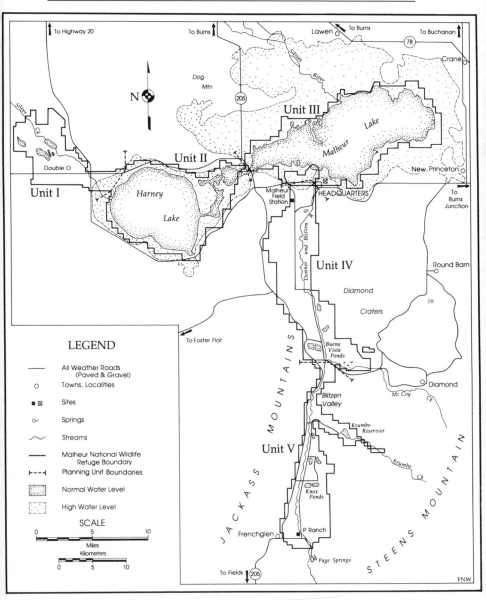

Malheur National Wildlife Refuge

About half of the unit consists of uplands (10,530 acres) and there are 7,530 acres of wetlands. Little riparian vegetation is present except east of Warbler Pond and adjacent to the Double O substation. Recent high water levels have killed all but a few of a row of planted willows about 1 mile west of Harney Lake. Hardstem bulrush grows in the deep freshwater ponds, sloughs, and channels, and isolated alkali bulrush stands are found east, north, and west of Derrick Lake. Baltic rush, spikerush, sedges, and arrowgrass dominate wet meadows. Alkaline soils predominate in the eastern portion of the unit and plant life becomes scant west of Harney Lake. Outcrops are adjacent to wetlands south of the unit, with smaller outcrops south of Derrick and Stinking lakes.

The Lake Regions

Harney Lake

Harney Lake (see map of Unit II) is the lowest point in the basin and, since there is no outlet to the sea, soils and water are high in alkalinity. Prevailing winds have created extensive dunes along the northeast shore. Most water enters Harney Lake from Silver Creek. The lake rarely exceeded 24 inches in depth in recent years until the 1980s. Generally maximum depths occurred in May; as summer progressed, most water evaporated, leaving a 30,000-acre white alkaline playa. Little water generally persisted after July, except around freshwater springs and near the Silver Creek inlet. Severe dust storms occurred frequently in spring when the lake contained little water. However, depths began increasing in 1983 and 21 feet of water had accumulated in the lake by 1985.

A long narrow island located near the southwest shore in the 1940s and 1950s provided nesting sites for American White Pelicans, Snowy Plovers, California Gulls, and Caspian Terns. However, water depths were not sufficient to create the island from 1960 through 1982. Water inundated the island after 1983 and this condition has persisted through 1988.

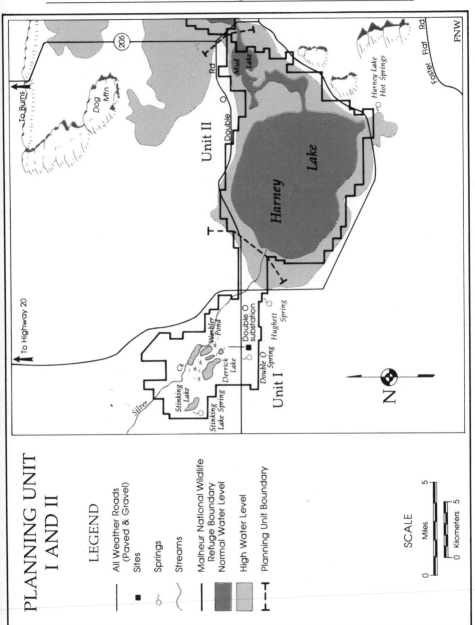

PLANNING UNIT
I AND II

LEGEND

All Weather Roads
(Paved & Gravel)
■ Sites
୧ Springs
Streams

Malheur National Wildlife
Refuge Boundary
Normal Water Level
High Water Level
Planning Unit Boundary

SCALE

0   Miles   5

0 Kilometers 5

Malheur Lake

During high-water periods such as occurred in the 1980s, Malheur Lake (see map of Unit III) reaches depths which prevent emergent plant growth. At these times the lake consists of large expanses of open water with a few isolated emergent stands in peripheral zones. Except for colonial nesters, bird populations are generally reduced. When water levels are lower, Malheur Lake is one of the largest freshwater marshes in North America. From at least the 1870s through 1982, lake levels fluctuated from dry (in 1934) to 64,000 surface acres (average 45,000 surface acres). Average east-west and north-south distances are 20 and 12 miles, respectively, with maximum depths to 6 feet. In the early 1980s, Malheur Lake joined with Mud and Harney lakes, covering an area of 180,000 surface acres.

When Malheur Lake is vegetated, habitats vary from east to west. The eastern portion is shallow and alkaline. Extensive areas of open water are generally present: further east, water becomes shallower until a series of small islands emerge. This island chain is vegetated with Baltic rush, and appropriately called Juncus Ridge. About one-quarter mile east of the ridge, Pelican Island is a high sand-dune complex vegetated primarily with greasewood and saltgrass. From this upland east to the shoreline, water is shallow or in dry years absent. When water is available, alkali bulrush thrives, but in drier years foxtail barley covers the subalkaline flat. Along the northeast shore low dunes covered with greasewood had built up during dry periods, but most washed away during the high-water years of the 1980s. Much of this portion of the lake is bordered by greasewood, with saltgrass growing on moist sites. In areas of shallow water, dense sago pondweed beds generally provide excellent feeding habitat for thousands of ducks in July and August, while shorebirds concentrate east of Pelican Island from July through September.

The lake's deepest water is in the central portion, and fresh water entering the lake from the Blitzen and Silvies rivers

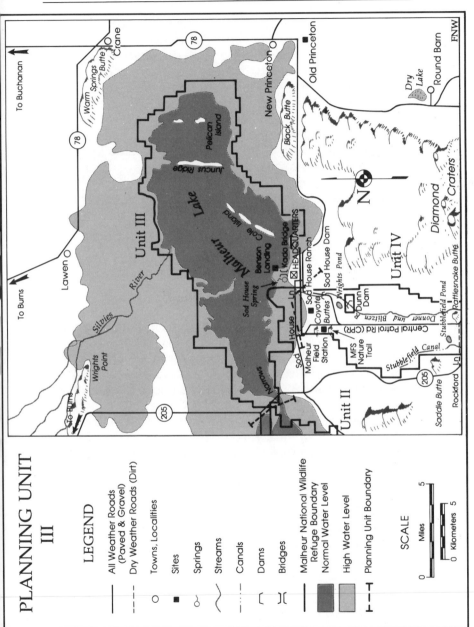

PLANNING UNIT III

LEGEND

All Weather Roads (Paved & Gravel)

Dry Weather Roads (Dirt)

○ Towns, Localities

■ Sites

⚲ Springs

⌇ Streams

⌇ Canals

[Dams

][Bridges

▬ Malheur National Wildlife Refuge Boundary

Normal Water Level

High Water Level

┬ Planning Unit Boundary

SCALE

0   Miles   5

0   Kilometers   5

reduces alkalinity. Hardstem bulrush is the dominant emergent in this area, but burreed dominates along the south shore. Near Cole Island and the north shore, dense Baltic rush stands are generally found. Extensive sago pondweed beds occur in the central and northern portions when the lake is productive. A few small islands covered with saltgrass and greasewood are present near the north shore.

The lake's western one-third consists of a series of ponds varying in size from 10 to 500 acres, separated by grease-wood and saltgrass uplands on the drier sites and Baltic rush on moist sites. These uplands form islands in periods of high water. In the late 1960s this was a major waterfowl nesting locality, and from 1984 through 1988 the uplands provided nesting sites for pelicans, herons, egrets, gulls, and terns. After the ponds, sloughs, and channels fill, water flows west-ward through the Narrows toward Mud and Harney lakes.

Blitzen Valley

The narrow Blitzen Valley extends from Page Springs 35 miles north to Malheur Lake, and covers an area of 66,000 acres (see maps of Units IV and V). Several tributary streams join the Blitzen River as it flows northward toward Malheur Lake. Bridge and Mud creeks irrigate refuge lands northeast of the P Ranch substation; Krumbo Creek enters the Blitzen River north of Krumbo Road after providing water to Krumbo Reservoir and Krumbo Valley, while Kiger, McCoy, Swamp, and Cucamonga creeks irrigate Diamond Valley, joining the Blitzen River northeast of the Buena Vista substation. In addition, a few large springs occur within 5 miles of Frenchglen.

There are two refuge substations in the Blitzen Valley. P Ranch substation (about 1 mile east of Frenchglen) was the former headquarters for the ranching empire of Peter French, and Buena Vista substation is about 21 miles south of refuge headquarters.

Blitzen Valley consists mostly of wetlands (29,650 acres) interspersed with shrubby uplands (31,900 acres). The

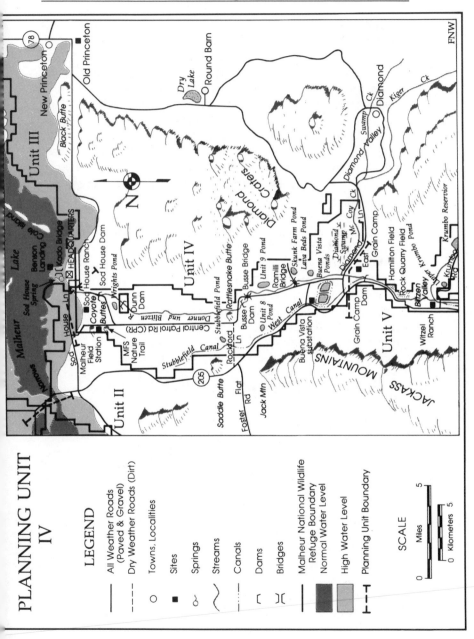

PLANNING UNIT
IV

LEGEND

— All Weather Roads (Paved & Gravel)

--- Dry Weather Roads (Dirt)

○ Towns, Localities

■ Sites

᧞ Springs

⌇ Streams

⋯ Canals

[Dams

)(Bridges

▬ Malheur National Wildlife Refuge Boundary

▬ Normal Water Level

▬ High Water Level

⊤ Planning Unit Boundary

SCALE

Miles

Kilometers

deeper channels, ponds, and depressions have extensive hardstem bulrush, burreed, and cattail stands. There are several artificial ponds in the valley, including Knox, Benson, Buena Vista, Unit 9, Unit 8, Skunk Farm, Wright's, and Dredger. Dense emergent vegetation grows in most ponds, with hardstem bulrush the dominant in deeper water, while cattail or burreed dominate in the shallower portions.

Riparian vegetation grows profusely along water courses, especially at the valley's southern regions. From Page Springs north and northwest for about 10 miles, small water-loving trees form dense thickets, but farther north these grow in isolated, widely scattered groves.

Rimrocks border both the valley's east and west sides from near Buena Vista south to Page Springs. Between Buena Vista and Frenchglen, a high escarpment known as the Jackass Mountains lies west of Highway 205. This escarpment is vegetated primarily with big sagebrush, cheatgrass, and juniper, and is composed almost entirely of Steens Mountain Basalt which was deposited during a period of extensive volcanic activity in the late Miocene.

Vegetation and Bird Habitat

The variety of habitats on Malheur NWR account for the large number of bird species which have been recorded. In a region characterized by shrub-steppe desert, the key to this avian diversity is water. Several species reach the northwestern extremity of their nesting range on or near the refuge. These are primarily marsh-dwellers, including the Great and Snowy egrets, White-faced Ibis, Black-necked Stilt, and Franklin's Gull, but also the Black-throated Sparrow, one of the most characteristic birds of the hot southwest desert regions.

Large planted trees around human habitations create an oasis effect, especially at refuge headquarters where not only regular migrants but also many eastern vagrants congregate.

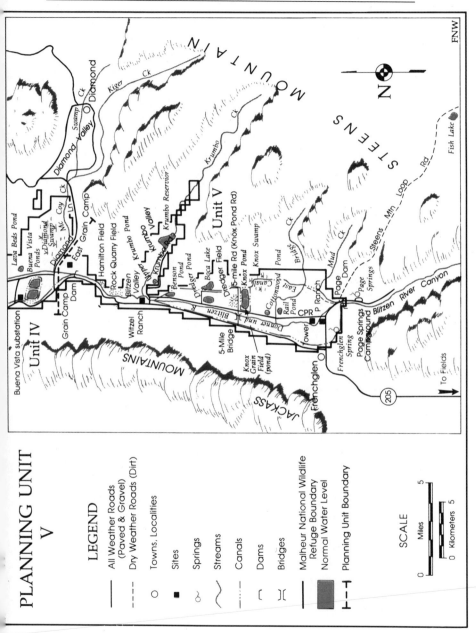

PLANNING UNIT V

LEGEND

All Weather Roads (Paved & Gravel)

Dry Weather Roads (Dirt)

○   Towns, Localities

■   Sites

δ   Springs

〜   Streams

⋮   Canals

[Dams

)(Bridges

    Malheur National Wildlife Refuge Boundary

    Normal Water Level

⊢--⊣   Planning Unit Boundary

SCALE

0   5
Miles

0   5
Kilometers

Several first state records have occurred here since the late 1950s. Banding of small birds at Malheur NWR was in progress from 1960 through 1984, and produced much of the information contained in this report. This banding station was one of the few in the Great Basin region, and provided considerable information on the status, arrival, departure, and migrational peaks of the many bird species which migrate through the Intermountain West.

The plant communities on Malheur NWR are typical of other northern Great Basin regions except for the many acres of wetland habitat found on the refuge. The interspersion of deep marshes, saline flats, wet meadows, grass-shrub uplands, riparian zones, and xeric slopes provides the contrasts necessary for the large assortment of birds which occur. This section describes twelve major vegetative communities on the refuge, but many other minor plant associations can also be found.

Submergent Community

Although mostly inconspicuous, several submergent plant species occur on the refuge, with their center of abundance in the deeper sloughs, canals, channels, and lakes. Sago pondweed, one of the most important, is widely distributed but is especially prevalent in some years in Malheur Lake. Sago is a favored food plant for molting and migrant waterfowl, particularly Tundra Swans, Mallards, Northern Pintails, Redheads, and Canvasbacks. Invertebrates thrive in dense sago stands, providing food for the young of Eared Grebes, Franklin's Gulls, and waterfowl. At least nine other pondweed species are found on the refuge. Richardson's pondweed is sometimes abundant in the canals and ponds, and horned pondweed occurs in dense stands at Sod House Spring and in portions of Malheur Lake.

Muskgrass grows profusely near the north shore of Malheur Lake, but this species is detrimentally influenced, as are the pondweeds, by turbid water resulting from the swimming activities of the accidentally introduced carp. When sunlight is unable to reach the substrate, plant growth is hindered. Also aeration of the bottom sediments is necessary for maximum submergent plant growth. After a pond or lake has dried, submergent plant growth is usually stimulated for at least 3 years but declines rapidly thereafter.

Derrick and Malheur lakes and Unit 8 Pond have dense stands of water milfoil. In Derrick Lake, this plant becomes so dense that birds have difficulty swimming through it. One species which benefits is the Western Grebe, as grebes wait until milfoil grows to the surface and then use it for nesting material.

Two water-buttercups occur on the refuge: white water-buttercup grows extensively in Malheur Lake (at normal lake levels) and at other scattered localities, while yellow water-buttercup is a showy aquatic which grows in canals and ditches throughout the refuge. This latter species grows profusely south of Wright's Pond and is often browsed upon extensively by Canada Geese and American Coots.

Mares-tail is sometimes abundant and is especially evident in isolated dense stands between the Double O substation and Harney Lake; however, few birds are ever seen in these stands. Bladderwort, another important species, is found among the stands of hardstem bulrush in Malheur Lake and Knox Pond and is often associated with the large heron, egret, ibis, and cormorant colonies in the lake.

Emergent Community

Three important emergent species grow extensively on Malheur NWR. Broad-fruited burreed flourishes in shallow water along the south edge of Malheur Lake (at normal lake levels) and in the Blitzen Valley, though few stands are found in the Double O region. This abundant emergent is a favored species for nesting Greater Sandhill Cranes and Soras. In addition, Canvasbacks and American Coots also regularly use the plant for nesting purposes.

In the deeper channels, canals, ponds, and lakes, hardstem bulrush grows in dense stands throughout the refuge. This plant is the most important emergent on the refuge for marsh-dwelling birds. It provides a suitable nesting habitat for colonial nesters, Redheads, Canvasbacks, Ruddy Ducks, Northern Harriers, Greater Sandhill Cranes, Virginia Rails, Marsh Wrens, Common Yellowthroats, and Yellow-headed Blackbirds, and migrating swallows congregate in dense bulrush stands at night to roost.

Common cattail also occurs throughout the refuge but is not as abundant as either burreed or hardstem bulrush. From Wright's Pond south for about 2 miles, narrow-leafed cattail occurs in the canals, ditches, and depressions. Both species of cattail are often seen growing together in this area and they regularly hybridize. Avian species inhabiting this emergent are generally the same as those in burreed and hardstem bulrush.

Common reed is the least common of the tall emergents and grows in isolated stands, particularly in Diamond Swamp and north of Buena Vista. This large emergent has increased in recent years on the refuge and receives very little bird use.

At least four species of spikerushes grow in shallow water in the Blitzen Valley and Double O. The bulrushes are also well represented with eight species; except for hardstem bulrush, most are widely distributed but uncommon. Alkali bulrush is generally found in east Malheur Lake, west Harney Lake, and north of the Double O substation in soils having high alkalinity. Both Snow and Ross' geese and several species of ducks feed extensively on the seeds and roots of this valuable emergent.

Wapato, or broad-leafed arrowhead, is found at isolated locations, particularly in canals near Boca Lake and Buena Vista. Certain species of diving ducks, especially Canvasbacks, feed on the tubers (also called duck potato) and Trumpeter Swans in winter often concentrate near arrowhead stands. Wapato has increased on the refuge in recent years, but has declined elsewhere in the Pacific Northwest.

Also important as waterfowl food are the smartweeds. Duck and American Coot autumn use of an area is often determined by the presence or absence of these aquatic forbs. As ponds and lakes recede in late summer, extensive stands of smartweeds often establish on the moist soil. Boca and Malheur lakes and the Knox Pond area are important smartweed regions on the refuge. Another aquatic forb often used by waterfowl is American speedwell, which grows in the shallow water areas of Malheur Lake and in the Blitzen Valley.

Alkali Playa Community

Except around freshwater springs little or no vegetation is found on the alkali playas which occur in the closed basins of Malheur NWR. The largest, and the sump for the Malheur-Harney Lakes Basin, is Harney Lake. With normal precipitation, Harney Lake is primarily a large alkaline flat virtually devoid of vegetation. Exceptions are around several springs near the south and east shores where alkali bulrush and Baltic rush occur and along the western shore where Silver Creek enters the lake. Desert saltgrass covers the south shoreline in moist-seep areas, while greasewood is the dominant shrub along the margins of the lake.

Green-winged Teals, Northern Shovelers, Northern Pintails, and shorebirds gather in Harney Lake during migration. When Harney Lake reached record depths in the 1980s, nearly two thousand Common Mergansers spent the autumn months. Migrating ducks and Snow Geese favor the alkali bulrush along the western margin of the lake, and it is not uncommon to see over ten thousand Snow Geese here in March. Along Harney Lake's southeast, east, and northeast shores the majority of the refuge's population of Snowy Plovers nest. Harney Lake has been classified as a Research Natural Area (RNA), and entrance is by permit only.

Stinking Lake, at the northwest extremity of the refuge, is fed by a large freshwater spring along the south shore. Currants grow in dense tangles at the spring, providing habitat for not only resident species such as the Song Sparrow but migrants as well. Warblers and Rufous-sided Towhees are regularly seen here and an adult male Rose-breasted Grosbeak was observed on July 4, 1976. Along the margins of the small stream which extends from the spring into the closed lake, a profusion of flowering plants grow. These include western water hemlock, Indian paintbrush, yellow monkey flower, and Oregon sidalcea. In the stream, hard-stem bulrush and watercress provide habitat for Virginia Rails, Marsh Wrens, Common Yellowthroats, and Yellow-headed Blackbirds. In addition to the characteristic big sage-brush and greasewood shrubs surrounding the lake, a few willows and squaw-currants are found near the northwest shore. During the high-water years of the early 1980s, much of this vegetation was lost or damaged when the lake inundated the surrounding uplands. It is hoped that this vegetation will return to its original condition in the future. Stinking Lake has also been designated an RNA.

The alkali playas usually provide excellent shorebird habitat. Generally Stinking Lake is the most important location for shorebirds on the refuge, with thousands congregating during autumn migration. Beginning in June, shoreflies hatch, and the shores and exposed flats become covered with millions of these insects. This unlimited food source attracts shorebirds, waterfowl, and gulls from late June through late September.

Desert Saltgrass-Greasewood Community

Saltgrass and greasewood find ideal growing conditions where the water table is near the surface, and the lowland desert surrounding Malheur, Mud, and Harney lakes is dominated by these two species. In isolated locations, wada or seablite grows in dense stands and in autumn these plants turn black, giving the impression of a recent fire. Wada seeds were once an important food source for the Indians who inhabited the Malheur-Harney Lakes Basin.

The Double O region has many acres of this association, with smaller areas near Malheur Field Station, south of Wright's Pond, and along the margins of Mud and Malheur lakes. Loggerhead Shrikes, Sage Thrashers, and Brewer's and Sage sparrows are summer residents. Long-billed Curlews regularly find suitable nesting sites on saltgrass hummocks in the Double O region.

Dunes Community

Little vegetation grows on the continually shifting sand of the dunes. At Malheur NWR dunes are rather alkaline and greasewood is the dominant shrub, though the dune complex northeast of Stinking Lake is dominated by saltbushes. Horsebrush occurs sparingly with the more abundant greasewood at the Harney Lake dunes. Few other plants grow, but in some areas Indian ricegrass can be found. The continual shifting of the Harney Lake Dunes exposes the large greasewood root systems and many die annually, but new plants grow rapidly in the moist soil. The fringes of the Harney Lake Dunes had been stabilized from wind action by these shrubs, but recent high water has now eroded extensive areas. These vertical wave-eroded dunes provide Bank Swallow habitat, and 67 nesting burrows were noted in 1985 and several hundred in 1986, 1987, and 1988.

Few birds will be seen on refuge dunes. Sage Sparrows are occasionally found among the denser shrubs and White-crowned Sparrows are regularly seen during migration. Long-billed Curlews are also encountered occasionally as individuals sometimes feed on insects found at the Harney Lake Dunes, and Golden Eagles frequently perch on the summits of the taller dunes.

Xeric Slope Community

A combination of desert shrubs thrives on the warm south-facing slopes. This community can be seen on North and

South Coyote, Saddle, and Rattlesnake buttes, and many of the characteristic species are identified along the Malheur Field Station Nature Trail on South Coyote Butte. Saltbush, greasewood, spiny hopsage, horsebrush, and budsage are the dominants, with Indian ricegrass and the introduced cheatgrass commonly interspersed among the shrubs. In addition to growing on south-facing slopes, this community is also found on a small alkali flat east of the Center Patrol Road near Busse Dam and more abundantly on the slopes adjacent to the refuge.

Bird species are limited in this plant community, but it is the regular nesting habitat for the Black-throated Sparrow. Horned Larks, Sage Thrashers, and Sage Sparrows are occasionally encountered, and Poorwill and Common Nighthawk nests have been found.

Meadow Community

The moist or flooded meadows are one of the most important habitats on the refuge, and it is here that numerous bird species feed, rest, and nest. Plant composition varies, but some important grasses include creeping wildrye, redtop, little meadow foxtail, timothy, sloughgrass, meadow barley, and Kentucky bluegrass. Sedges are an important component of the community and include such species as slender-beaked, Nebraska, beaked, awned, and several others. At some wetter sites Baltic rush grows in almost pure stands. Interspersed among the grasses, rushes, and sedges, several flowering plants add their colors. Widely distributed species are serrated and great swamp senecios, curly dock, blue-eyed grass, penstemons, golden pea, silver weed, and slender cinquefoil. In the Double O region, water hemlock is sometimes abundant. Canada thistle abounds on disturbed sites throughout the refuge and is an important food plant for Mourning Doves, White-crowned Sparrows, American Goldfinches, and other seed-eating birds.

Cinnamon Teals nest primarily in this habitat, as do Common Snipes, Wilson's Phalaropes, Red-winged Blackbirds,

Bobolinks, and Savannah Sparrows. In spring, wet meadows are important feeding areas for White-faced Ibises, Canada, Snow, and Ross' geese, Mallards, Northern Pintails, American Wigeons, Sandhill Cranes, Long-billed Curlews, Willets, and Ring-billed, California, and Franklin's gulls.

Sagebrush Uplands-Rabbitbrush-Great Basin Wildrye Community

Interspersed among the meadows are upland islands vegetated with either big sagebrush-Great Basin wildrye, or green rabbitbrush-wildrye. In deep soils, sagebrush grows to heights exceeding 6 feet, particularly on the upland ridges north of P Ranch. Uplands become covered with dense stands of wildrye after a fire, and it may be many years before shrubby vegetation reestablishes.

Mallards, Gadwalls, and Western Meadowlarks use these uplands for nesting and in the past both Swainson's and Ferruginous hawks have nested in the taller sage. Most refuge Short-eared Owls also nest in this habitat, particularly on the grass-covered uplands north of P Ranch and near both Buena Vista and Malheur Field Station.

Sagebrush-Native Bunchgrass Community

The sagebrush-bunchgrass association is found at only a few locations on the refuge, and sagebrush is the dominant feature. Throughout southeast Oregon, much of the original habitat is now occupied by extensive stands of cheatgrass, while big sagebrush has increased since European settlement. Only on the steep slopes protected from livestock grazing do the native bunchgrasses persist with any regularity. Overgrazing by livestock and fire suppression have favored sagebrush and cheatgrass at the expense of the native bunchgrasses. With fire suppression, sagebrush—which has low fire tolerance—has thrived while bunchgrasses have mostly disappeared. Cheatgrass was introduced into North America in the 1890s, spreading and growing profusely on disturbed sites. Overgrazing provides ideal conditions for this annual grass while eliminating the more palatable native species. Principal among the native bunchgrasses are bluebunch wheatgrass, Sandberg's bluegrass, Thurber's needlegrass, Idaho fescue, prairie junegrass, squirreltail, and Indian ricegrass.

In years with sufficient winter and spring precipitation, flowering plants can become very conspicuous. Indian paintbrush, narrow-leafed phacelia, tansy-leafed evening primrose, larkspurs, globe mallows, numerous mustards, yellow-bell, several composites, monkey flower, among others, dominate the landscape.

The diversity of birds in this association is rather limited, but Sage Thrashers, Western Meadowlarks, and Brewer's, Sage, and Vesper sparrows are evident. Common Nighthawks also nest in this habitat. In migration, warblers, Western Tanagers, Rufous-sided Towhees, and several sparrow species can be seen moving through the sagebrush expanses.

Western Juniper-Sagebrush Community

On the refuge, this association is found primarily west of Highway 205 between Diamond Lane and Frenchglen Spring. Western junipers grow in dense stands, especially in canyons, with sagebrush scattered among them. The understory is mostly cheatgrass with some remnant bunchgrasses. In some locations, yellow balsam-root is abundant, especially on the slopes north of Frenchglen.

The variety of birds is greater here than in other sagebrush associations. Black-billed Magpies, American Robins, Bushtits, Green-tailed Towhees, and Lark, Chipping, and Brewer's sparrows commonly nest. Mountain Quail and Black-throated Gray Warblers have also been found here in summer. In winter, Red-tailed Hawks, Townsend's Solitaires, American Robins, and Bushtits may be common, and in some years Mountain Bluebirds are abundant. Long-eared Owls, Rock Wrens, Cedar Waxwings, and Evening Grosbeaks have also been found in this habitat in recent years.

Riparian Community

At some refuge locations dense thickets of small trees occur along streams and channels. Willows are most commonly found, but at the southern extremity other tree species grow along permanent water. Thin-leafed alder and blue elderberry are found at Page Springs northward along the East Canal to Bridge Creek, and red-osier dogwood occurs around Page Springs. A few introduced box-elders and cottonwoods grow along the Blitzen River near P Ranch.

Most common are the willows, with at least five species. Willow groves are especially prevalent around P Ranch and north to Knox Pond. Usually found among the willows are golden currant and Wood's rose, particularly along the Center Patrol Road from Bridge Creek to Knox Pond Road, and near Wright's Pond. Herbaceous species in the riparian zones include cow parsnip, Canada thistle, and goldenrod.

This habitat has the greatest bird diversity of any community on the refuge. During spring and autumn migration Sharp-shinned and Cooper's hawks, Mourning Doves, woodpeckers, flycatchers, Ruby-crowned Kinglets, vireos, warblers, sparrows, and finches use the riparian zones. A Yellow-billed Cuckoo and Chestnut-sided Warbler have been observed in the riparian zones north of P Ranch, and Willow Flycatchers, Eastern Kingbirds, Yellow Warblers, and Song Sparrows nest commonly among the thickets. Both Bank and Northern Rough-winged swallows nest in the vertical stream banks, and all large bridges have their complement of Barn and Cliff swallows. Bewick's Wrens have been seen annually in the dense thickets northeast of P Ranch in recent years. In the past, the Gray Catbird and Black-headed Grosbeak have been seen in summer north of P Ranch, and Swainson's Thrushes at Page Springs. Most large groves at

Malheur NWR have a resident pair of Great Horned Owls, and Long-eared Owls are occasional, laying their eggs on abandoned Black-billed Magpie nests. Rough-legged Hawks and Northern Shrikes use the trees for loafing, lookout perches, and roosting in winter.

Canyons Community

Small segments of Bridge and Mud Creek canyons are within the refuge boundary. Here, permanent water with willow thickets, Wood's rose tangles, and in places, large western junipers provide habitat for several species of birds, particularly in winter. Unfortunately, overgrazing by livestock and recent fires have been detrimental to vegetation in portions of the canyons.

Dippers can often be seen along the streams in the winter months, while Hairy Woodpeckers and both Sharp-shinned and Cooper's hawks occasionally frequent the canyons during the colder months. Also in winter, Bushtits, Townsend's Solitaires, American Robins, Ruby-crowned Kinglets, and Winter Wrens are regularly seen. California Quail seek the tangles for wintering habitat while both Canyon and Rock wrens are permanent residents. Turkey Vultures, Red-tailed Hawks, and Golden Eagles can be seen along the rimrocks in summer.

Bird Finding

The greatest number of species per day can be seen at Malheur NWR during spring migration. If the majority of habitats on the refuge are investigated, about 110 species can be seen in mid-May. Autumn migration is more prolonged, beginning in late June and extending through November; even though the same number of species migrate through the refuge, they do not congregate as in the spring.

Because of the tendency for small birds to trickle through in autumn, it is unusual to obtain a lengthy species list in a single day. In addition, water has receded and many areas which had open water in spring are dry by August, while tall dense vegetation tends to conceal marshbirds and waterfowl after June.

Spring Migration

Spring migration actually begins in mid-winter with the arrival of Canada, Greater White-fronted, and Snow geese, Northern Pintails, Green-winged Teals, American Wigeons, and other waterfowl in mid-February. Although all of these species occur on the refuge, major concentrations occur on the flood-irrigated meadows south and east of Burns. The Double O region of the refuge is most active at this time, as spring-fed waters are diverted into ponds and lakes, providing some ice-free water. These early migrants are mostly from wintering regions in the California Central Valley.

By mid- to late March several species of waterfowl reach their peak numbers. Tundra Swans can be seen in mid-March on Boca Lake and Knox, Unit 9, and Buena Vista ponds as they move northward toward Malheur Lake. In late March 1975, over twenty thousand Tundra Swans were observed on Malheur Lake, mostly near the eastern shore. Snow Geese and Northern Pintails also reach peak numbers at this time but most use occurs on the meadows near Burns. Bald Eagles associate with these immense waterfowl concentrations, and over two hundred have been recorded in late March, mostly in the vicinity of Burns. However, Double O, Malheur Lake, and the Blitzen Valley all support several eagles at this time.

While waterfowl are peaking in abundance, a few shorebirds begin to arrive, but do not reach their migration peak until late April and early May. The scarcity of mudflats somewhat restricts shorebird use, but Black-bellied Plovers, Pectoral Sandpipers, and Long-billed Dowitchers may be seen feeding in the newly flooded meadows of the Blitzen Valley and Double O. Commonly nesting species such as Long-billed Curlews, Willets, Common Snipes, and Wilson's Phalaropes can be seen performing their courtship rituals in these same meadows. The Double O region, especially at Stinking Lake, attracts the greatest number of shorebirds, with American Avocets being most prominent.

Also beginning in March, a few of the colonial marshbirds make their appearance. The majority enter the refuge near Frenchglen and move north toward Malheur Lake. Great Blue Herons and Double-crested Cormorants are the first to arrive. In the Blitzen Valley, Great Blue Herons are seen at most fish-supporting water systems, while Double-crested Cormorants occur primarily in the larger ponds and lakes. As the season progresses most activity by these two species occurs on or adjacent to Malheur Lake. By late April both are engaged in nesting. Black-crowned Night-Herons, Great and Snowy egrets, White-faced Ibises, and Franklin's Gulls generally arrive in April. Egrets, particularly Great Egrets, are conspicuous throughout the Blitzen Valley, feeding on fish in the shallower canals and ponds. Snowy Egrets are less commonly seen and appear to confine most of their activity to the canals in the Blitzen Valley and the shallow-water areas of Malheur Lake. Since night-herons are mostly nocturnal, observations are often limited, but two or three can usually be seen daily in the Blitzen Valley and Double O in hardstem bulrush stands, and in the riparian zones. They regularly concentrate at Sod House Dam where they feed on barrier-stranded migrant carp. The White-faced Ibis usually first appears on the meadows near headquarters in late April. In May, it is often seen feeding on soil invertebrates on the irrigated meadows in the southern one-half of the Blitzen Valley. Recently, ibises have been most common in the vicinity of Knox Pond.

Greater Sandhill Cranes arrive usually in late February and go immediately to their nesting territories. From March 1 through April 15, pairs can be seen in the open meadows at Double O, near headquarters, and in the Blitzen Valley, but they are most abundant from Buena Vista south to P Ranch. If favorable feeding areas are available near Buena Vista cranes will form large feeding flocks consisting mainly of subadults. If conditions are unfavorable on the refuge, they move to the Diamond Valley where over four hundred have been seen on the meadows north and west of Diamond. Smaller subadult flocks are often present southwest of refuge headquarters and south of Benson Pond in late March and April.

Songbirds are most evident in May, but a few hardy species arrive in February. Male Red-winged Blackbirds appear around February 20, and early Say's Phoebes are first seen at either headquarters or Malheur Field Station at about the same time. Through March, additional species make their appearance and by April Ruby-crowned Kinglets, Yellow-rumped Warblers, Rufous-sided Towhees, and White-crowned Sparrows are conspicuous among the planted trees and shrubs, and in or adjacent to the willows throughout the refuge. With the exception of the Bank Swallow, all swallow species are present after mid-April and often congregate around headquarters and Malheur Field Station.

Most warbler species migrate through the region between late April and early June. Headquarters and Benson Pond attract large numbers of warblers, and by mid-May Orange-crowned, Nashville, Yellow, Townsend's, MacGillivray's, and Wilson's warblers are frequently encountered at these locations. Even in the sagebrush expanses, warblers are occasionally seen at the peak of migration, and they can be common throughout the riparian zones.

Many other migrant songbirds are moving through the region at this time. Solitary and Warbling vireos, Western Tanagers, Black-headed Grosbeaks, Lazuli Buntings, Chipping Sparrows, and many others occur throughout the refuge, but their center of abundance is at headquarters. The eastern vagrants usually appear in late May. Examples of species recorded include Blue Jay, Northern Parula, Yellow-throated, Black-throated Green, Blackpoll, Black-throated Blue, Black and White, Magnolia, Hooded, Cape May, Chestnut-sided, and Bay-breasted warblers, Summer and

Scarlet tanagers, Rose-breasted Grosbeak, and Painted Bunting.

In mid-May, a trip should begin at Malheur Field Station for the largest daily species list. From Malheur Field Station a leisurely drive to headquarters frequently produces Sage Thrashers and Brewer's Sparrows among the sagebrush expanses near the station, and Great Blue Herons, Great Egrets, White-faced Ibises, Greater Sandhill Cranes, Long-billed Curlews, Willets, and Black-necked Stilts in the marsh and meadow habitats. A Cattle Egret was seen here on July 16, 1976, and Red-winged Blackbirds and Savannah Sparrows are regularly encountered. A stop at headquarters is essential as numerous migrant songbirds stop and linger for a few days. A pair of Great Horned Owls frequent the taller trees here and an occasional Common Barn-Owl is seen, while Northern Saw-whet and Flammulated owls can occasionally be found. Information and bird-lists are available at the visitor center where staff are on duty from 7:00 a.m. to 4:00 p.m. except on weekends. The museum at headquarters contains specimens of most species found on the refuge.

From headquarters, south down the Center Patrol Road, Pied-billed Grebes, American Bitterns, waterfowl, American Coots, Soras, Virginia Rails, Eastern Kingbirds, Marsh Wrens, and Song Sparrows are seen in the meadows, marshes, thickets, or uplands adjacent to the road. At Wright's Pond, Eared Grebes, Ruddy Ducks, and Forster's and Black terns frequent the marshes. Between Wright's and Buena Vista ponds, Northern Harriers are regularly encountered and at dusk, or on cloudy days, Short-eared Owls can be seen hunting over the meadows. Among other waterfowl a pair of Trumpeter Swans is usually seen at Buena Vista Pond. A stop at Buena Vista substation often produces American Kestrels, Say's Phoebes, Western Kingbirds, and Northern Orioles, and along the rimrocks watch for Red-tailed Hawks, Common Ravens, and Canyon Wrens. Both the Cape May Warbler and Northern Waterthrush have been seen at the substation.

From Buena Vista, travel Highway 205 south to Frenchglen. Along the way watch for Red-tailed Hawks, Golden

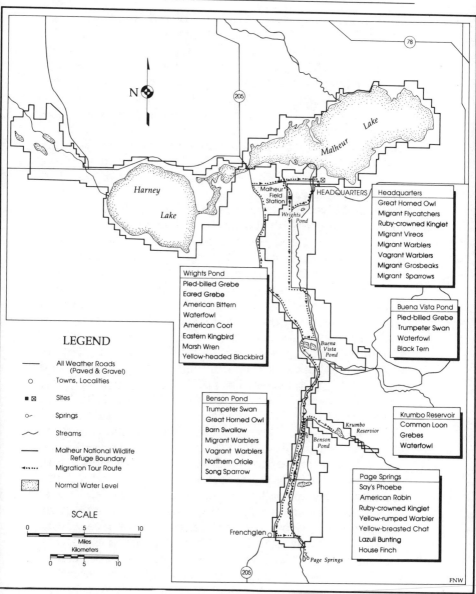

N

78

205

Malheur Lake

Harney Lake

Malheur Field Station

HEADQUARTERS

Wrights Pond

Buena Vista Pond

Krumbo Reservior

Benson Pond

Frenchglen

Page Springs

205

Headquarters
Great Horned Owl
Migrant Flycatchers
Ruby-crowned Kinglet
Migrant Vireos
Migrant Warblers
Vagrant Warblers
Migrant Grosbeaks
Migrant Sparrows

Buena Vista Pond
Pied-billed Grebe
Trumpeter Swan
Waterfowl
Black Tern

Wrights Pond
Pied-billed Grebe
Eared Grebe
American Bittern
Waterfowl
American Coot
Eastern Kingbird
Marsh Wren
Yellow-headed Blackbird

Krumbo Reservoir
Common Loon
Grebes
Waterfowl

Benson Pond
Trumpeter Swan
Great Horned Owl
Barn Swallow
Migrant Warblers
Vagrant Warblers
Northern Oriole
Song Sparrow

Page Springs
Say's Phoebe
American Robin
Ruby-crowned Kinglet
Yellow-rumped Warbler
Yellow-breasted Chat
Lazuli Bunting
House Finch

LEGEND

— All Weather Roads
(Paved & Gravel)
o Towns, Localities
■ ⊠ Sites
o- Springs
〜 Streams
— Malheur National Wildlife
Refuge Boundary
◄••••• Migration Tour Route
Normal Water Level

SCALE

0   5   10
Miles
Kilometers
0   5   10

FNW

Spring Migration

Eagles, Prairie Falcons, Chukars, Belted Kingfishers, and House Finches. At Frenchglen, Western Kingbirds, Northern Orioles, House Finches, and House Sparrows are seen among the trees. The tree grove northwest of the hotel has produced several eastern vagrants as well as common migrants. From Frenchglen proceed to Page Springs Campground. In the junipers, American Robins, Brewer's Blackbirds and an occasional Lesser Goldfinch can be seen, and on the rimrocks Say's Phoebes, Rock and Canyon wrens, and Cliff Swallows occur. Northern Rough-winged and Violet-green swallows concentrate over the Blitzen River and migrant Green-tailed Towhees are occasionally seen around the campground. In the riparian habitat, Ruby-crowned Kinglets, Yellow, Yellow-rumped, and Wilson's warblers, Yellow-breasted Chats, Lazuli Buntings, and Song Sparrows are regularly found, while Cinnamon Teals and Gadwalls use the small stream which runs from Page Springs to the Blitzen River.

From Page Springs drive to P Ranch where Lewis' and Hairy woodpeckers are occasionally seen. In the meadows north of P Ranch, Bobolinks are frequently observed after mid-May. Among or adjacent to the dense willow thickets, songbirds congregate during migration, particularly White-crowned and Lark sparrows. Continue north to Benson Pond and stop at the trees near the pond. Many regular migrants congregate here and the rare Northern Parula and Black and White and Blackpoll warblers have been recorded in the past. Cedar Waxwings and Evening Grosbeaks are often observed in late May and early June, and Ospreys are occasionally seen over the pond. If time permits, drive to Krumbo Road and turn right toward Krumbo Reservoir. After descending into Krumbo Valley, a small pond can be seen on the left. Nearly all duck species which occur on the refuge use the pond in the spring, including an occasional Barrow's Goldeneye. A variety of water-birds may be present at Krumbo Reservoir. Among these are Common Loons, Western, Eared, Horned, and Pied-billed grebes, Common Goldeneyes, Common Mergansers, and several other duck species. Return to Highway

205 and drive back to Sod House Lane-Highway 205 junction. North of Buena Vista, shrub-steppe nesting species are often encountered in the sagebrush expanses.

Summer Birds

As late spring migrants are leaving in the first half of June, most resident birds are involved in nesting activities. Canada Geese and Greater Sandhill Cranes already have young, as do Double-crested Cormorants, Great Blue Herons, Golden Eagles, Red-tailed Hawks, and Great Horned Owls.

Several species nest around human habitations, including American Kestrels, Northern Flickers, Say's Phoebes, Western Kingbirds, Barn, Cliff, and Tree swallows, European Starlings, American Robins, Yellow Warblers, Northern Orioles, Brewer's Blackbirds, House Finches, House Sparrows, and an occasional House Wren pair. Birdlife abounds in the meadows and marshes. Mallards, Gadwalls, Cinnamon Teals, Northern Shovelers, Redheads, Canvasbacks, Ruddy Ducks, along with smaller numbers of other waterfowl, all nest in these wetlands. Trumpeter Swans nest on several of the larger ponds such as Benson, Buena Vista, Skunk Farm, Rail, and Unit 8 ponds, and Diamond and Knox swamps, but the species becomes elusive during the incubation period and is sometimes difficult to see. Greater Sandhill Cranes occur in this habitat, and American Coots are everywhere in the ponds, channels, and sloughs; in late June their "red-topped" young are seen in the open water along the Center Patrol Road. Soras nest commonly and Virginia Rails can sometimes be heard, but their secretive nature provides few observations. Marsh Wrens and Common Yellowthroats can be heard and occasionally seen among the dense emergent vegetation. At Wright's and Warbler ponds, Yellow-headed Blackbirds can be found nesting and Red-winged Blackbirds nest in the meadows throughout the refuge.

In the riparian zones, summer residents include the Great Horned Owl, Eastern Kingbird, Willow Flycatcher, Black-

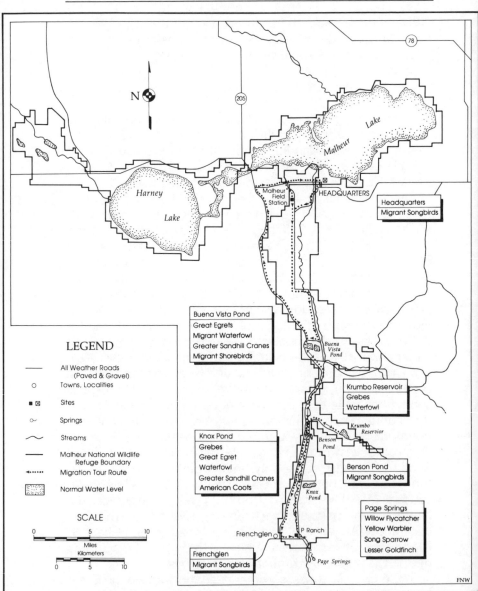

LEGEND

	All Weather Roads (Paved & Gravel)
o	Towns, Localities
■ ⊠	Sites
o~	Springs
~	Streams
	Malheur National Wildlife Refuge Boundary
◄·····	Migration Tour Route
	Normal Water Level

SCALE

Miles
0   5   10

Kilometers
0   5   10

Headquarters
Migrant Songbirds

Buena Vista Pond
Great Egrets
Migrant Waterfowl
Greater Sandhill Cranes
Migrant Shorebirds

Krumbo Reservoir
Grebes
Waterfowl

Knox Pond
Grebes
Great Egret
Waterfowl
Greater Sandhill Cranes
American Coots

Benson Pond
Migrant Songbirds

Page Springs
Willow Flycatcher
Yellow Warbler
Song Sparrow
Lesser Goldfinch

Frenchglen
Migrant Songbirds

Autumn Migration

billed Magpie, American Robin, Yellow Warbler, Red-winged Blackbird, and Song Sparrow. Northern Flickers and Tree Swallows will occasionally nest in the large willows near P Ranch, and at the southern extremity of the Blitzen Valley Yellow-breasted Chats occur in the dense tangles, particularly near Page Springs Dam.

Common Nighthawks, Horned Larks, Sage Thrashers, Loggerhead Shrikes, and Brewer's and Sage sparrows find suitable nesting habitat in the expanses of sagebrush and greasewood. Male Northern Harriers regularly hunt these expanses in June, although their nests may be several miles away in the emergent stands of the Blitzen Valley. Turkey Vultures are commonly seen soaring over the shrub-steppe regions, particularly near P Ranch where they roost among the large cottonwoods and loaf in the mornings and early evenings on the P Ranch tower.

Autumn Migration

Autumn migrations begin in late June with the arrival of waterfowl and shorebirds and extend into December when the last waterfowl depart for their southerly wintering regions. During this prolonged period birds concentrate where favorable habitat is available but, unlike in spring, habitat can be somewhat limited, as many marshes and all meadows are dry after mid-August. However, receding ponds and lakes create additional shorebird and marshbird feeding areas and species among these groups are often more evident in autumn than in spring. The larger duck aggregations are rarely seen because they occur in the inaccessible regions of Malheur and Harney lakes.

Southbound Mallards, Northern Pintails, both Green-winged and Cinnamon teals, American Wigeons, Redheads, and Greater Yellowlegs have usually arrived in late June. Western and Least sandpipers, Long-billed Dowitchers, and most other shorebirds become common after early July. East Malheur Lake regularly has large shorebird concentrations, but their center of abundance is in the Double O region. Several thousand American Avocets and Wilson's Phalaropes can usually be seen at Stinking and Harney lakes, along with several species which have nested at far northern latitudes. Peak of passage is in late July and August, with populations declining in early September, but a few linger into October and, in mild autumns, well into November.

The ponds, sloughs, canals, and ditches attract good concentrations of waterbirds by late July. West Wright's Pond is usually an excellent location to see Pied-billed Grebes, waterfowl, Black and Forster's terns, and other species. When emergent vegetation becomes landlocked, Soras and Virginia Rails are sometimes seen on the mudflats in the early evening. Other ponds in the Blitzen Valley and Double O usually have their complement of waterfowl. As ponds recede, fish-eating birds concentrate to feed on entrapped carp. Pelicans, cormorants, herons, egrets, and Common Mergansers are the principal species, but on occasion Western Grebes, Ring-billed Gulls, and Forster's Terns contribute to the diversity. Rarities are sometimes seen among these feeding aggregations, as was the Sabine's Gull observed on Buena Vista Pond on September 25, 1987.

Grainfields near Buena Vista become attractive to Canada Geese and Greater Sandhill Cranes in August. Cranes generally peak in mid-October, but a few sometimes linger into November. Mallards, with lesser numbers of Northern Pintails and American Wigeons, use these fields in autumn. Yellow-headed, Red-winged, and Brewer's blackbirds are in immense flocks from late July into September, and associated with these masses are the raptors. Bald and Golden eagles, Red-tailed Hawks, Northern Harriers, and Prairie Falcons can usually be seen, dependent on seasonality and prey availability.

Among the smaller birds, Cliff Swallows begin staging in early July as their young fledge. Several hundred can often be seen around headquarters, Malheur Field Station, Center Patrol Road-Diamond Lane junction, and on the power-lines between Diamond Lane and Frenchglen. These Cliff Swallow flocks have been joined by Northern Rough-winged, Bank, and Barn swallows by mid-July, with Tree and Violet-green swallows arriving in August. Beginning in late July and continuing into September, desert shrub species move through the refuge in great numbers, with both the Sage Thrasher and Brewer's Sparrow often abundant between Wright's Pond and Rattlesnake Butte. Other passerines begin moving through the refuge in late July. The planted trees at refuge headquarters, Benson Pond, and Frenchglen have the greatest number and diversity, but at the migration peak members of this large diverse group can be seen throughout the refuge. Yellow Warblers are usually the first to arrive, and by mid-August most migrant species have made their appearance. These birds continue to be commonly seen into early October, but the majority have left by mid-October. A Blackburnian Warbler was at headquarters for at least 3 days in September 1986 for the first state record. Most vagrants which have been seen in spring have also been recorded in autumn.

For the greatest autumn species list a similar trip to that of spring is recommended in late August or early September. Drying ponds should be examined closely as shorebirds can sometimes be seen in large numbers. Among the large concentrations of Western Sandpipers and Long-billed Dowitchers, Pectoral, Least, and Baird's sandpipers, Lesser Yellowlegs, Red-necked Phalaropes, and others can occasionally be seen. Also, numbers of Great Egrets may be present, particularly at Buena Vista Pond. Adjacent to the Center Patrol Road, dry meadows provide habitat for migrant raptors. Red-tailed Hawks, Northern Harriers, American Kestrels and, after late October, Rough-legged Hawks hunt these grasslands for small mammals. The dense willow thickets near Page Springs Dam regularly contain a large number of passerines, particularly Willow Flycatchers, Yellow and MacGillivray's warblers, Common Yellowthroats, Song Sparrows, and American and Lesser goldfinches. A Northern Waterthrush was banded here in August 1984.

Winter Season

The diversity and density of birds is greatly reduced on Malheur NWR in winter, but with some effort sixty or more species can be seen in a single day. Along the Center Patrol Road, Rough-legged Hawks, Northern Harriers, Common Ravens, and Northern Shrikes are regularly encountered. Golden Eagles are permanent residents and are occasionally seen on the refuge. Prairie Falcons are often observed, particularly near rimrocks and grain fields, while wintering Bald Eagles concentrate near ponds and lakes at the south end of the refuge. Several eagles regularly perch in the large cottonwoods near P Ranch and Cottonwood Pond. Red-tailed Hawks spend the winter months primarily near and among the junipers west of Highway 205 from Frenchglen to Krumbo Road.

Canada Geese can sometimes be abundant near Buena Vista, headquarters, Knox Pond, and in the Double O area, while Mallards can be common at the warm water springs at Double O. Usually any open water has a variety of ducks, but Common and Barrow's goldeneyes and Hooded Mergansers concentrate their activities on the ice-free waters of the Blitzen River.

Dippers regularly move from the higher elevations of Steens Mountain in November and are often seen along the Blitzen River (near Page Springs) and in Bridge Creek Canyon. Riparian zones at Page Springs attract a few hardy passerines, including Marsh Wrens, Ruby-crowned Kinglets, and Song Sparrows. American Tree Sparrows are also found in riparian thickets at scattered locations throughout the refuge, particularly in recent years in dense willows south of Busse Dam. Among the junipers, American Robins can be abundant or virtually absent, depending on the berry crop. Townsend's Solitaire numbers are also dependent on this crop. In the protected canyons and in the dense junipers west of Highway 205, Cooper's and Sharp-shinned hawks, Hairy

Woodpeckers, Northern Flickers, Mountain Chickadees, Bushtits, Ruby-crowned Kinglets, and Dark-eyed Juncos can usually be found. Both Canyon and Rock wrens regularly winter among the rimrocks, talus slopes, and rocky outcrops throughout the refuge.

Species Accounts

Following is an annotated list of the birds recorded on Malheur NWR through 1988. Common and scientific names are from The American Ornithologists' Union Checklist of North American Birds (sixth edition) and subsequent A.O.U. revisions which have appeared in the Auk since 1983.

Records included in this report are from numerous U.S. Fish and Wildlife Service personnel and by persons known to be reliable in field identification. For commonly encountered species credit is not given, but for more unusual birds the observer's name often follows their record. Many records are from birds banded on the refuge. Since several service employees were involved in the banding program after 1966, these records are not credited to the bander. Before 1966, most banding was accomplished by E. Kridler. Records from the 1800s and early 1900s are cited as most are from published accounts. U.S. Fish and Wildlife Service employees who contributed greatly to the following accounts include the following: R. Erickson, D. Marshall, E. Kridler, W. and B. Anderson, J. Anderson, W. and M. Radke, S. Furniss, B. and K. Deuel, J. Scharff, F. Zeillemaker, S. Thompson, E. McLaury, G. Ivey, D. Paullin, M. and S. Rule, D. Severson, K. Faber, M. Barnes, M. Jess, T. Downs, C. Sooter, G. Benson, R. Voss, L. Ditto, S. Jewett, J. Mazzoni, and J. Fleisher.

Status is based on the following criteria.

Abundant: Can be seen daily in season and proper habitat throughout the refuge.

Common: Almost certainly seen daily in suitable habitat and season.

Uncommon: Present but not certain to be seen.

Occasional: Irregularly seen.

Rare: Known to be present, but not every year.

Accidental: Species seen five or less times.

Vagrant: A wandering bird outside its normal range.

Colonial: A group of individuals or species nesting together or in close association.

Winter, spring, summer, and autumn designations are not based on calendar quarters. For example, autumn migrant describes any southbound bird even if seen in June.

A few records are not included in this report as no details were provided to the refuge staff. I take full responsibility for those records which were omitted or overlooked.

ORDER: GAVIIFORMES
FAMILY: GAVIIDAE

Common Loon
Gavia immer

Uncommon spring and autumn migrant. The Common Loon's avoidance of smaller bodies of water helps account for the lack of refuge records; however, the species can sometimes be seen on the larger water areas such as Malheur, Harney, and Boca lakes and Krumbo Reservoir. Since the turn of the century, Common Loons have only been seen in spring and autumn migration, but Bendire (1877) listed the species as a probable nester on Malheur Lake in the 1870s.

Common Loons have arrived in mid-March (1985); most records are from April (April 18, 1966-April 27, 1974). There are four records for May, with the latest on May 24 (1984). Spring migrants usually appear alone, but 24 were on Boca Lake on May 11, 1964. Autumn migrants have arrived in August (earliest August 16, 1972), but most move through the refuge in October and November (latest November 30, 1983). As in spring, autumn migrants usually occur alone; however, M. Archie observed seven on Krumbo Reservoir on November 3, 1985. When passing through this region, Common Loons are likely traveling to or from the Pacific coast, though recent records from southern Nevada reclamation projects indicate some individuals could be migrating north or south through the western Great Basin.

Pacific Loon
Gavia pacifica

Accidental. There are three records for the refuge; one in spring, two in autumn. The spring record occurred June 3, 1968, when E. McLaury collected an adult on Skunk Farm Pond (Littlefield and McLaury 1973). The first autumn record was on December 4, 1983, when an individual was observed at the Narrows. M. Archie obtained the third record when he saw a lone bird at Krumbo Reservoir on November 3, 1985.

ORDER: PODICIPEDIFORMES
FAMILY: PODICIPEDIDAE

Pied-billed Grebe
Podilymbus podiceps

Common in spring, summer, and autumn; uncommon in winter. Pied-billed Grebes nest solitarily throughout the refuge where suitable habitat is available in lakes, ponds, channels, and sloughs with emergent vegetation. When threatened, individuals of this elusive species submerge with hardly a ripple, remaining motionless with only their heads protruding above water. Therefore, Pied-billed Grebes may appear more uncommon than they actually are. During spring evenings, the "yelping" call of territorial grebes can be heard from most wetlands on the refuge.

In spring, the species arrives on the average date of March 9. The earliest record was on January 19 (1984). No pronounced spring migration peak has been noted. Nesting begins in late April or early May, and peaks in late May and early June. Flightless young can be seen through August. Pied-billed Grebes begin leaving Malheur NWR in mid-August, with the autumn peak in September. Most have left by late October, with the latest record on December 4 (1971). The species has been seen during fifteen Christmas counts in the southern Blitzen Valley. The most recorded in late December was thirteen on December 17, 1983. The absence of open water prevents the species from wintering in large numbers, but a few can usually be seen in January and February around freshwater springs and at isolated areas of open water on the Blitzen River.

Horned Grebe
Podiceps auritus

Uncommon in spring and summer; rare in autumn; accidental in winter. Malheur NWR lies southwest of the principal Horned Grebe nesting range; however, it has increased as a nesting species since Marshall (1959) first reported a nest near Rockford Lane on June 24, 1958 (first state nesting record). Presently, there are usually four or five pairs which spend the summer on the refuge. Nowhere do Horned Grebes nest consistently, but pairs can usually be seen on semipermanent ponds such as Buena Vista, Wright's, Warbler, and Knox.

The earliest spring arrival was April 8 (1969), and the average is April 24. Migration peak is in mid-May, with most migrants gone by May 25. A few pairs remain to nest; the earliest eggs were found on June 7 (1979), and the earliest young July 10 (1972). Shortly after the young fledge, individuals begin migrating from the area. There are few autumn records, but single birds were seen on September 30, 1940; October 30, 1965; September 22, 1970; October 4, 1975; and September 30, 1977. Other autumn migrants include two individuals at Sod House Spring on October 16, 1979; ten at Krumbo Reservoir on December 7, 1981 (this represents the largest concentration recorded); and two at Sod House Spring on October 12, 1986. Two were on Dredger Pond on December 15, 1974, and one was at Sod House Spring on February 5, 1985, for what I consider winter records.

Eared Grebe
Podiceps nigricollis

Common in spring, summer, and autumn; rare in winter. Eared Grebe numbers on the refuge are largely dependent on the productivity of Malheur Lake. Aquatic insects are an important food component for the species; if insects are scarce in the lake Eared Grebes will not nest. During these times there have been no noted increases in nesting pairs elsewhere on the refuge, except in 1979 when twelve hundred pairs nested on west Harney Lake. During most years, smaller colonies occasionally occur on Derrick and Boca lakes, Krumbo Reservoir, and Knox and Wright's ponds, depending on water and feeding conditions. Nests are anchored to submergent aquatic vegetation, as are those of other grebe species.

Eared Grebes have arrived on January 19 (1956), but the average spring arrival is not until March 31. The migration peak usually falls between April 15 and May 15 and most migrants have departed by May 20. Upon spring arrival, Eared Grebes congregate on Stinking Lake before moving to other refuge locations. An estimated 4,400 were there on April 21, 1982, but usually their numbers do not exceed 2,500. Nesting begins in late May and peaks from late June to early July; individuals have been noted incubating in August. Finley (1912) reported 2,465 nests on Malheur Lake on July 4, 1912, but in recent years approximately eight hundred nests has been the maximum number. During the late 1960s and early 1970s, the species nested with Franklin's Gulls, the aggressive gulls apparently providing protection from potential predators. In years when the Double O area has substantial water, the species nests there in flooded rushes, but unfortunately most of these nests are unsuccessful, as water levels recede before eggs hatch or young fledge. The species starts leaving the refuge in early August, and peak numbers occur between August 20 and October 5. The latest autumn record was November 23 (1971). No large Eared Grebe flocks have been noted in autumn, as most migrate rapidly south to Mono Lake in eastern California, where a large percentage of North America's Eared Grebes congregate. The species has been recorded during five refuge Christmas counts. The most seen in winter was 25 on December 9, 1960, and sixteen on December 17, 1983.

Red-necked Grebe
Podiceps grisegena

Accidental. The first southeast Oregon record for the Red-necked Grebe was obtained on June 20, 1980, when a single bird appeared at Sod House Spring. The individual was seen daily through June 29, but was found dead on July 4, 1980 (Littlefield et al. 1985).

Western Grebe
Aechmophorus occidentalis

Common in spring, summer, and autumn. Malheur Lake is the principal use area for Western Grebes, but the species also regularly occurs on Derrick and Boca lakes, Krumbo Reservoir, and Knox Pond. Solitary pairs will sometimes nest away from others of their kind, but several pairs usually nest together in loose colonies. When nesting habitat is limited,

Western Grebe and Clark's Grebe

nests are often placed in dense aggregations. One such colony was located in west Harney Lake in 1983, where a 1-acre bulrush mat held an estimated 850 nests.

The earliest spring migrant was seen on February 22 (1979), but their average arrival is not until March 18. Peak of spring passage is between April 15 and May 5, and most migrants have moved on by May 15. Nesting begins in mid-May and extends well into August. Nest initiation is usually dependent on submergent plant growth. Nests are anchored to this aquatic vegetation and little or no nest construction can occur until it has grown to near the water's surface. Therefore, flightless young can still be seen in mid-September. Autumn migration begins in mid-August and peaks in mid-September, with the latest record on November 18 (1985).

Clark's Grebe
Aechmophorus clarkii

Occasional in spring, summer, and autumn. The Clark's Grebe was considered a light-phased color-form of the Western Grebe from 1886 until 1985. Originally described in 1858, the Clark's Grebe was designated a full species until 1886 when the American Ornithologists' Union Checklist of North American Birds (first edition 1886) combined the two forms into a single species. Lack of interbreeding, behavioral differences, and differential call notes have recently been examined and described (Nuechterlein 1981). Based on this new information, Clark's Grebe is now back to its original 1858-1886 status.

Until recently, Clark's Grebe had not been seen on Malheur NWR. The species apparently prefers deeper water than do Western Grebes; as Malheur Lake levels began increasing in the early 1980s, so did observations of Clark's Grebe. The first record occurred in 1983 when a lone bird appeared on Buena Vista Pond. In 1984, two pairs were seen through the summer at the Narrows, and in 1985 several pairs were seen near refuge headquarters and the Narrows, and on Harney Lake. In 1985, successful reproduction occurred on Malheur Lake and possibly Harney Lake. In July 1986, about sixty adults and several chicks were seen near the northeast shore of Harney Lake. Others were noted on Harney Lake in June 1987, and one pair was seen on Skunk Farm Pond on June 7, 1987.

ORDER: PELECANIFORMES
FAMILY: PELECANIDAE

American White Pelican
Pelecanus erythrorhynchos

Abundant in spring, summer, and autumn; accidental in winter. Historically, American White Pelicans were common breeders on the refuge. Bendire (1877) found the species nesting on a small island in Malheur Lake on April 16, 1874, but by 1912 pelicans no longer used islands, having switched their nesting sites to extensive bulrush mats. This habitat was used until pelicans abandoned the refuge as a nesting site in the drought years of the late 1920s and 1930s. The drought culminated in 1934 when the lake became completely dry. In 1938, after water returned to the lake, pelicans again nested, using unique nesting sites. During the dry years, vegetation had been mowed and stacked within the lake bed. After water returned to the lake, these haystacks provided ideal pelican nesting platforms and were used extensively until the structures disintegrated after the 1940 nesting season. Thereafter, the species used islands in both Malheur and Harney lakes. From 1960 through 1984, pelicans abandoned the refuge as a nesting locality, though several thousand nonbreeders annually summered. High water levels in Malheur Lake in the mid-1980s created several small islands, and in 1985 a few pairs nested near the Narrows, producing three young, the first on the refuge in 25 years. In 1987, an estimated eight hundred young were produced, and in 1988 fifteen hundred pairs nested on Malheur Lake. For a more complete review of the American White Pelican on the refuge through the 1979 nesting season see Thompson et al. (1980).

The species has arrived as early as February 28 (1963), but the average spring arrival is not until March 29. Abundant carp populations continue to attract pelicans through early summer, and peak numbers are usually present in mid-July and August. Color-marking data (in the 1960s) indicate these summer birds are from Lower Klamath and Clear Lake NWRs, California, and Pyramid Lake, Nevada. Numbers remain relatively stable through August, but in September and October many leave the refuge. Few remain by mid-November. The latest autumn observation was on December 19 (1981). There are five winter records: one wintered in 1958-59 and one the following year; ten were at headquarters in January 1987, one on December 21, 1987, and seven on December 21, 1988. Most winter records were of individuals which had probably been injured, as several have been found in the past with broken wings and other injuries after collisions with fences or powerlines. An unusual collision occurred in 1971, when a pelican was temporarily stunned after colliding with the headquarters flag pole.

FAMILY: PHALACROCORACIDAE

Double-crested Cormorant
Phalacrocorax auritus

Common in spring, summer, and autumn; rare in winter. Most Double-crested Cormorant activity is confined to the vicinity of Malheur and Harney lakes during the nesting season, but once young have fledged the species disperses to other refuge locations. Depending on food supplies, cormorants are regularly seen on Knox, Benson, and Wright's ponds, Boca Lake, and Krumbo Reservoir in August and

September. An average of eighty pairs nested from 1966 through 1981, but as water levels in Malheur Lake increased, cormorant numbers also increased. In addition to older nesting sites in bulrush stands in Malheur Lake, flooded homesites provided new nesting habitat as large trees became water-bound. From 1982 through 1985, an average of 565 pairs nested on or adjacent to the refuge, and in 1986 and 1987 this number increased to over nine hundred pairs. Feeding flocks flying over Malheur Lake in the mid-1980s were reminiscent of the immense cormorant flocks seen along the Pacific coast throughout the year.

The species arrives shortly after the larger lakes become free of ice. The earliest spring record was February 5 (1984) and the average is March 17. Nesting begins soon after arrival. The earliest nesting record was on March 28 (1972), but usually nesting does not begin until the first week in April. The nesting season is rather protracted and flightless young have been seen as late as August. During the nesting season, cormorants are closely associated with Great Blue Herons which also nest early. The species remains through mid-September, but begins leaving the refuge in late September, though 1,285 were still present on November 7, 1983. The latest record occurred on December 9 (1971). Banding returns indicate cormorants migrate from the refuge in two directions. One route is northwest toward the Pacific Ocean, where two have been recovered, one from Anacortes, Washington, and the other from Ruggs Junction, Oregon. The second route is south, with returns from Carson City and Stillwater NWR, Nevada, and Guaymas, Sonora, Mexico. Other than one record in late December 1940 and one in late December 1976, winter records on the refuge were nonexistent until the early 1980s. Since that time, a few cormorants have wintered each year. Four were at Krumbo Reservoir on December 19, 1981; two wintered in 1980; six wintered in 1984; and nine attempted to winter in 1985 (by February 1985 only six remained). In 1987, eleven were seen near headquarters on December 21, and ten wintered in 1988.

ORDER: CICONIIFORMES
FAMILY: ARDEIDAE

American Bittern
Botaurus lentiginosus

Common in spring, summer, and autumn; rare in winter. Cryptic plumage, elusive behavior, and its habitat preferences make the American Bittern seem more uncommon on the refuge than it really is. Commonly known as "slough-pumper," because of its unique spring vocalizations, the species usually is heard more often than seen. To know its true abundance, one has to visit the marshes and wet meadows away from regularly traveled roads.

In spring the American Bittern usually arrives in early April (average April 4), but has been reported as early as February 22 (1981). The peak of spring migration is normally between April 15 and 30, with most migrants gone by May 5. I have found two nests in the Blitzen Valley, both in late May, and one north of the refuge in early June. C. Foster examined eight nests north of the Double O substation in 1979 and 1980. Completed clutches were present from May 28 through June 11, and one nest had hatched on June 18. Average clutch size was 5.4; most nests were located in Baltic rush. As wetlands dry in July and August, birds start leaving the refuge. Autumn migration peaks between September 10 and October 1, with a few individuals lingering into November. What I consider late autumn migrants were seen on December 9 in 1959, 1960, and 1982. The species has been seen several times in the winter. A lone bird was observed from December 1 through 20 (Gabrielson and Jewett 1940), and another on January 24, 1942. Single individuals were recorded during the 1943, 1964, and 1976 Christmas counts in the southern Blitzen Valley. Since the establishment of a new Christmas count in the northern Blitzen Valley in 1979, American Bitterns have been recorded in 1980 (five), 1981 (one), and 1983 (one).

Least Bittern
Ixobrychus exilis

Rare in spring and summer. Bendire (1877) recorded the Least Bittern on two occasions in Malheur Lake, and Willett (1919) found it a rather common nester there, building its nest in the taller bulrush toward open water. Few records have accumulated since these early accounts; however, the species is shy and it could be more common than records indicate. Individuals have been seen from May 27 through September 8, with most reports from Malheur Lake. Single birds were seen repeatedly in June and July 1975, and again on April 29, 1977, and May 26, 1986, along the Center Patrol Road, 3 miles south of Malheur Field Station; and a male was seen at Buena Vista Pond on May 24, 1988 (G. Ivey). D. Paullin and I saw a pair in a large heron and egret colony in Malheur Lake on June 13, 1975. S. Thompson and D. Davis watched two immatures and at least one adult in the center of the lake on June 30, 1981. Brief glimpses of this small bittern have occurred in the lake since 1969, usually from a speeding airboat. In 1982, as Malheur Lake was increasing in size, Least Bitterns were heard and seen almost daily between Kado Bridge and Benson Landing. Deep water in the center of the lake had inundated their normal habitat, apparently pushing individuals into peripheral zones. A similar situation existed in 1983, but as the lake continued to increase in size, the species disappeared from that area.

Great Blue Heron
Ardea herodias

Common in spring, summer, and autumn; uncommon in winter. Great Blue Herons have had a similar history on Malheur NWR to that of several other colonial species. First recorded by Bendire (1877) in the 1870s, herons nested in close association with pelicans and cormorants. Early in the 20th century about one hundred pairs nested, except in 1918 when Willett (1919) reported over six hundred pairs. This was the largest number ever recorded nesting on the refuge. From one to two hundred pairs occupied territories until the early 1980s, but as Malheur Lake increased in size in the mid-1980s pair numbers also increased. From 1966 through 1981 pair numbers averaged 174, and from 1982 through 1985 pair numbers averaged 456. Around flooded home-sites, inundated trees provided new nesting sites and, like cormorants, Great Blue Herons immediately responded. Most nesting has been confined to or adjacent to Malheur Lake; however, other sites have been used sporadically. From 1938 through 1948, J. Scharff reported a few pairs nested in Diamond Swamp. Eighteen pairs nested on an island in Boca Lake in 1951, and twelve pairs have nested consistently the past several years in willows near the west end of Harney Lake (96 pairs nested there in 1986).

Spring migrants begin arriving in mid-February, becoming common in early March. Migrants continue to arrive through mid-April, and most transients have departed by late April. Upon arrival, resident Great Blue Herons move onto nesting sites. Nesting is often in progress by late March, and by mid-April nest initiation is at its peak. A few young are flying by mid-June. Until high water in Malheur Lake eliminated most emergent habitat, the majority of pairs nested on hardstem bulrush platforms in the northern portion of the lake. In this colony, Great and Snowy egrets, Black-crowned Night-Herons, and White-faced Ibises all nested in close proximity with blue herons. Once nesting has been completed, the species begins migrating in late August. Migration peaks in September; however, herons are still common through October. Most migrants have left by mid-November. Band recoveries from locally produced herons indicate some birds move south while others migrate southwest. Southern migrants have been recovered near Yuma and Phoenix, Arizona, and 25 miles southwest of Denio, Nevada. Southwest migrants have been recovered at Richvale, Dixon, and Nelson, California. Although many leave the refuge for the winter, others remain. Most open waters which contain fish usually support Great Blue Herons. Highest winter numbers, based on Christmas counts, occurred in 1943 (55), 1967 (57), 1979 (58), 1984 (58), and 1987 (53). In December 1983, ninety were seen in the southern Blitzen Valley for the largest winter number, and 75 were near headquarters on December 18, 1981.

Great Egret
Casmerodius albus

Common in spring, summer, and autumn; accidental in winter. Great Egrets were virtually extirpated from the refuge at the turn of the century. Plume hunters killed most nesting birds in 1898, and only two individuals were seen in 1908. The species, however, made a rapid recovery and by 1912 egrets were again occupying nesting sites in Malheur Lake (Thompson et al. 1980). Their numbers continued to increase through the 1920s, but the drought years of the 1930s temporarily eliminated the species as a refuge nester. Once sufficient water returned to Malheur Lake, Great Egrets returned, and 107 were seen in 1935. Matted bulrush provided nesting sites, and this habitat was used almost exclusively until high water inundated most emergent stands in the 1980s. No other nesting habitat was used on Malheur NWR between 1935 and 1982, except that a few pairs nested in willows in Diamond Valley in the 1930s and 1940s. Increases in Great Egret numbers were noted in the 1940s, and by 1947 about three hundred pairs nested. Numbers were again reduced in the drier 1950s and early 1960s, but from 1966 through 1981 there were an average of 253 pairs. As high water in Malheur Lake developed, an average of 603 pairs nested from 1982 through 1985. Willows along the Silvies River became flooded, and many pairs nested in this newly created habitat. Unlike Great Blue Herons and Double-crested Cormorants, few egrets used the larger trees around flooded homesites for nesting.

Average spring arrival is March 24, with the earliest observation on February 20 (1981). Most local pairs have arrived by May 1. Nesting is in progress by late April and continues through most of June. Most young have fledged by the end of July. Once young fledge, both adults and young disperse throughout the Malheur-Harney Lakes Basin. Many are seen north of the refuge, feeding in drying ponds and sloughs. Peak numbers are usually present in September and early October. Over nineteen hundred have been seen on aerial surveys in autumn. Great Egrets start leaving the area in September, and by November few remain. On December 3, 1981, one was seen at Double O for the latest autumn record. Locally banded birds have provided sixteen returns. Eleven recoveries are from Mexico, with most from Sonora. The southernmost record was from Jamay, Jalisco, Mexico. There are returns from Lissie, Texas; Madras and Paisley, Oregon; Fallon, Nevada; and Chandler, Arizona. There are no returns from California, so the majority apparently migrate south through the western Great Basin. There is one refuge winter record. A lone bird was seen at Harney Lake on January 3, 1984.

Snowy Egret
Egretta thula

Uncommon in spring, summer, and autumn; accidental in winter. Little information is available on the Snowy Egret from the time C. Bendire reported the species as a moderately common summer resident in the 1870s (Bendire 1877) to the local extirpation of the species by plume hunters in 1898. From 1898 to 1935 there was but one record: a lone bird was seen on May 24 and 26, 1914. A few Snowy Egrets reportedly migrated through the refuge in 1935, but sightings increased in 1940. In 1941, fifteen were seen and three nests located. By 1945 their numbers had increased to 95 individuals, and 120 nested in Malheur Lake in 1946. Drought conditions in the early 1960s resulted in the species disappearing as a breeder from 1960 through 1962, but 25 pairs were again nesting in 1963. From 1966 through 1981, an average of 86 pairs nested annually. As Malheur Lake increased in size in the 1980s, Snowy Egret pairs also increased. From 1982 through 1985, an average of 161 pairs nested annually. The largest number ever recorded on the refuge occurred in 1985 when 227 pairs nested.

The average arrival date is April 19, and the earliest record occurred on March 12 (1984). The nesting population has usually arrived by May 15. Upon arrival Snowy Egrets usually move immediately to Malheur Lake. Few are seen in the Blitzen Valley (except at Knox Pond where pairs nested in 1986 and 1987), but the species can often be observed north of the lake, which is the favored feeding location for most colonial nesters. Fifty-two nests were located on May 16, 1972, for the earliest nesting record. Nesting is in progress through June, and young fledge in July and August. Their only known refuge nesting localities have been Malheur Lake and Knox Pond. Snowy Egrets begin leaving in late August, and few are seen after September. The latest autumn record was on November 20 (1985). There is only one winter record; a single bird was seen on January 1, 1937. To date there are no band recoveries from locally produced Snowy Egrets.

Tricolored Heron
Egretta tricolor

Accidental. A male Tricolored Heron was collected by G. Benson on October 31, 1945, at Benson Pond (Scharff 1944). To my knowledge this was the first Oregon record.

Cattle Egret
Bubulcus ibis

Rare in late spring, summer, and autumn. The Cattle Egret is a new species to the refuge. It was first recorded on August 13, 1974 (Littlefield 1980), and several records have accumulated since. In 1976, one was seen near refuge headquarters on July 16, and another individual was near the Narrows from April 30 through May 7, 1977. Three were recorded on September 5, 1979, north of Malheur Lake, and three additional observations occurred in 1980—August 1, August 14, and October 10. The first nesting record for the Malheur-Harney Lakes Basin, as well as the first Oregon nesting record, occurred on July 9, 1982, when five young were found in a nest adjacent to Malheur Lake (Thompson and Paullin 1985). There were two nesting pairs on June 8, 1984, and two pairs were also present in 1985. No known nesting has occurred since 1985, but one individual was seen near P Ranch on May 3, 1987 (J. Bolsinger); six near Knox Pond on May 21, 1987; one pair north on Malheur Lake on May 30, 1987 (G. Ivey); one in Diamond Valley on April 26, 1988 (G. Ivey); and one at Buena Vista Pond on May 8, 1988.

Green-backed Heron
Butorides striatus

Accidental. There are three refuge records for the Green-backed Heron. W. and B. Anderson obtained the first when they observed one near Cole Island on June 12, 1971. D. Davis and S. Lindstedt saw the second individual about 3 miles southwest of headquarters on June 16, 1982. The third record occurred on July 11, 1984, when G. Ivey located a bird about 3 miles northeast of Frenchglen.

Black-crowned Night-Heron
Nycticorax nycticorax

Abundant in spring, summer, and autumn; occasional in winter. The Black-crowned Night-Heron is both presently and historically one of the more abundant colonial nesters on the refuge, though no noticeable increase in numbers occurred during the high water years of the 1980s. Annual fluctuations in population numbers are a characteristic trait for night-herons on the refuge. In some years the species is abundant, while in other years their numbers are minimal. For example, only 78 individuals were present in 1940, but five thousand pairs were nesting 7 years later. Generally, five to six hundred pairs nest annually, but one thousand pairs nested in 1974 for the recent peak. Although the species is a common nester on the refuge, observations are often limited because of their nocturnal behavior. Elsewhere within the breeding range of the species, night-herons concentrate at fish hatcheries if they are available, and here the species comes into direct conflict with humans. In the past many were shot, and as a result the only band return of a Malheur bird came from a hatchery near Ruby Lake, Nevada. Although no winter returns are presently available, there are indications that many local birds winter along the west coast of Mexico, in the states of Sinaloa and Nayarit.

The earliest the species has arrived in the spring was March 1 (1985), but the average arrival is not until March 29. Most breeding birds are on territory by May 15. Nesting is in progress by mid-April, and some young have hatched by May 14. The species habit of nesting low to water often results in some nests being inundated. Nesting is mostly confined to Malheur Lake, but recently there were small colonies at Double O and Knox Pond. Recently fledged young have been seen well into August, but the majority are flying in July. Once nesting has been completed, birds disperse in all directions. Birds in nonbreeding plumage can be seen in the Blitzen Valley during the nesting season, but most adults are absent from the valley until postbreeding dispersal. Night-herons begin leaving the refuge in late August and continue to migrate from the area through November. Fifty were still on the refuge on December 2, 1981, but normally only stragglers remain after November. What I considered to be a late migrant was seen on December 13, 1963. Wright's and Knox ponds, Boca and Derrick lakes, and Diamond Swamp are favored autumn haunts for the species; however, night-herons are found throughout the refuge, particularly from August through October. In winter, the species has been seen during six Christmas counts in the southern Blitzen Valley. Six were seen in 1958, but usually only single individuals are recorded during the winter months.

FAMILY: THRESKIORNITHIDAE

White-faced Ibis
Plegadis chihi

Fairly common in spring, summer, and autumn; accidental in winter. Coues (1874) was the first to report the White-faced Ibis in Harney County; however, C. Bendire did not see the species during his stay in the basin in the mid-1870s. In the early 1900s it was well established on the refuge, as Willett (1919) reported one hundred individuals nesting in Malheur Lake in 1918. The species has been seen annually since, but its numbers have fluctuated depending on water conditions. Until recently about sixty pairs nested in Malheur Lake, but beginning in 1979 White-faced Ibis numbers have increased. On May 7, 1981, I counted 1,335 individuals flying over Benson Landing toward roost sites in the lake, and from 1982 through 1985 an average of 913 pairs have nested on or adjacent to the refuge. Presently, the refuge supports the largest ibis colonies in the state, and until 1985 few had been seen in Oregon outside Harney County.

The earliest the species has been seen in spring was on April 9 (1972), but its average arrival is not until May 3. The summer population is on the refuge by May 20. Before nesting, ibises are regularly seen in meadows feeding on soil invertebrates. In 1985, B. Ehlers observed individuals feeding in grasses on the Burns Union High School track field. Mowed meadows are also intensively used in autumn, with most use south and east of Burns. The earliest nest was found on May 16, 1972, but normally nesting does not begin until late May and early June. All nests I have seen on the refuge were in scattered stands of hardstem bulrush. The most nests recorded was over 1,900 in 1986 and 2,500 in 1987. Young fledge from mid-July through mid-August. All nesting has been in Malheur Lake except for ten pairs which nested near Wright's Pond in 1962, and 120, 300, and 2,100 pairs which nested in Knox Pond in 1985, 1986, and 1987, respectively.

White-faced Ibises begin migrating in early August; however, many remain in the basin through September. More birds are sometimes present in autumn than can be accounted for from the local nesting population. On August 29, 1974, 335 were seen in Malheur Lake and 351 were north of the lake on September 11, 1975, but only sixty pairs were present during the 1974 and 1975 nesting seasons. Colonies near Fallon, Nevada, and northern Utah may account for the autumn increases on the refuge. By the end of September most have left, but occasionally a few remain as late as November. The latest autumn record was on November 28 (1976). A single bird was seen on January 3 and February 2, 1964, providing a very unusual winter record.

ORDER: ANSERIFORMES
FAMILY: ANATIDAE

Tundra Swan
Cygnus columbianus

Abundant spring and autumn migrant; uncommon in winter; rare in summer. A large percentage (45-65 percent) of the Tundra Swans which winter in California migrate through the refuge in both spring and autumn. Spring congregations are dependent on weather conditions. If unfavorable weather persists departures are delayed. For example, on March 20, 1975, 22,000 swans were seen in east Malheur Lake after several days of stormy weather. Normally, eight to nine thousand birds are on the refuge during the peak of migration. The first migrants generally arrive in mid-February (earliest January 29, 1984), but the peak of abundance does not occur until March 15 to 30. Most birds have left by May 10. This species is rarely seen in summer, usually associating with resident Trumpeter Swans. One individual spent the summer on Wright's Pond from 1972 through 1976. In 1974 and 1975, it was apparently mated with a trumpeter, but in 1976 it was replaced by another Trumpeter Swan. Lone birds have recently been seen on Sod House Spring, Buena Vista Pond, Malheur Lake, Dredger Field, and Knox Pond during the summer. Southbound migrants first appear in early October. All ponds and lakes containing water and submergent food plants attract individuals but, as in spring, Malheur Lake usually has the largest concentration. Peak numbers are present between November 10 and 25, and by mid-December migrants have left the refuge. Food supply has an influence on the wintering status of the species. If dense stands of sago pondweed persist in Malheur Lake, swans commonly winter. Their swimming activity keeps water open even at subzero temperatures. Many ducks also use these bodies of open water, feeding on plant fragments pulled from the substrate by swans. The species has been recorded during all but five Christmas counts. In the southern Blitzen Valley count area, highest numbers were in 1957 (189), 1958 (107), 1969 (217), and 1975 (594).

A neck-collared Tundra Swan was observed on Wright's Pond from March 5 through March 7, 1974, by J. Fleisher. The individual had been banded as a juvenile at Seward Peninsula, Alaska, on August 25, 1971, and had subsequently been sighted at San Luis NWR, California, on November 30, 1971, and February 11, 1972. The bird was seen again near Willows, California, on February 9, 1973.

Trumpeter Swan
Cygnus buccinator

Uncommon permanent resident. Bendire (1877) first recorded the Trumpeter Swan on the refuge when he collected a bird from Malheur Lake on March 24, 1877. In addition, one pair was seen on the Blitzen River from May 25 through June 15, 1921 (Prill 1922). These were the only records until the species was successfully reintroduced in 1958 after two earlier unsuccessful attempts. Presently, the refuge nesting population is decreasing.

Trumpeter Swans begin nesting in early May and young hatch in June. Normally cygnets number three to five, but one pair hatched seven young in 1976. Young have usually fledged by late August. Cygnets have been produced each year since reintroduction except 1977, but where the young go remains a mystery. One cygnet banded in 1970 was found dead near Vale, Oregon, in 1971, and other locally produced birds have also been recorded near Fallon, Nevada, and at Lake Almanor, California. The refuge population consists of about sixty birds, of which twelve to fifteen pairs regularly nest. Two pairs have nested in Malheur Lake and one pair on Warbler Pond; the remainder nest in the Blitzen Valley. Traditional nesting locations include Benson, Knox, Unit 8, Unit 9, Skunk Farm, Wright's, Buena Vista, and Cottonwood ponds, Knox and Diamond swamps, and Boca Lake. The "bumper" swan year on the refuge was 1979, when 32 cygnets fledged, but normally seven to ten are produced annually. Breeding adults and young of the year are sedentary, finding winter habitat where there is open water and submergent vegetation. On February 5, 1982, I found 51 swans together on the East Canal near Boca Lake, but typically flocks number only about ten to twelve individuals.

Greater White-fronted Goose
Anser albifrons

Uncommon spring and autumn migrant; rare winter visitor. Like many other waterfowl species, white-fronted geese migrate from the southwest into the Double O area, continuing northeast to the meadows and grainfields near Burns. The species has been recorded as early as February 4 (1964), but the average arrival is not until February 21. Spring migration peak is between March 15 and 25, and the latest spring record was for sixty birds on May 19, 1962. White-fronts are early autumn migrants, arriving in late August (earliest August 21, 1980) or early September. Peak of autumn migration occurs between September 20 and October 20, and most have left by mid-November. The latest the species has been seen was December 7 (1963). There are a few winter records: ten were seen from December 17 through 30, 1961; one on December 21, 1977; one wintered in 1978-79; and eight wintered in 1979-80. While on the refuge, the species is seen at scattered locations but nowhere consistently. In autumn a few can sometimes be seen in grainfields near Buena Vista.

White-fronted geese seen in the basin are either on their way to or returning from California's Central Valley. Subspecific status has yet to be determined for these birds. Tule Geese (*A. a. gambelli*) color-marked at Cook Islet, Alaska, have been seen near Burns, as have Pacific White-fronted Geese (*A. a. frontalis*) color-marked at Tule Lake NWR, California. Other individuals appear intermediate between these two forms.

Snow Goose
Chen caerulescens

Abundant spring and autumn migrant; rare in winter and summer. The Snow Goose is the most abundant member of its subfamily in the basin. The species has arrived as early as January 29 (1970, 1980), but its average arrival is 16 days later (February 14). Peak of spring migration is between March 15 and April 5. During this period its numbers have exceeded 113,000 (in 1982). Most depart in March and April, but 150 birds were seen on May 12, 1962. Harney and Malheur lakes are regularly used; Snow Geese are often seen feeding in alkali bulrush stands. Moist meadows are also important feeding habitat in the spring, especially near Double O and headquarters. Most birds use the Double O to Malheur Lake corridor, with little use in the Blitzen Valley south of Wright's Pond. From the basin, Snow Geese migrate northeast toward Montana, and thence north to southeast Alberta, then northwest to Alaska and Siberia; others migrate north to northern Canada. Color-marked birds from northwest Canada, Alaska, and Siberia have been seen on or near the refuge since 1975. A few Snow Geese sometimes summer here. Three were observed from May 29 through June 4, 1960; one was seen from May 26 through August 3, 1963; one was seen near Double O on June 18, 1973; two summered at Double O in 1977; three were seen on August 12, 1980; seven were reported from Harney Lake on June 16, 1982; two were on Malheur Lake on July 3, 1985; one summered on Malheur Lake in 1987; and one was seen on Malheur Lake on May 27, 1988. The earliest autumn record was on September 3 (1961), with the peak of migration in late October. Rarely are there more than thirty thousand birds in the basin at one time, and their migration is rapid. Usually little feeding habitat is available. The latest record was on December 20 (1958). Most birds will nest in Alaska and Siberia, migrating through the refuge in spring, but bypassing the area in autumn. These individuals migrate over the Gulf of Alaska, and this change in migration route further reduces their autumn numbers on the refuge.

Since Marshall (1959) first reported the "Blue Goose" in the basin, several additional records have occurred. Like Marshall's record, most observations have been in the vicinity of Burns. These dark morphs have been seen on March 22, 1956 (one bird), November 8-11, 1962 (one), March 7, 1963 (one), November 8, 1963 (one), March 30, 1971 (two), April 8, 1971 (one), April 16, 1971 (one), March 9, 1972 (one), March 25, 1972 (one), April 22, 1975 (two), November 8, 1976 (one), March 21, 1979 (three), and one summer record on June 16, 1982 (one).

Ross' Goose
Chen rossii

Fairly common spring and autumn migrant; accidental in summer. Ross' Geese, like other members of the subfamily, arrive in the spring from the southwest after spending the winter months in California's Central Valley. Most bypass the refuge and congregate on the mowed-grazed meadows south and east of Burns, where the species often becomes abundant. The Ross' Goose arrives later than its larger relative the Snow Goose; as Snow Geese are decreasing, Ross' are increasing. February 2 (1979) is the earliest refuge record, and the average spring arrival is March 13. Their greatest abundance occurs between April 1 and 15. Unlike other species of migrant geese, Ross' Geese spend only a short time here, and by May most are on their way to their Perry River, Northwest Territory, nesting areas via western Montana. The largest number seen in the region was four thousand on April 16, 1976, about 1 mile south of Burns. If one examines the flocks carefully, rarely a blue-phase color morph can be seen. In 1982, M. Archie saw eight such morphs among a flock 5 miles south of Burns. There is one Ross' Goose summer record; J. Cornely and G. Ivey captured an individual on Malheur Lake in July 1979. In autumn, Ross' Geese arrive from the northeast, occurring on the refuge between October 27 and November 16. The peak of migration is between November 3 and 12. Often the smaller Ross' Goose can be seen among the massive flights of Snow Geese. At the peak of migration mixed flocks can be seen passing over the Narrows as both species are rapidly moving to favorable winter climes southwest of the refuge.

Emperor Goose
Chen canagica

Accidental. There is one refuge record for this Bering Sea nesting species, that of a single bird observed by G. Benson on December 14, 1939. Birds south of Alaska have mostly been seen along the coast; however, several records presently exist from the Klamath Basin, and one was present near Burns on March 7 and 8, 1988.

Western Canada Goose
Branta canadensis moffitti

Abundant permanent resident. This large goose is a conspicuous bird on the refuge during spring and summer. In autumn and winter the subspecies can also be abundant, but is generally concentrated in the vicinity of refuge grainfields. Western Canada Geese which do leave the refuge for the winter are early spring migrants, usually beginning to return in early February and reaching peak numbers between March 1 and 15. By April 1 most migrants have moved northward. In mid- to late February, pairs become aggressive as the nesting season approaches. Nesting begins in mid-March, with the peak of nesting in April. Nesting pairs are distributed throughout the refuge, but the greatest densities are found on Benson, Knox, Buena Vista, Skunk Farm, Warbler, and Wright's ponds. Young usually hatch in late April and early May, and nearly all ponds have broods present in May and June. Four to six goslings normally hatch per nest, but broods containing ten or more are often seen. These are likely the result of two to several family groups joining; while one pair "baby-sits," the other pairs leave the gaggle to feed elsewhere. As the season progresses, adults with young move from smaller ponds and sloughs to larger, permanent water bodies; Boca Lake and Knox, Buena Vista, and Wright's ponds have been important brooding areas. Young fledge in July, and families join together and move to favorable feeding spots. Grainfields near Buena Vista and Double O, and north of Malheur Lake usually have the largest congregations in autumn. The subspecies reaches its peak numbers in late November and early December, after a continual buildup which begins in mid-August. Numbers decline when water becomes ice covered. Double O supports the largest concentration after freeze-up, as numerous warm-water springs keep some water open.

Yearlings and unsuccessful nesting pairs concentrate at scattered locations on the refuge in late May and June. From late May to mid-June these birds leave for northern molting areas. Banding data indicate the birds move to northern Canada. Many autumn returns from refuge-banded geese have been from Saskatchewan and Alberta. Those leaving the refuge in the autumn move south to warmer climates in western Nevada and the California Central Valley.

Lesser Canada Goose
Branta canadensis taverneri

Uncommon spring and autumn migrant; rare in winter. Lesser Canada Geese migrate through the region, but few use the refuge. Meadows south and east of Burns, Happy Valley (north of Diamond), and Catlow Valley support the majority of birds. In spring, this medium-sized Canada Goose arrives in mid-February and peaks in March, leaving the basin for arctic nesting grounds in early April. Small flocks can occur anywhere on the refuge during migration as no particular area is consistently used. Usually they are seen feeding on new green shoots in mowed, wet meadows. Lesser Canada Geese arrive in the autumn in mid-October and peak in November. The latest autumn record was on December 8 (1975). Occasionally a few of these smaller geese can be seen among the wintering flocks of Western Canada Geese, but they are never common.

The Cackling Goose (*B. c. minima*), the smallest North American goose, is occasionally seen on the refuge. Willett (1919) reported this Mallard-sized goose as common on Malheur Lake. The normal migration route from their nesting areas on the Yukon Delta, Alaska, to California Central Valley wintering regions is mostly west of Malheur; most concentrate at Tule Lake and Lower Klamath NWRs, California. However, a flock of 45 was seen near headquarters on February 13, 1971; one hundred birds were seen on Malheur Lake on March 5, 1972; and one hundred wintered near headquarters in 1979-80. Usually "cacklers" are seen intermingled among other geese and their numbers rarely exceed ten individuals.

Wood Duck
Aix sponsa

Occasional in spring, summer, and autumn; rare in winter. The Wood Duck has increased on Malheur NWR in recent years and there are now records for every month. The majority of Wood Ducks seen on the refuge are likely migrating to or from California Central Valley wintering areas and northern Idaho, northwestern Montana, and southeastern British Columbia nesting regions. However, increased summer records may have resulted from the Oregon Department of Fish and Wildlife and Bureau of Land Management's program of artificial house placement. Nesting boxes have been placed along the Silvies River north of Burns and in other eastern Oregon regions, and these are being used by the species.

Wood Duck numbers decrease on the refuge in September and there are few winter records. However, two were seen during the 1944, 1963, and 1987 Christmas counts, and five on December 24, 1960, and at least one pair wintered near headquarters in 1964-65. In 1970-71, a free-flying female and flightless male wintered on Sod House Spring. No refuge nesting has been recorded, even though a few artificial houses were formerly provided. An adult male and female with several fledged young were captured and banded at Benson Landing on September 12, 1973. However, considering the date, these birds were probably migrants. Interestingly, on September 12, 1974, the same male with a different female (again accompanied by fledged young) was captured at the same location. Wood Ducks have been seen throughout the refuge; no particular location appears to be favored. The largest groups seen were 13 (15 miles south of headquarters) on July 28, 1983, and 27 (at Krumbo Reservoir) on November 13, 1980.

Green-winged Teal
Anas crecca

Abundant in spring and autumn; uncommon in summer and winter. This smallest of the North American dabbling ducks occurs abundantly in migration, but usually concentrations are in the remote areas of the Malheur-Harney Lakes Basin. Up to fifteen thousand have been seen in spring migration feeding in shallow ponds between Lawen and Buchanan. Green-winged Teals arrive in mid-February and peak in mid-March. Most migrants have moved on toward nesting areas (primarily in the Canadian boreal forest) by mid-May. While on the refuge, the greatest concentrations occur along the north and east shores of Malheur Lake; however, small groups can be seen at widely scattered points in the Blitzen Valley and Double O. As in other Oregon regions, few green-wings remain during the nesting season. Generally, about 150 pairs nest and, while pairs or broods can occasionally be seen in the Blitzen Valley, the species is more common in the Double O unit. Of four nests examined by C. Foster at Double O, nest initiation ranged from May 1 through June 7. Average clutch size was 10 eggs. Young usually hatch in June and fledge in July and August. Autumn migrants appear in late July as males arrive from northern nesting regions. The migration peak usually occurs between October 1 and 15 and most have left by mid-December. Both Malheur and Harney lakes are important autumn use areas. Banding data indicate most migrants are heading for the California Central Valley; however, there is some evidence that a few are moving southeast. One bird was recovered in 1964 from Seabrook, Texas, and another in 1972 near Lake Charles, Louisiana. Both birds had been banded about 2 months earlier on the refuge. When suitable winter habitat is available a few Green-winged Teals winter. The species has been recorded during all but one Christmas count. Highest counts were 1941 (117), 1958 (101), 1963 (97), and 1972 (85).

In March 1964, Jarvis (1966) collected a Eurasian Green-winged Teal (*A. c. crecca*) on the refuge. This represented one of the few records for western North America outside the Aleutian Islands, Alaska. The bird, an adult male, was captured during banding activities and is now deposited at Humboldt State University (HSU No. 898).

American Black Duck
Anas rubripes

Accidental. There are two refuge records for this eastern North American species. An adult male was captured and banded on November 14, 1930, near headquarters by G. Benson. The second record was on May 5, 1977, when R. Sjostrom and C. Talbot observed a black duck at Benson Landing. Coincidentally, both refuge records are from the same location.

Mallard
Anas platyrhynchos

Abundant in spring, summer, and autumn; common in winter. Once the most common nesting duck on the refuge, the species has now dropped in rank to third or fourth. In the late 1940s about fifty thousand young were produced annually, while in recent years production has dropped to around two thousand. In addition, agricultural developments in southwest Idaho and northeast Oregon have attracted many Mallards which would normally have migrated through this area. This has been partially responsible for a decline in the number using the refuge in spring and autumn. During the 1980s, ten to fifteen thousand have usually been present at the peak of migration.

Spring migration is usually in progress by mid- to late February, as northeast-bound migrants arrive from California. Peak numbers occur in late March, with most migrants gone by mid-April. Among pairs that remain on the refuge to nest, egg laying begins in late March (earliest 29 March), with incubation beginning in earnest during late April. Average clutch size based on 84 nests was 8.1 eggs. Their nesting peak is in May, but young can sometimes be seen in late April. If a female loses her first clutch she will renest, explaining the presence of small young in July. A variety of nesting habitats are used. Nests are most often found among shrubs, grasses, and emergents, but have also been found in haystacks and trees. In late July, males from other nesting regions move onto the refuge to molt; peak numbers occur in early October with migrants leaving by mid-December. In some winters Mallards are common on the refuge, but generally they do not occur in large numbers. The warm-water springs at Double O usually have wintering Mallards and in some years the grainfields on the refuge support several hundred individuals.

Northern Pintail
Anas acuta

Abundant spring and autumn migrant; uncommon in summer and winter. The Northern Pintail is the most abundant waterfowl migrant in the Malheur-Harney Lakes Basin, with as many as one-quarter million present in the spring. In migration the species can be seen throughout the refuge, but the majority use the Double O-Malheur Lake migration corridor. The newly flooded meadows around Malheur Lake, Double O, and near Burns attract thousands of pintails in the spring, while areas of shallow water in Malheur and Harney lakes are most important in autumn. Most spring migrants are heading northeast to nesting areas in Montana and southern Canada after spending the winter in California's Central Valley. The species is one of the earliest spring migrants; in autumn the migration period is rather prolonged.

In spring, Northern Pintails usually appear in mid-February (earliest January 21, 1971), when ponds first begin to thaw and snow starts to melt. Spring migration is rapid with peak numbers in early to mid-March. Thereafter numbers decline and, except for the few pairs which remain to nest, all have migrated by early May. Usually fewer than four hundred pairs nest on the refuge. Unlike other ducks, pintails prefer short, open vegetation for nesting sites; therefore, predation rates are often high. Like the Mallard, pintails nest early: nesting is in progress by mid-April and usually peaks in May. The latest known initiation date was on June 16 (Foster 1985). Average clutch size is 7.5 (n = 24). Young hatch after about 23 days. If the first clutch is destroyed, most hens will renest and many young are still flightless in late July and August. When Malheur Lake is at normal levels, drake pintails begin congregating (particularly in east Malheur Lake) in early June. Many males are believed to have originated from nesting regions in Alaska, Canada, and the northern Great Plains states. Here, among dense emergent vegetation, birds molt into their eclipse plumage, remaining flightless for 3 to 4 weeks. Pintail numbers usually peak between 25 August and 10 September. By early December most migrants have left. Although uncommon in winter, pintails have been seen during all but one southern Blitzen Valley Christmas count. Highest counts were in 1962 (69), 1963 (143), 1969 (68), and 1975 (99). The highest refuge winter count was in 1963, when fifteen hundred were observed.

Blue-winged Teal
Anas discors

Uncommon in spring and summer; occasional in autumn; accidental in winter. The Blue-winged Teal is an uncommon nesting dabbler on the refuge. In summer, while in eclipsed plumage, the species cannot be safely identified from the abundant Cinnamon Teal, and female differentiation is difficult throughout the year. Therefore its true status in summer and autumn is imperfectly known. Weather conditions east of Oregon often dictate Blue-winged Teal numbers on Malheur NWR: the species usually increases on the refuge when drought persists in the northern plains states.

The average spring arrival is April 11, the earliest February 27 (1983). Most arrive paired and no spring peak has been noted. Usually no more than two hundred pairs are present during the nesting season. Nesting habitat is similar to that of the Cinnamon Teal, usually in moist zones in the ecotone between marshes and uplands. The autumn peak and departure dates are unknown; however, since the species generally avoids cold climatic conditions, the Blue-winged Teal likely migrates about the same time as the Cinnamon Teal. Although the species normally overwinters much further south than southeast Oregon, there are two winter records—one during the 1960 Christmas count and one on December 31, 1965. One individual banded at the refuge on July 27, 1961, was later recovered in April 1963 at Maracaibo Zulia, Venezuela.

Cinnamon Teal
Anas cyanoptera

Abundant in spring and summer; common in autumn; rare in winter. The Cinnamon Teal usually ranks either first or second in waterfowl abundance on Malheur NWR during the nesting season, and by May nearly all water bodies have pairs of Cinnamon Teal. It has an average arrival date of March 3, somewhat later than other duck species. The earliest record was on February 4 (1972). Like the Blue-winged Teal and Gadwall, the majority arrive paired and no migration peak has been detected. The earliest recorded nest initiation was on April 18 (1972); most nesting does not begin until mid-May. The latest nest initiation is in late June, and recently hatched young are often seen into August. Young are most evident in late June and July. Nesting habitat is in moist meadows; as water in the meadows recedes, broods are regularly seen in ditches adjacent to the Center Patrol Road. Most young have fledged by early September and begin migrating from the region shortly afterward. Males gather on Malheur and Harney lakes after mid-July and peak numbers are present from August 15 through 30. Most have left by mid-October, but a few sometimes linger into November.

There are a few winter records—1960 Christmas bird count (four); January 1, 1961 (two); December 23, 1962 (three); January 1, 1963 (one).

Most local Cinnamon Teals winter along Mexico's west coast. Malheur band return locations include Durango (one), Baja California (one), Sonora (one), Sinaloa (two), and Michoacan (one). All other returns have been from California as birds are migrating.

Northern Shoveler
Anas clypeata

Abundant in spring and autumn; common in summer; occasional in winter. During migration small groups of shovelers occur in bodies of shallow water throughout the refuge, while major concentrations occur on the larger ponds and lakes. Malheur, Boca, Derrick, and Harney lakes have had the greatest number in recent years. More than other dabbling ducks, the Northern Shoveler consumes large quantities of small aquatic invertebrates. When Harney Lake has favorable autumn water conditions and high invertebrate populations, shovelers can be the most abundant duck on the refuge. In the late 1950s, their numbers approached one-quarter million, feeding on the immense populations of crustaceans which were present in the lake at the time. Numbers have not been comparable since, as most shovelers now either bypass or rapidly migrate through the region.

Northern Shovelers arrive in late February or early March, and peak in mid- to late April. Most migrants have left by mid-May. Birds remaining on the refuge to nest vary annually, but usually five to seven hundred pairs are present during the summer. Nesting is in progress by early May; however, nest initiation dates range from March 25 through June 19 (Foster 1985). Based on 61 nests, average clutch size was 9.3 eggs. Male shovelers are considered the most territorial of dabbling ducks, and many are still defending the territory at the time of hatching. Young are regularly seen from June through July.

Autumn migrants begin arriving in mid- to late August, and peak numbers are present in early September. Most move from the region early, but a few are still present in mid-November. Small numbers of shovelers have been seen in winter where open water occurs. Greatest wintering numbers were recorded during Christmas counts in 1958 (69) and 1963 (24).

Gadwall
Anas strepera

Abundant in spring, summer, and autumn; uncommon in winter. The Gadwall is an abundant nesting species on the refuge. Most arrive in the spring as pairs, and few large flocks are seen. The species is the most difficult of the ducks to identify, as males do not have the bright nuptial plumage found in other species; but while somber in coloration, the males' gray and black attire is most attractive. The white speculum at the wing's trailing edge provides easy identification when birds fly. In the spring and summer, the species is seen in flooded meadows, canals, and ponds throughout the refuge; in the autumn many congregate on Malheur, Boca, and Derrick lakes, and on Unit 8 Pond.

The species begins arriving in April with the migration peak in early May. About two thousand pairs remain on the refuge to nest. Nesting is in progress from mid-May through late July. Gadwalls nest on dry sites in dense vegetation, often among greasewood stands. Average clutch size for 35 nests located on the refuge is 9.1 eggs. The hatching peak is in July, and young still unable to fly are regularly seen in early September. Males begin arriving on Malheur Lake to undergo their eclipse molt in mid-July. Accompanied by American Wigeons and American Coots, the majority of molting male Gadwalls spend their flightless days in the deeper portions of Malheur Lake, where they feed on filamentous algae and other submergent aquatic plants. Birds begin leaving in late August and early September, shortly after molt completion. The species again increases in late September as northern migrants move onto the refuge. Peak numbers occur in mid- to late October, and most have left by mid-November. Band return data indicate many Gadwalls migrate from the refuge southwest to California, while other locally banded birds migrate south through western Nevada to wintering areas in Sonora, Sinaloa, and Nayarite, Mexico. Wintering Gadwalls are usually found in Double O and the southern Blitzen Valley. The most seen in winter was 1,545 on January 1, 1964, but rarely do their numbers exceed one hundred.

Eurasian Wigeon
Anas penelope

Rare in spring, autumn, and winter. Several records for this Old World species have accumulated since it was first recorded on December 13-19, 1959. Shortly thereafter another was seen on January 26, 1960. Since these early observations, the species has been seen on numerous occasions at scattered localities throughout the refuge. Single individuals were seen on March 1, 1960; April 18, 1968; in April 1969, April 1976, and October 1976; on February 12, 1981; June 24, 1982; March 9-14, 1984; March 9, 1987; February 10, 1988; and April 4, 1988. Two Eurasian Wigeons were recorded on January 14, 1966; April 28, 1966; May 14, 1982; and May 23, 1987. The most observed at one time was five on April 2, 1966. The two individuals seen on May 14, 1982, appeared to be a mated pair. One bird which was banded on the refuge on April 18, 1968 was later shot near Gustine, California, on December 20, 1969.

American Wigeon
Anas americana

Abundant spring and autumn migrant; uncommon in summer and winter. During migration the American Wigeon is one of the common ducks on the refuge. In spring, the species can be seen on newly flooded meadows, but Malheur and Derrick lakes receive the most use. Wigeons often associate with American Coots on the larger ponds and lakes, where they commonly feed on submergent aquatic plants. The species also regularly grazes on new grass shoots, in a similar way to several species of geese.

Migrants first appear in mid-February and reach their peak in mid-April. Most have moved on to their Canadian parkland and Alaskan nesting regions by May 20. Usually between two and four hundred pairs remain on the refuge to nest. Pairs are widely scattered with the highest densities along streams and ponds bordered by dense willows, which appear to be their favored habitat. Nesting is in progress by late May with young being seen from mid-June through July. In late July, adult males from northern nesting areas begin arriving at Malheur Lake to molt. Peak numbers are usually present in late September and early October. Unlike other duck species, which concentrate in east Malheur Lake, American Wigeons use the extensive hardstem bulrush stands near the lake's center (when present). Most have left for wintering areas by early December. Band returns indicate the majority migrate southwest to California's Central Valley, with a minor number moving south through western Nevada. The species has been recorded during all but one Christmas count. Highest counts were in 1957 (243), 1958 (450), 1961 (350), 1963 (124), 1979 (142), and 1983 (117).

Canvasback
Aythya valisineria

Common in spring and autumn; uncommon in summer; occasional in winter. Overall, Canvasbacks have decreased over much of their range in recent years. Habitat losses in the northern Great Plains have been primarily responsible for the declines; in addition, Canvasbacks are the major host species for parasitic female Redheads (see below). Studies have shown lower nesting success for parasitized nests compared to those which were not parasitized. On Malheur NWR, the species is still common, particularly when submergent food plants are available and when Malheur Lake is in a productive state. Canvasbacks begin arriving in late February and the spring peak usually occurs in mid-April. Most migrants have left by early May. In early spring, the species associates with Tundra Swans, as swans keep water from freezing by their swimming and feeding activities. Canvasbacks also surface feed on vegetation which has been pulled from the substrate by the feeding swans. Malheur and Boca lakes and Krumbo Reservoir are important concentration areas, but small flocks are often seen on the smaller ponds and sloughs throughout the refuge. These same areas are also used by autumn migrants. Depending on habitat conditions, from one to eight hundred pairs nest on the refuge, with nest initiation from mid-April (earliest April 18) through mid-June. The species prefers hardstem bulrush for nesting sites, but nests have also been found in burreed and cattail. Wright's and Knox ponds, and Boca, Malheur, and Derrick lakes have been important nesting localities. Autumn migrants begin arriving in mid-September, and peak in mid- to late October. On October 2, 1968, E. McLaury observed the arrival of over four thousand Canvasbacks from the northeast. About two thousand landed on Malheur Lake, while the remainder continued southwest. Only three hundred remained on October 3. If sago pondweed is available the species will linger on Malheur Lake until it freezes. If food is lacking, Canvasbacks rapidly migrate from the refuge to San Pablo Bay, California, and other wintering regions. Most migrants have left by mid-December. The species has been recorded during eighteen Christmas counts, with highest counts in 1975 (108) and 1976 (75).

Redhead
Aythya americana

Abundant in spring, summer, and autumn; occasional in winter. The number of Redheads using the refuge varies annually, depending on the productivity of Malheur Lake. Generally, the species is the third most common breeding duck with two to three thousand pairs. In 1979 an estimated seven thousand pairs nested, making it the most abundant nesting duck. Most nesting occurs on Malheur Lake among bulrush stands when this vegetation is available.

Redheads have arrived as early as February 9 (1981), but usually do not appear until late February. Numbers slowly build and regularly peak just before nest initiation. Earliest nest initiation occurs in mid-May, reaching a peak in late May. Nests have been located in spikerush, Baltic rush, burreed, and cattail, but most are in hardstem bulrush. Average clutch size on Malheur NWR is 9.3 eggs, but since many Redhead females are nest parasites some eggs may have been contributed in this way. Redheads parasitize their own species; in addition, Redhead eggs have been found in Canvasback, Ruddy Duck, Mallard, Lesser Scaup, Northern Pintail, Cinnamon Teal, Northern Shoveler, Gadwall, American Bittern, and American Coot nests. Newly hatched young are seen from mid-June through mid-July. Adult Redheads are poor parents as there is no indication of males defending a territory, and females do not defend broods and often abandon their young. However, since most broods are produced in the deeper ponds and lakes, many survive without parental care. Fledging usually occurs in July. Adult males begin congregating in July, and Redheads peak in early August. Migration from the refuge is underway by August, and most have left by late October. Banding data indicate Redheads migrate from the refuge in a south or southeast direction, with direct recoveries from Utah, Texas, Arizona, Baja California, Sonora, and Sinaloa. Occasionally the species has been recorded on the refuge in winter. Usually only a few are present, but on January 4, 1959, one hundred were recorded.

Redheads have been recorded during eighteen Christmas counts, with the greatest number seen in 1975 (23).

Ring-necked Duck
Aythya collaris

Uncommon in spring and autumn; rare in summer; occasional in winter. The Ring-necked Duck reaches its greatest nesting densities in the closed boreal forest of Canada, with a few nesting in grassland habitats further south. Most migrate to the Atlantic coast and along the Mississippi River to the Gulf coast. West coast migrants make up a small percentage of the total population; however, as many as two thousand have been seen on Malheur Lake at one time.

The species is an early spring migrant, arriving in mid-February and peaking in March. The latest date was on May 24 (1971). Pairs rarely nest on Malheur NWR. A female with young was observed 4 miles south of Malheur Field Station in the summers of 1964 and 1965, providing the first Oregon nesting record (Marshall and Duebbert 1965). A nest was located at Double O on June 1, 1979, and R. Johnstone found a brood of two young on July 21, 1980, in Stubblefield Pond. I observed a territorial pair near Buena Vista in May 1986, but no nest or brood was located. These represent the only known refuge nesting records although a few pairs probably nest annually. The earliest autumn migrant was noted on August 24, 1974 (J. Wittenberger), but usually the species does not arrive until late September. Greater numbers migrate through the region in October, but the species does not peak until November. Most migrants have disappeared by early December. Ring-necked Ducks have been seen during 21 Christmas counts, with highest counts in 1963 (41), 1975 (93), 1981 (41), and 1983 (115).

The species is usually seen on the larger lakes and ponds throughout the refuge, but occasionally it appears in canals, ditches, and smaller ponds. Boca and Malheur lakes and Krumbo Reservoir are important resting and feeding areas when submergent aquatic food plants are available.

Greater Scaup
Aythya marila

Rare in spring and autumn. The Greater Scaup confines most summer activities to arctic and subarctic nesting regions, with the majority wintering along the Atlantic and Pacific coasts. The species primarily uses offshore migration routes and there are few inland Oregon records. The species has been seen on Malheur NWR on few occasions. Four males and three females were banded by P. DuMont between October 23, 1936, and November 19, 1937. On November 18, 1960, an immature male was collected, representing the first specimen for eastern Oregon (Kridler and Marshall 1962). Other records are of two males seen May 7-8, 1977 (D. DeSante); three males at Sod House Spring November 6, 1982 (M. Archie); and one male at Buena Vista Pond on March 18, 1984.

Bendire (1877) reported the Greater Scaup as a common migrant in the Malheur-Harney Lakes Basin. Either this was a case of mistaken identity, or the species has changed its migration patterns during the past century.

Lesser Scaup
Aythya affinis

Common spring and autumn migrant; uncommon in summer and winter. Lesser Scaups seen on the refuge are mostly migrants, with few remaining to nest. Major migration corridors for this species are east of Malheur; therefore, their numbers rarely exceed five thousand individuals. While Lesser Scaups are on the refuge, Malheur and Boca lakes and Krumbo Reservoir usually have the largest concentrations, but at the migration peak a few birds use smaller ponds throughout the refuge. Like other duck species, the Lesser Scaup arrives in mid- to late February. Peak period occurs in mid-April, and most have migrated by mid-May. Usually fifteen to eighty pairs remain to nest. Unlike other diving ducks, which place their nest over water, the Lesser Scaup prefers drier sites with nest placement on moist meadows, dry uplands, or islands. Nesting begins in late May, and young are present in late June and July. Southbound migrants appear in late August and are at their peak of abundance in mid- to late October. Most migrants have left by early December, but during mild autumns migrants will remain until after December. Banding data indicate most migrants are moving toward California's Central Valley; however, a few may move south, as there is one recovery from Sonora, Mexico. Lesser Scaups have been recorded during 23 Christmas counts, with highest counts in 1957 (45), 1962 (130), 1963 (67), and 1973 (47). About three hundred were on Malheur NWR on December 31, 1959, and in 1965 for the greatest winter numbers.

Oldsquaw
Clangula hyemalis

Accidental. This circumpolar species nests in the subarctic and arctic regions of Canada and Alaska, and winters primarily along the Atlantic and Pacific coasts. There are few inland Oregon records, but Oldsquaws have been recorded five times on the refuge. R. Erickson observed the first on January 28, 1954. The second bird was seen for several days before it was collected on November 17, 1956 (Marshall 1959). Other records were an immature collected on Malheur Lake on November 9, 1958; one found dead at headquarters on December 8, 1958; and one recorded during the 1960 Christmas count.

Surf Scoter
Melanitta perspicillata

Accidental in autumn. This sea duck has been recorded six times on the refuge. Sooter (1942) observed and subsequently collected a female Surf Scoter along 5-mile Road on

November 10, 1941. J. Scharff obtained the second record when he found a dead male at Benson Landing on December 16, 1943. Additional records include an immature male at the Narrows on October 15, 1981; a male on November 6, 1982 (M. Archie); a female at the Narrows on November 2, 1985 (M. Archie); and a female at Malheur Lake on October 17-18, 1987 (M. Denny).

White-winged Scoter
Melanitta fusca

Accidental in spring; occasional in autumn. The White-winged Scoter was first noted on April 6, 1942, when J. Scharff observed a group of three. Presently, this is the only spring record. Autumn records include single birds on October 13 and November 5, 1957; in autumn 1958 (no date given); on October 21, 1965; November 2, 1967; October 10, 1970; November 6, 1982 (M. Archie); and September 25, 1987 (P. Pickering).

All refuge records have been from Malheur Lake, and it is possible the White-winged Scoter migrates regularly through this region but uses isolated areas where chances of being seen are remote. Birds using Malheur NWR probably originate from the southern extremity of their nesting range in North Dakota and southern Canada.

Common Goldeneye
Bucephala clangula

Common in autumn, winter, and spring; accidental in summer. This species, which nests in tree cavities, is strictly a migrant or winter resident on the refuge, generally arriving in late autumn. The earliest record was on September 23 (1975), but usually the species is not seen until late October or November. Peak of autumn migration occurs in early December, and numbers decline after mid-December. Where water remains unfrozen, Common Goldeneyes can often be seen through the winter. The Blitzen River (between P Ranch and Page Springs) and Sod House and Double O springs provide favorable winter habitat. The species has been recorded during all but two Christmas counts. Highest counts were in 1957 (101), 1964 (495), 1979 (135), 1981 (108), 1982 (174), 1983 (150), 1984 (152), and 1987 (211). When ponds, lakes, and rivers become free of ice in February, Common Goldeneyes are usually the first duck to appear. Increasing numbers occur in mid-February, with peak numbers in March and early April. In spring, their elaborate courtship displays can sometimes be observed. These displays often occur at Krumbo Reservoir, but are likely anywhere the species concentrates. The last spring record was on May 18 (1963). The only summer record occurred on June 20, 1979, when an adult male was located. In North America, nesting distribution is confined to boreal coniferous forest; therefore, any Common Goldeneye seen on Malheur NWR in the summer months is far from its nearest nesting habitat and probably represents a sick or injured individual.

Barrow's Goldeneye
Bucephala islandica

Occasional in autumn and winter; rare to occasional in spring. C. Sooter was the first to observe the species on Malheur NWR, when he recorded an individual near Cole Island on November 1, 1942. Kridler and Marshall (1962) reported on the first specimen for southeast Oregon, when an immature was collected on November 18, 1960. Since then, the Barrow's Goldeneye has been recorded on several occasions between October 20 (1972) and April 28 (1987). Abundance peak is in December, January, and February, with individuals often being seen in the ice-free reaches of the Blitzen River near Page Springs. Twenty-three were seen in this area on December 18, 1986. Migrants are occasionally seen in spring and autumn on ponds and rivers throughout the refuge.

No Barrow's Goldeneyes have been banded on the refuge, and the origin of birds wintering here remains unknown. Since the species regularly nests in the Cascade Range of Oregon and Washington, individuals wintering on the refuge may originate from that region.

Bufflehead
Bucephala albeola

Common in spring and autumn; uncommon in winter; rare in summer. Buffleheads arrive in late February, peak in early to mid-April, and have left for their northern nesting regions by May 28. Migrants move through the refuge in small flocks and no large congregations have been noted. Usually the species is seen on the larger ponds and lakes throughout the refuge. On rare occasions, males can be seen performing their courtship displays in March and April. Marshall (1959) first reported on the Bufflehead summering at the refuge, as four or five individuals were seen on Boca Lake on May 28 and July 31, 1957. Since these dates, there have been several additional summer records. About fifty were present on July 2, 1965, and 25 were on Boca Lake on June 15, 1973, for the highest summer counts. Most summer records are probably subadults as it takes 2 years to reach sexual maturity; however, there have been summer records of males in adult plumage. The earliest autumn record was on September 22 (1964). The peak occurs in late October and most migrants have left by early December. In winter, the species has been recorded during all but two Christmas counts. Greatest numbers were seen in 1958 (61), 1973 (60), and 1983 (116). Where calm ice-free water is available, a few Buffleheads usually winter. Several usually winter on or near Sod House Spring; however, when Malheur Lake levels are high, few remain in the northern portion of the refuge.

In migration, Buffleheads are regularly seen on Boca, Derrick, and Malheur lakes, Knox and Krumbo ponds, and Krumbo Reservoir.

Hooded Merganser
Lophodytes cucullatus

Occasional in spring, winter, and autumn; accidental in summer. This cavity-nesting species is nowhere common on Malheur NWR, but those which are present inhabit the deeper lakes, ponds, and sloughs, and open water in the Blitzen River, feeding on small fish and invertebrates. The earliest autumn date was October 9 (1960), but in most years the species is not seen until November. Peak numbers occur in late November. Migrants in this region are most likely on their way to the Snake River in Idaho, a favored wintering locality. In winter, Hooded Mergansers have been seen during all but one Christmas count. Highest counts were in 1970 (43), 1974 (36), 1983 (35), 1984 (54), and 1987 (39). On December 31, 1965, an estimated two hundred were on the refuge for the greatest number recorded. A spring influx occurs in February, with the peak in early March. Late spring records occurred on April 22 in both 1961 and 1965.

A few pairs presently use artificial nestboxes about 60 miles north of headquarters, but no nesting has been noted on the refuge. However, G. Ivey found a dead juvenile female at Knox Pond on July 28, 1988. A brood containing two young was located in 1975 about 15 miles northwest of headquarters but this probably represented a family group which had moved down the Silvies River from north of Burns, where nestboxes have been placed.

Common Merganser
Mergus merganser

Common in spring and autumn; uncommon in summer; common to uncommon in winter. Common Mergansers, while on the refuge, are regularly seen on water bodies which contain adequate populations of food fish. In spring, the species is regularly encountered on the larger lakes and ponds, while in summer, canals, sloughs, and rivers are also used as feeding sites. In autumn, Common Mergansers are most common on Malheur and Harney lakes, but can also be seen on drying ponds and sloughs feeding on entrapped carp. Often during these drying periods the species is found associating with American White Pelicans. Once water becomes ice covered, Common Mergansers concentrate on fast-flowing open water and warm-water springs. Although the species is present throughout the year, greatest concentrations are usually found during autumn migration.

Common Mergansers arrive in mid-February and peak in late March and early April. Most migrants have moved northward by early May. The few pairs (five to twenty) which remain on or near the refuge to nest initiate nesting in April, but to date no nesting site has been located. Likely these females nest among boulders along the Blitzen River and in Mud and Bridge Creek canyons. Broods appear in May, particularly in the Blitzen River and in the East and West canals at the southern extremity of the refuge. Here, mayfly larvae are common and probably provide an important food source for the young. Autumn migrants appear in late September and peak numbers are present between late October and late November. The greatest concentration occurred on November 18, 1982, when 1,735 were counted on Harney Lake. Most migrants have left for warmer regions by mid-December; however, Common Mergansers regularly winter. The species has been recorded during all but two Christmas counts. Highest counts were in 1943 (40), 1958 (110), 1974 (77), and 1984 (65). On December 19, 1986, 759 were on Harney Lake for an extraordinary wintering concentration.

Red-breasted Merganser
Mergus serrator

Accidental. The Red-breasted Merganser is a recent addition to the Malheur NWR list. Off the refuge, one was recorded on November 23, 1976, at Dry Lake (about 6 miles east of the refuge), but the first refuge record did not occur until

October 10, 1983, when M. Archie observed a single bird near Double O. The next year, a second record occurred as three males appeared at Boca Lake on April 16, 1984.

Ruddy Duck
Oxyura jamaicensis

Abundant in spring, summer, and autumn; occasional in winter. The Ruddy Duck is a characteristic species of the deeper ponds, lakes, and sloughs on the refuge. During spring and autumn migration, concentrations of Ruddy Ducks can sometimes be seen on Malheur, Harney, Derrick, Boca, and Stinking lakes, Krumbo Reservoir, and Knox Pond.

Ruddy Ducks first appear in late February, but do not reach their peak of abundance until late April or early May. Migrants have left the refuge by May 20. In summer, Ruddy Ducks can be abundant, particularly if Malheur Lake is productive. Recent pair counts were over 2,500 in 1979 and 1980, with most in Malheur Lake. Other nesting localities include Boca and Derrick lakes, and Knox, Buena Vista, Warbler, and Wright's ponds. Nesting begins in mid-May and continues through June. Young, present in June and July, fledge in August and September. Males are often seen accompanying hens with young broods in June, but by July most males have deserted family groups, and by late July females also have usually abandoned the young. Like young Redheads, Ruddy Ducks are capable of surviving without parental care. In autumn, numbers increase in early August and peak between October 1 and November 10. If submergent food plants are available, many birds linger into November. An estimated fifty thousand were on the refuge November 8, 1959, but generally most have departed by late October. Large rafts regularly occur in Malheur Lake in both spring and autumn. These rafts consist almost entirely of Ruddy Ducks, and rarely do other duck species associate with these compact flocks. A few remain through the winter and have been recorded during all but six Christmas counts. The highest count was in 1983 (174). Usually ten to seventy birds winter on the refuge.

ORDER: FALCONIFORMES
FAMILY: CATHARTIDAE

Turkey Vulture
Cathartes aura

Common in spring, summer, and autumn; accidental in winter. One of the main attractions on Malheur NWR are the Turkey Vultures at P Ranch. In the afternoon, vultures congregate at the P Ranch Tower before flying to adjacent cottonwoods to roost. Over two hundred birds have been seen there during migration, but normally sixty to one hundred can be expected in summer. During migration in August and September, a few dark-headed juveniles can be seen, but generally the summer population seems to consist of subadults.

The earliest spring record was on February 18 (1976) and the average is March 16. Peak of spring migration occurs between April 5 and 25, and most migrants have left by May 15. It is doubtful any Turkey Vultures nest within the refuge boundaries, as nesting sites are located in rimrock shelters. A pair was found in a small cave near Page Springs on April 23, 1970; no eggs were present and the site was not rechecked to determine if nesting later occurred. In summer, adjacent to the refuge, pairs or singles are frequently seen near Buena Vista, Diamond Craters, Mud Creek Canyon (where a nest was located in 1978), and Page Springs. These areas contain ideal rimrock nesting habitat. Autumn migration gets underway in August, and peak numbers are present between September 1 and 15. Most have left for unknown wintering areas by October. The latest autumn record was on October 20 (1965). A single vulture was seen near P Ranch through

November 25, 1975, and a local rancher reported one bird had spent the winter of 1975-76 roosting in trees near Frenchglen Spring. This represents the only winter record.

FAMILY: ACCIPITRIDAE

Osprey
Pandion haliaetus

Occasional in spring; rare in autumn; accidental in summer. Ospreys visit Malheur NWR annually, but their numbers are limited. Normal habitat while here is the larger lakes and ponds where there is an abundance of fish. Ospreys have been regularly seen near headquarters, Benson Pond, the Narrows, Malheur Lake, and Double O. Nesting locations for birds which migrate through the Malheur-Harney Lakes Basin are presently unknown, but a few probably nest around lakes and reservoirs in the Blue Mountains. Wintering areas include southern Nevada, western Arizona, and western Mexico.

The earliest spring arrival was March 15 (1956) and the average is April 15. Most commonly, Ospreys are seen from April 20 to May 10. The latest record occurred on June 10 (1978). There are four summer records: June 20, 1971, headquarters; June 21, 1975, Benson Pond; one summered in 1982; and one was seen July 26, 1984. Historically, Ospreys were found nesting by C. Bendire in the 1870s near the north shore of Malheur Lake. The species is scarce in autumn, but it has been seen between August 10 (1984) and October 14 (1985). Most records fall between September 10 and 20.

Black-shouldered Kite
Elanus caeruleus

Accidental. The Black-shouldered Kite has recently undergone a range expansion into Oregon, but presently there is only one record for Malheur NWR. This record occurred on October 7, 1977, when a single bird was seen near headquarters where it remained through November 10. It was seen repeatedly within 2 miles of headquarters, feeding in mowed meadows (Littlefield 1980).

Bald Eagle
Haliaeetus leucocephalus

Common in spring; uncommon in autumn and winter. In the 1870s, the Bald Eagle was a nesting species in the Malheur-Harney Lakes Basin (Brewer 1875). C. Bendire found a nesting pair near the present town of Burns in 1875, but as a result of subsequent disturbance and habitat destruction nesting Bald Eagles disappeared shortly after European settlement. Today, the species is strictly a migrant and winter resident.

Bald Eagles usually arrive in October; an immature was seen near Boca Lake on August 31, 1981, for the earliest record. After late October, eagles are regularly seen around the larger lakes and ponds. Malheur Lake has the largest number, but Derrick and Boca lakes and Krumbo Reservoir support a few individuals. Numbers decline in early December, but a few winter on the refuge. Bald Eagles have been seen during all but six Christmas counts. Highest counts were in 1943 (eleven), 1980 (seventeen), and 1987 (ten). Bald Eagles can regularly be seen in the cottonwood tree near Cottonwood Pond. Most eagles in the northern portion of the refuge roost in tall pines along Rattlesnake Creek about 12 miles north of Malheur Lake, but the roost site for individuals wintering in the southern Blitzen Valley has not yet been located. Possibly large black cottonwoods along the Little Blitzen River (10 miles south of Page Springs) could be providing roosting sites. Bald Eagles increase with the late February arrival of waterfowl. Peak of spring migration occurs between March 5 and 30. Although regularly seen on the refuge at this time, most concentrate on the flooded meadows east and south of Burns. As waterfowl numbers decline, so do Bald Eagles. Nearly all have left by April 5, with the latest record on April 28 (1983). The majority of Bald Eagles seen here in migration likely winter near Klamath Falls, Oregon, with a minor contribution from eagles wintering in west-central Nevada and Lake Tahoe, California. Limited banding and radio-telemetry data have shown that at least some of these birds are on their way to nesting territories in Alberta and Saskatchewan, Canada.

Northern Harrier
Circus cyaneus

Abundant in spring, summer, and autumn; common in winter. Northern Harriers typically hunt a few feet above dense marshes, meadows, and grassy uplands throughout the refuge. Recent studies have shown that harriers, like owls, are capable of locating their prey by sound (Rice 1982), and this ability enables them to hunt successfully over dense vegetation. Refuge marsh and meadow habitat is largely abandoned in May and June, and individuals are seen hunting over the shrubland expanses surrounding the refuge. Harassment by territorial Red-winged Blackbirds is likely responsible for this habitat change and, once blackbirds have completed nesting, harriers again return to their preferred habitat, where they feed primarily on meadow voles and other small mammals. Occasionally the species takes larger prey such as jackrabbits, ducks, and American Coots; the larger female usually captures larger food items, while the smaller male concentrates his efforts on smaller prey. On rare occasions a female will be seen floating on water with extended wings, and after a short period swims to shore dragging a drowned coot behind. This is probably typical behavior when capturing all large aquatic prey.

Northern Harriers increase in numbers in late February and peak between March 15 and April 15. Transients have left the refuge by May 5. Nesting is in progress by late April and continues through June. Most nest in ungrazed dense

Northern Harrier

emergent stands; nests have also been located in weedy fields and among shrubs. Generally males have a single mate, but on occasion males with two or more nesting females have been found. Dark-backed, cinnamon-breasted, fledged young appear in July (earliest June 25, 1987). Autumn migration begins in late August and usually peaks between September 15 and October 15. Migrants have left the refuge by December 1. Northern Harriers are the second most commonly encountered wintering hawk. The species has been recorded during all Christmas counts, with highest counts in 1941 (56), 1968 (51), 1979 (68), 1980 (59), and 1982 (63).

Sharp-shinned Hawk
Accipiter striatus

Uncommon in spring and autumn; occasional in winter. Sharp-shinned Hawks are most often seen at headquarters, near or among willow thickets, and in junipers throughout the refuge. Individuals occur alone and if a good food source is available birds will remain at one location for several days. Small birds usually are inactive when they are present, as any bird from kinglet to quail size is a potential meal for this small woodland hawk. The species has been seen feeding on such species as California Quail, Mourning Dove, Varied Thrush, American Robin, Red-eyed Vireo, and House Sparrow at headquarters.

Sharp-shinned Hawks arrive early, with the earliest autumn record on August 3 (1981). Migration is at its peak between September 15 and October 15. Nearly all migrants have left by late November. The species has been recorded during ten Christmas counts. In 1973 and 1977, three were seen, but usually only one has been observed. In winter, individuals have occurred at headquarters where California Quail and House Sparrows provide ample food, and in junipers, particularly in Mud and Bridge Creek canyons. Sharp-shinned Hawks again increase on Malheur NWR in late February and peak of spring migration takes place in mid-April. Most have left the refuge by the second week of May. The latest spring record was on May 17 (1976).

Cooper's Hawk
Accipiter cooperii

Uncommon in autumn, winter, and spring; accidental in summer. This medium-sized accipiter is generally found at lower elevations than either the Sharp-shinned Hawk or Northern Goshawk. The species regularly nests on Steens Mountain and there is one summer record for Malheur NWR, a single bird at Malheur Field Station on June 20, 1971. In autumn, Cooper's Hawks arrive early (earliest August 9, 1981) and peak between September 20 and October 10. Most migrants have left the refuge by November 15 (latest December 1, 1970). The species has been recorded during eighteen Christmas counts. Greatest numbers were seen in 1941 (three), 1943 (three), 1957 (three), 1963 (five), 1978 (four), 1987 (four), and 1988 (four). Migrants begin returning in late February and are most evident in late March and early April. The latest spring record is May 28 (1974). While on the refuge, Cooper's Hawks prefer the trees at headquarters, willow thickets (particularly in south Blitzen Valley), and Mud and Bridge Creek canyons, but at the migration peak the species is to be expected anywhere on the refuge.

Northern Goshawk
Accipiter gentilis

Occasional in autumn, winter, and spring. Northern Goshawks commonly nest in the Blue Mountains, north of Burns, and occasionally on Steens Mountain. Those which move onto the lowlands in autumn spend much of their time in sagebrush expanses and along rimrocks, where they likely feed on Sage Grouse and Chukars. Often goshawks are seen near Jack Mountain and in the Warm Springs Mountains, northeast of Crane.

The species has been recorded between August 8 (1982) and April 29 (1980). Most records have occurred in January and February, and goshawks have been seen during six Christmas counts. All records have been of single birds except in 1967 and 1987 when two were observed. Willows and open sagebrush were the preferred habitats for the few individuals which have been recorded on the refuge, and most records have been of immatures.

Red-shouldered Hawk
Buteo lineatus

Accidental. On August 8, 1976, S. Herman located a Red-shouldered Hawk near the Blitzen River at P Ranch. S. Croghan and I returned with Herman to the same location on August 9. The individual was watched for some time as it attempted to roost in a cottonwood grove. Eight Red-tailed Hawks were also roosting and continually harassed the Red-shouldered Hawk. Eventually it was driven away and was last seen flying southwest over P Ranch (Littlefield 1980). In addition, M. Smith observed an adult and immature near Frenchglen on August 27, 1987. These represent the only refuge records; however, C. Bendire collected three eggs from two nests near Camp Harney (10 miles north of Malheur Lake) in April and May 1878. In addition, Bendire (1892) collected an adult female on April 17, 1878.

Broad-winged Hawk
Buteo platypterus

Accidental. A subadult Broad-winged Hawk was observed and photographed by T. Crabtree, J. Gilligan, O. Schmidt, and H. Nehls on May 30, 1983, as it flew low over headquarters. This represented the first Oregon record. A few Broad-winged Hawks winter in coastal southern California and this individual might have originated from there.

Swainson's Hawk
Buteo swainsoni

Uncommon in spring and autumn; occasional in summer; accidental in winter. The Swainson's Hawk has declined on Malheur NWR and in other southeast Oregon regions in recent years (Littlefield et al. 1984). Reasons for the decline have yet to be determined, but the species was once the most common nesting buteo. No Swainson's Hawk has nested on the refuge since 1979, when a pair unsuccessfully nested in a juniper tree south of Krumbo Valley.

Since Swainson's Hawks winter principally in Argentina, it is surprising the species arrives on the refuge so early in the spring. The average arrival is April 5 (earliest March 14, 1970). Peak of migration is between April 10 and 25, and most transients have moved on by May 10. In 1941, an estimated 150 individuals spent the summer on Malheur NWR; however, few pairs have nested since 1970. In the past, nest construction has been observed in late April, with some eggs being deposited by early May. Nest sites have been in willow thickets, junipers, and sagebrush. Fledged young are usually present in mid-July. Autumn migration begins early (July 15) and continues through September. Peak of autumn migration is between August 20 and September 10. The latest migrant was recorded on October 1 (1964), but Gabrielson and Jewett (1940) list the latest state record as October 25 (from Harney County). Unfortunately these authors did not list the location or year. A single bird was present on the refuge December 31 (1964), for a rare winter record. Individuals seen in the northern United States in winter are likely sick or injured, but the bird observed in 1964 appeared normal.

Red-tailed Hawk
Buteo jamaicensis

Common permanent resident. The Red-tailed Hawk is the most common nesting buteo on the refuge. Nesting sites vary and include large trees, rimrocks, and power-poles. Headquarters, P Ranch, and Sod House Ranch consistently have nesting pairs. Nests at these locations are usually used only for 1 year and Great Horned Owls take them over the next year. Most nesting pairs are permanent residents and are regularly seen on or near their territories throughout the year.

The spring influx occurs in late February and the species peaks between March 15 and April 15. Most migrants have left by May 15. Nest initiation is in progress by late March with egg laying in early April. Eggs hatch in early May to early June and young fledge in June and July. From ten to twenty pairs nest annually, and numbers appear to be increasing. Garter snakes are an important food source for several of the pairs, particularly during the nesting season. Autumn migration begins in September and peak numbers occur from mid-September to mid-October. Migrants have left the refuge by late November. Red-tailed Hawks have been recorded during all Christmas counts. Highest counts were in 1963 (40), 1970 (35), 1971 (81), 1979 (21), 1981 (17), and 1987 (21). In winter, the species frequents juniper-covered slopes west of Highway 205 between Buena Vista and Frenchglen.

Ferruginous Hawk
Buteo regalis

Occasional in spring, autumn, and winter; rare in summer. Like Swainson's Hawks, Ferruginous Hawks have declined on Malheur NWR since the 1940s. There are no recent nesting records on the refuge, while in 1941 an estimated ten pairs nested. Until 1955, the species was considered a permanent resident. Presently a few pairs still nest in the Malheur-Harney Lakes Basin. Pairs have recently nested between Crane and Buchanan, near Riley, east of Boca Lake, southeast of Princeton, 4 miles southeast of headquarters, and east of Burns.

The species is most common in spring in April and May. When Malheur Lake is at normal levels, Ferruginous Hawks are regularly seen west of headquarters feeding in alfalfa fields; recently the species has also been seen southeast of headquarters feeding in crested wheatgrass seedings. In autumn, Ferruginous Hawks have been recorded as early as July 26 (1978), but generally the species moves through the refuge from September through mid-November. Most autumn records are in October. As in spring, alfalfa fields are commonly used. After mid-November, the species declines, but it has been recorded during ten Christmas counts. All counts have been of single birds except in 1941 (three), 1949 (two), and 1975 (two).

Rough-legged hawk
Buteo lagopus

Abundant in autumn, winter, and spring. The Rough-legged Hawk nests in subarctic and arctic regions and moves onto the refuge in October, after which it becomes the most abundant wintering hawk. While here, its activities are centered on or near ungrazed meadows, where there is an abundance of meadow voles. Most wintering birds are of normal light plumage, but usually around 7 percent are dark phased. Identifiable individuals are seen year after year, indicating that many birds return to the same wintering area. Specific rough-legs have been seen using their same refuge wintering localities for at least 7 years.

The earliest autumn record occurred on September 25 (1985). The species becomes abundant in November, with peak numbers in late November and early December. Rough-legged Hawks have been recorded during all Christmas counts, with highest counts in 1941 (101), 1943 (124), 1963 (84), 1978 (86), and 1980 (83). On a few Christmas counts, Malheur NWR has recorded the greatest number in North America, indicating the abundance of this species in some years. In spring, Rough-legged Hawk numbers appear to be influenced by weather. In mild springs, birds return north early, while in colder springs migration is delayed. Usually peak numbers occur between April 1 and 20. The latest spring record was on May 11 (1978).

Golden Eagle
Aquila chrysaetos

Common permanent resident. Golden Eagle pairs remain in the Malheur-Harney Lakes Basin throughout the year, and the nesting population has remained relatively stable the past two decades. Electrocution on power-poles continues to kill many annually, but the most important limiting factor is probably food supply. In years of low jackrabbit numbers, few Golden Eagles nest. In 1973 and 1974, only four of 23 pairs were known to have nested. All pairs nested in 1976 after rabbit numbers had increased. In 1984, again a year of low rabbit densities, only two pairs nested.

If food is available, pairs return to their nesting territories in January and February. Most nest on rimrocks, but one pair has nested on a haystack north of Malheur Lake and another in a juniper northwest of the refuge. Only one pair nests within the refuge boundary, but thirteen pairs nest on adjacent rimrocks. The earliest nesting record was February 26 (1971) when one egg was found in a nest near Harney Lake. The nest contained two eggs on February 28. Nearly all eggs are laid in March and hatch from mid-April through early May. Fledged young have been seen in late June, but usually are not recorded until July. In August, many Golden Eagles move to favorable hunting areas (e.g., Steens Mountain) where there is an abundance of ground squirrels. These birds move back to the lowlands in September and remain through the winter if food is available. Thompson et al. (1984) have reviewed the nesting history and present status of the species in the Malheur-Harney Lakes Basin.

FAMILY: FALCONIDAE

American Kestrel
Falco sparverius

Uncommon in spring, summer, and autumn; occasional in winter. Though fairly common in other regions of Oregon, the American Kestrel is usually an uncommon nester on the refuge, and even in migration the species is widely scattered. Lack of large trees for nesting cavities probably accounts in part for their low densities here. In past years, several nests have been found in rimrocks and in buildings; three pairs have nested in attics at Malheur Field Station. Many former nesting sites are presently occupied by European Starlings. In the mid-1980s there were from ten to fifteen pairs nesting on the refuge.

In spring, kestrels increase in late March and reach their peak from April 1 to 25. Most migrants have departed by May 5. A few pairs remain to nest. Pairs have nested at headquarters, Buena Vista, Page Springs, P Ranch, Malheur Field Station, and Double O. Nesting is in progress by early May and continues through the month, with young hatching in June and fledging in July or early August. In autumn, the peak occurs between August 20 and September 15, but most migrants bypass the refuge and in some years move to Steens Mountain and the Warm Springs Mountains. Over one hundred were seen on Steens Mountain on September 4, 1971 (W. Anderson). Most transients have left Malheur NWR by November 1. The species has been recorded during all but six Christmas counts. Highest counts were in 1977 (eight), 1979 (seven), 1980 (seven), 1981 (twelve), and 1988 (seven). In recent years, Buena Vista, headquarters, Frenchglen, Malheur Field Station, and P Ranch have been favored wintering locations.

Merlin
Falco columbarius

Occasional in spring and autumn. The Merlin has been known to nest in Oregon, but there are no known nesting records for Harney County since Bendire (1892) took eggs near Camp Harney on April 20, 1876. The species has been recorded in spring from March 18 (1983) through May 2 (1966), with most records from April 11 to 27. Merlins are more common in autumn. Willett (1919) listed two taken near Malheur Lake in August, while others have been seen between August 26 (1980) and November 7 (1987). Although Harney County is well within the winter range for this species no records exist from early November through mid-March.

Peregrine Falcon
Falco peregrinus

Rare. The Peregrine Falcon is presently the only federally listed endangered avian species which occurs on the refuge. Bendire (1877) considered it rare in the Harney Valley, but did collect a three egg set from a basaltic cliff near Malheur Lake on April 24, 1877 (Bendire 1892). No known nesting has occurred in the lowlands since that date. Observations have declined during the past twenty years. Up until the early 1970s it was not uncommon to see six or seven individuals annually during migration, but presently one appears about every 3 years.

The majority of spring records have been in March and April, with the latest record on May 16 (1971). Like Bald Eagles, peregrines are more likely to be seen at the peak of waterfowl migration. Summer records are of single birds seen on June 11, 1969 (Malheur Lake); July 20, 1977 (Stinking Lake); and July 9, 1979 (1 mile east of headquarters). Most recent records have been in autumn. When Malheur Lake is at normal levels, the species concentrates along the eastern shore where it feeds on molting, sick, or weak waterfowl and shorebirds. The earliest autumn record occurred on August 28 (1975), and migrants have left the area by late November. Peregrine Falcons have been recorded on seven Christmas counts, the last in 1975. All have been of single birds except for two seen on the 1944 count.

Prairie Falcon
Falco mexicanus

Uncommon permanent resident. Bendire (1877) listed the Prairie Falcon as common in the Harney Valley in the 1870s, and Gabrielson and Jewett (1940) reported it as common in eastern Oregon. An estimated 35 individuals resided at Malheur NWR from May through June 1940, but since these early reports the species has declined in the area. A few pairs still nest on or adjacent to the refuge and individuals are seen regularly throughout the year, but numbers do not compare with those from the past. Agricultural areas, rimrocks, sagebrush uplands, and mudflats are preferred feeding sites, and rimrocks provide nesting platforms.

In spring, a small influx occurs between March 15 and April 15. Eggs have been found as early as March 27, but generally nesting does not begin until mid-April. Young usually fledge in late June and early July. Prairie Falcons are more common in autumn as fledged young and migrants join with resident pairs. The species can be seen throughout the refuge from mid-August through November. Grainfields attract Prairie Falcons, particularly when large concentrations of blackbirds are present. Peak numbers occur from August 20 through October 25. Individuals are usually seen alone and have been recorded during all but seven Christmas counts. Five birds were recorded on the 1983 count for the highest number.

ORDER: GALLIFORMES
FAMILY: PHASIANIDAE

Gray Partridge
Perdix perdix

Rare permanent resident. The Gray Partridge was once a common resident on the refuge, but there have been few recent records. In the 1930s and 1940s Gray Partridges were frequently seen, but a reduction in refuge grain farming, which is an important habitat component, resulted in their virtual disappearance. By 1957, thirty to fifty birds were present, and in 1959 this number had been further reduced to ten to thirty individuals. Four were observed on July 4, 1967, and six on November 13, 1970. These were the last records until B. Ehlers found two birds south of refuge headquarters on February 27, 1986, and I saw two near Boca Lake on September 21, 1987.

A few still occur elsewhere in the Malheur-Harn Basin. There have been recent records south of B and Princeton, Wright's Point, and other locales. T cent agricultural developments are providing a necessary habitat component for this European species, and at the present time the Gray Partridge appears to be increasing.

Chukar
Alectoris chukar

Common permanent resident in suitable habitat. Since Chukars were first introduced into the Malheur-Harney Lakes Basin in 1952 and 1953, they have increased in numbers and are now common to abundant among the rimrocks and rocky slopes throughout the county. This Asian species is regularly found west of Highway 205 from Buena Vista to Frenchglen, near Page Springs, in Mud and Bridge Creek canyons, and among rimrocks at Double O and Krumbo Reservoir. Chukars have also recently established on Rattlesnake Butte and Diamond Craters.

No information is available on nesting chronology on Malheur NWR as no nest has ever been located. Nesting habitat is limited and is confined to Mud and Bridge creeks, Page Springs, and Rattlesnake Butte. Often in the hot months of July and August individuals can be seen along Highway 205 from Buena Vista to Frenchglen as birds move from dry rocky slopes down to the West Canal for water. Chukars also occasionally appear away from their normal habitat, as was the case when five and thirty were seen at refuge headquarters on January 30, 1971, and in January 1977, respectively.

Ring-necked Pheasant
Phasianus colchicus

Common permanent resident. Ring-necked Pheasants were first introduced into the Malheur-Harney Lake Basin in 1913, with additional releases in 1936, on November 25,

1939, and on September 12, 1940. Like other transplants in the United States, pheasants responded by rapidly increasing only to decline a few years later. After the last introductions, 506 pheasants were recorded during the 1941 Christmas count. By 1960, 172 were reported from the same area and in 1970 numbers had dropped to 98. Although 185 Ring-necked Pheasants were seen in the southern Blitzen Valley on December 18, 1986, their numbers today are nothing to compare with those from the past.

In February, males become aggressive and by April, as the nesting season approaches, male to male conflicts are common. Nesting begins in mid-May and continues into July. Generally broods are most evident in June, but recently hatched chicks have been seen as late as July 19 (1974). Late broods probably represent renesting efforts after the first clutch has been destroyed. The species becomes gregarious after the nesting season and remains in flocks through the winter. Most flocks remain sexually segregated from December through February.

Ruffed Grouse
Bonasa umbellus

Unsuccessfully introduced. Ruffed Grouse were introduced near P Ranch in 1936, but all apparently died during the severe winter of 1936-37. This species is still common north of Burns along streams which have adequate riparian habitat.

Sage Grouse
Centrocercus urophasianus

Uncommon spring, summer, and autumn; rare in winter. Sage Grouse have declined on Malheur NWR since the 1940s. Formerly about 100 individuals were regularly seen east of P Ranch, and an estimated 300 to 350 were on the refuge in 1941. Small groups still occasionally occur in summer at Double O; usually these groups do not exceed fifteen birds and more commonly number less than six. These consist primarily of family groups which have moved onto the refuge from the surrounding sagebrush expanses. In recent years, few grouse have been seen near P Ranch, but there are several recent records north of Buena Vista along the Center Patrol Road. Three factors have probably contributed to their decrease. First, increased nest predation by coyotes and Common Ravens has reduced the overall population. Second, livestock grazing and extensive crested wheatgrass seedings have resulted in loss of or damage to suitable habitat. Lastly, new cattle-watering developments on BLM lands now make it unnecessary for birds to move to refuge wetlands in late summer. "Strutting" grounds or leks occur within 3 miles of Malheur NWR, but generally most are at greater distances. On some neighboring grounds their numbers have decreased, while on others they have increased.

Sage Grouse begin moving onto the refuge in late May, remain through August, and usually move back into the surrounding uplands in September. Single Sage Grouse were observed on December 18, 1982, and December 17, 1984, representing the first winter records since the species was recorded during the 1944 Christmas count.

California Quail
Callipepla californica

Abundant permanent resident. I have been unable to determine when California Quail were first transplanted into the Harney Basin, but likely the first introduction was about 1914 when extensive releases occurred throughout the state. The local population was virtually extirpated in the severe winter of 1936-37, but forty birds were reintroduced in 1940 and the species was successfully reestablished.

California Quail have been recorded during all Christmas counts with the greatest numbers seen in 1958 (272), 1963

(286), 1965 (210), 1969 (214), and 1971 (207). Flocks of over eight hundred have been observed in winter, but as the nesting season approaches flock sizes diminish as pairs disperse to favorable nesting sites. The species nests over an extended period, and newly hatched broods have been seen from June 1 to August 26. Females lay large clutches and it is not uncommon to find nests containing as many as sixteen eggs. Broods often combine and occasionally twenty to thirty young will be seen accompanying an adult pair. California Quail associate with brushy tangles throughout the refuge, but are particularly common at headquarters, Buena Vista, Malheur Field Station, Page Springs, and along Mud Creek.

Mountain Quail
Oreortyx pictus

Rare permanent resident. Although the Mountain Quail has not been recorded on the refuge, it has been observed within half a mile, in Krumbo, Bridge, and Mud Creek canyons, and west of Highway 205 north of Frenchglen. Several were seen in the canyons during the winter of 1970-71 (E. McLaury, R. Toltzman), and W. Anderson located a calling male on the juniper-covered slopes west of Highway 205 near Krumbo Road on May 23, 1971. During severe, snowy winters the species should be looked for on the refuge, particularly near the East Canal from Page Springs to Bridge Creek.

ORDER: GRUIFORMES
FAMILY: GRUIDAE

Greater Sandhill Crane
Grus canadensis tabida

Abundant in spring, summer, and autumn; accidental in winter. The largest segment of the Central Valley population of Greater Sandhill Cranes nest on the refuge, with 181 pairs

in 1986. Pairs usually establish lifelong bonds, return annually to the same territory, and nest throughout the refuge
wherever suitable habitat is available. Nesting sites here are
usually among dense emergent vegetation where both pair
members construct the nest and share incubational duties.
All cranes that nest at the Malheur NWR winter in the California Central Valley, with the majority wintering about 30 miles
south of Sacramento.

The subspecies arrives early (average February 18), with
the earliest spring record on February 7 (1959). Peak of
migration occurs in late March and most transients have left
by early May. Nesting begins in early April and peak of nest
initiation is in late April. Generally, females lay two eggs
which hatch after 30 days. Young are present from early May
through early August. Greater Sandhill Cranes concentrate
at favorable feeding and roosting areas in autumn. Buena
Vista and East Grain Camp are traditional sites. In late July,
numbers increase and by late September or early October
2,500 to 3,000 birds can sometimes be found on the refuge.
Migration from Malheur NWR begins in late September and,
depending on weather, disturbance, roost site conditions, or
food supplies, many have left by mid-October. In some years
cranes remain well into November and there are three December records. A single bird was seen on December 11,
1964, and another on December 31, 1961. Four remained
through December 15, 1977. There are two winter records
(single birds wintered in 1980-81 and 1982-83).

Lesser Sandhill Crane
Grus canadensis canadensis

Uncommon in spring and autumn. Lesser Sandhill Cranes
congregate north of Malheur NWR in the meadows east and
south of Burns in March and April. Numbers sometimes peak
at over ten thousand in April. Few migrate through the
Blitzen Valley, with most migrating west of Double O. These
cranes can be separated from the Greater Sandhill Crane by

their smaller size, shorter bill, darker coloration, and pronounced forehead.

The subspecies usually arrives the first week of March (earliest February 16, 1983), and peaks in early April. Most have left for their southwestern Alaska nesting regions by early May. They generally move through the refuge rapidly, but on occasion groups can be seen flying over, loafing, or feeding in meadows and grainfields in the Blitzen Valley and Double O. In autumn, among the large flocks of greaters, a few lessers can be seen on the grainfields near Buena Vista and other scattered localities throughout the refuge. Lesser Sandhill Cranes are usually present from mid-September through mid-October. During 1980-81, one remained with a Greater Sandhill Crane in the Blitzen Valley for the only winter record. Lessers which migrate through this region winter from near Stockton, California, south through the California Central Valley. Greatest concentrations occur near Merced, California.

FAMILY: RALLIDAE

Black Rail
Laterallus jamaicensis

Accidental. The Black Rail is included on the refuge list on the basis of reports by C. Bendire from the 1870s. He observed a single bird on April 16 near Malheur Lake (Brewer 1875), and the species was seen later on two occasions ". . . in the swamps near Malheur Lake, where it unquestionably breeds" (Bendire 1877). There have been no confirmed reports from Malheur NWR since this time.

Virginia Rail
Rallus limicola

Common in spring, summer, and autumn; accidental in winter. Like other members of its family, the Virginia Rail is elusive and difficult to observe, preferring dense emergent stands, primarily hardstem bulrush. When at normal levels, Malheur Lake supports the majority of refuge Virginia Rails, but any extensive bulrush stand usually has its complement. Their presence is readily determined by the nasal "wank wank wank" calls which can often be heard at Wright's Pond, between Frenchglen and P Ranch, at Double O, and elsewhere on the refuge where there are extensive emergent stands.

Average arrival in spring is April 22, with the earliest on March 12 (1970). The peak of spring migration occurs between April 25 and May 5. Nesting is in progress in mid-May and young can be seen well into August. Nests are difficult to locate and I have little information on nesting chronology. One nest examined near Double O by C. Foster contained ten eggs on May 17, 1980. This nest was unusual in that it was on dry land, among creeping wildrye. Generally nests on Malheur NWR are in emergents, on wetland sites. Autumn migration begins in early August and peaks in late August. Most have left the refuge by late September. The latest record was at Malheur Lake on November 1 (1973). A few birds probably winter around open springs which contain dense emergent stands. Two were heard calling at Stinking Lake Spring on November 20, 1975, and these birds could have wintered. The only definite winter records were single birds near Page Springs on December 16, 1978 (E. Alfstad, B. Ehlers, J. Cornely), and December 18, 1986 (B. Ehlers).

Sora
Porzana carolina

Abundant in spring, summer, and autumn; accidental in winter. The elusive behavior of this species gives the impression that it is uncommon on Malheur NWR, but to realize its true abundance one has to wade the flooded meadows and marshes. Soras prefer wet meadows, but are regularly found in emergent vegetation, especially cattails, where their descending "whinny" calls can be heard frequently.

The earliest spring record was on April 4 (1979), and the average arrival is April 23. Peak of migration is from May 5 through 15. Migrants leave the refuge shortly after the peak period. Nesting usually is in progress by early May and peaks during the last half of May. For eight nests located near Double O average clutch size was 10.6 eggs (Foster 1985). As for other members of its tribe, incubation begins with the first egg laid; therefore, as young hatch they are cared for by the nonincubating bird while the other member continues to incubate the remaining eggs. Young are present from late May through early August. Autumn migration starts in late August, and peaks between September 1 and 15. Most have left by mid-October, but the latest record was on November 8 (1972). Single birds were seen on January 9, 1970, near Double O and December 10, 1986 near headquarters (G. Ivey), representing the only winter records.

Common Moorhen
Gallinula chloropus

Accidental. The Common Moorhen has been recorded four times on Malheur NWR. F. Zeillemaker, with members of the Corvallis Audubon Society, recorded the first on Cole Island on May 20, 1972. The second observation was obtained near the same location on May 22-23, 1981. The last records occurred from May 12 through 16, 1982, on Malheur Lake near headquarters and May 1984 (J. Beatty) at Buena Vista Pond. Since Malheur Lake has increased in both size and depth no additional observations have occurred there.

American Coot
Fulica americana

Abundant in spring, summer, and autumn; uncommon in winter. The American Coot can at times be the most abundant bird on the refuge, numbering up to 500,000 in autumn migration. Many pairs remain through the nesting season,

American Coot

occupying the deeper, open ponds and marshes in the Blitzen Valley and Double O. However, their center of abundance is in Malheur Lake, when it is at normal levels. Pairs mate for life and both birds participate in incubation with males doing the majority of the incubating. Indeterminate egg layers, coots have been known to lay 56 eggs in a season; therefore, the species is an important member of the wetland community, acting as a predator "buffer." Egg predation rates decline for other species once coots start to nest.

In spring, the species arrives early (mid-February), but peak numbers are not present until mid-April. Spring migrants have left the refuge by mid-May. Nesting begins in late April and reaches the peak in May. Incubation begins with the first egg and young hatch at 1-day intervals. While the male continues to incubate, the female tends the first young. Most young are hatched in June, but a few may be observed as early as May, and newly hatched young have also been observed well into July. The dark-downed, red-crowned chicks are regularly seen in the ditches and ponds, particularly adjacent to the Center Patrol Road. Chicks are usually abandoned before fledged as adults move to larger water bodies (especially Malheur Lake) before migrating. In August, a large percentage of coots seen along the Center Patrol Road are young. Migration begins in September and peaks between September 20 and October 10. Many remain until the lakes start to freeze, and then migrate rapidly from the refuge. In mild winters, many remain in the area. Coots have been seen during all but two Christmas counts. During the 1958 Christmas count, 1,230 individuals were recorded. Excluding 1958, highest counts were in 1963 (269), 1969 (106), and 1983 (102).

ORDER: CHARADRIIFORMES
FAMILY: CHARADRIIDAE

Semipalmated Plover
Charadrius semipalmatus

Uncommon in spring and autumn; accidental in summer. Kridler and Marshall (1962) were the first to record the Semipalmated Plover on the refuge, collecting one from a flock of five on May 4, 1959. This small plover nests primarily in the arctic-boreal regions, wintering on the west coast from San Francisco, California, south to Chile. Birds seen on the refuge are perhaps using an inland migration route through the western Great Basin to and from Salton Sea, California, and the Gulf of California. The species appears to be increasing on Malheur NWR. Where suitable mudflats and rocky shorelines occur, Semipalmated Plovers can usually be seen, particularly in autumn. Stinking and Harney lakes have been important use areas in the past. During the high-water periods of Malheur Lake, the species occurred regularly along the exposed portions of Sod House Lane, west of headquarters.

Semipalmated Plovers have been seen in spring between April 24 and May 30, with most records from May 1 to 15. Amazingly, G. Ivey found one pair nesting at Stinking Lake in 1987 and a flightless young was banded on July 16, representing one of the few nesting records for the continental United States. In autumn, the species returns early. The earliest autumn record was on July 10 (1982), and peak period of passage is between August 1 and 15. The latest autumn record was October 14 (1985).

Snowy Plover
Charadrius alexandrinus

Uncommon in spring, summer, and autumn. As in other regions of the Great Basin, on Malheur NWR the Snowy Plover inhabits barren alkali flats. This small plover is the most common nesting shorebird at Harney and Stinking lakes, but its cryptic light plumage blends well with the white alkaline soils, making the species appear less common than it really is. About four hundred individuals used the refuge in 1980 (primarily Harney Lake, S. Herman), but high water inundated much of their habitat after 1981.

Snowy Plover

The earliest spring Snowy Plover record was February 27 (1968), but the average arrival is not until April 26. Cryptic coloration and lack of observers likely account for the late average arrival. If Harney Lake were consistently surveyed in February and March the average date would certainly be much earlier. Nesting begins in May and continues into July. A nest with three eggs was located on May 14, 1967, and an adult with three young was seen on July 17, 1973. At Harney Lake, nests are usually placed among pebbles near the south shore. If the lake is dry, adults lead the newly hatched chicks to one of several freshwater springs one-quarter to a half mile from their nesting sites. In addition to Harney and Stinking lakes, the species has also been found in summer near Cole Island in southeast Malheur Lake. Little information is available on autumn migration. The late autumn record was on September 6 (1971) when ten were seen at Stinking Lake.

Killdeer
Charadrius vociferus

Common in spring, summer, and autumn; occasional in winter. The species commonly nests throughout the refuge on roads, dikes, and mud flats, often some distance from water. Its noisy, persistent calls make the Killdeer a conspicuous species during the nesting season. In addition, males perform a butterfly flight display when on territory, and these displays are particularly evident at headquarters in April. Both male and female incubate, and when disturbed will feign injury often within a few feet of their nest or young. Most pairs which nest on Malheur NWR appear to produce two broods annually and flightless young are seen well into July.

The species is the first shorebird to arrive in spring, appearing in mid-February (earliest January 31, 1971). Peak of migration occurs in mid-March, but flocks can be seen in late February. A few pairs initiate nesting in early April and one nest with four eggs was located on July 5, 1961. Although pairs nest on well-traveled roads, few are destroyed by vehicles; only one of eight such nests examined in 1973 was lost because of an automobile. Birds begin leaving the refuge in mid-July, with peak numbers present in late August and early September. Most have left for warmer climates by the end of November (75 at Boca Lake on November 21, 1986, were exceptional), but a few remain on the refuge through the winter. Individuals have been recorded during most Christmas counts, with the highest totals in 1964 (six), 1970 (nine), and 1980 (eight). During winter, birds inhabit open springs and ice-free waters along the Blitzen River.

Lesser Golden-Plover
Pluvialis dominica

Rare spring and autumn migrant. Lesser Golden-Plovers nest in tundra regions of northern Canada and Alaska, wintering primarily in the Southern Hemisphere. The majority use oceanic migration routes that are far removed from Malheur NWR, and thus there are few records.

Kridler and Marshall (1962) first reported on the Lesser Golden-Plover from the refuge. D. Marshall collected one at Malheur Lake on September 7, 1959, and observed another in the Blitzen Valley on August 24, 1959. P. DuMont reported seeing the species on May 28, 1959. The other refuge records are one seen at the Narrows on May 8, 1967; one 2 miles southwest of headquarters on May 23, 1967; one at Double O on September 19, 1983 (M. Archie); one near Cole Island on September 28, 1983; and one 2 miles southwest of headquarters on November 4, 1987.

Black-bellied Plover
Pluvialis squatarola

Uncommon spring and autumn migrant. Black-bellied Plovers nest in the far north from Baffin Island west to northwest Alaska. Most are coastal migrants, but a few migrate inland. Birds seen on Malheur NWR are probably using an inland route to and from wintering areas in the Gulf of California. In autumn and winter, the only black plumage visible is located in the wing pit which can only be seen when the bird flies. Even in spring, many plovers which are seen on the refuge have not attained their full breeding attire.

The earliest spring arrival was April 9 (1972); the latest record was May 24 (1970, 1982). Migration peak occurs in mid-May. The earliest autumn arrival was June 30 (1973); the latest record was November 7 (1987). Peak of autumn migration is usually in mid-September. While here, the species usually occurs in groups of two to five, with the highest numbers of fifteen recorded October 2, 1957, and 21 on November 7, 1987. The Black-bellied Plover is most often seen on Stinking Lake; however, the species has been observed throughout the refuge wherever suitable wetland habitat is available.

FAMILY: SCOLOPACIDAE

Greater Yellowlegs
Tringa melanoleuca

Common in spring and autumn; rare in winter. The Greater Yellowlegs is one of the earliest shorebirds to arrive in both spring and autumn. While on Malheur NWR, the species is commonly seen feeding in shallow water and on mudflats at scattered localities. In autumn, Malheur and Stinking lakes have the largest concentrations, but nowhere is the species found in large numbers.

The earliest spring record was February 27 (1964), and the average arrival is March 19. Peak of migration is from April 1 to 15, with the latest spring observation on June 2 (1970). Greater Yellowlegs return from their northern muskeg nesting areas early and linger well into autumn. The earliest record was June 21 (1969), peak is between September 1 and 25, and the latest autumn observation was November 25

(1976). The species has been seen rarely in winter. One was sighted on January 22, 1963; four on December 31, 1964; two wintered at Hughett Spring in 1974-75; and one was observed by J. Lemos and M. St. Louis at Harney Lake Hot Spring on December 17, 1984.

Lesser Yellowlegs
Tringa flavipes

Occasional in spring; uncommon in autumn. The major migration route for Lesser Yellowlegs lies east of the Rocky Mountains through the Great Plains states; however, a few migrants do pass through eastern Oregon. It is sometimes seen in spring, but more records exist from autumn. Records are from the entire refuge, but Double O, Buena Vista Pond and, when lake levels are normal, Malheur and Harney lakes are important use areas.

Of the few birds which migrate through Malheur NWR in spring, most are seen between April 15 and 30. The earliest record is March 29 and the latest May 9 (both 1972). In autumn, the species has arrived as early as June 22 (1940), but the peak is not until August. A few linger through September, and the latest record was November 7 (1987). The species has not been recorded in winter.

Solitary Sandpiper
Tringa solitaria

Occasional spring and autumn migrant. The Solitary Sandpiper, as its name implies, is usually seen alone, feeding along pond margins and streams throughout the refuge. The species does not migrate in flocks, but where favorable habitat is found several widely spaced birds can often be seen. Such was the case when six were observed at Dredger Pond on August 17, 1977. The species nests in the boreal forest of Canada and Alaska, and is unique among North American shorebirds, nesting in the old tree nests of American Robins, waxwings, Gray Jays, and Rusty Blackbirds.

In spring, Solitary Sandpipers have been recorded from April 25 (1942) through May 30 (1987). Records are so scanty that no spring peak has been noted. The species has been seen from July 31 (1979) through September 20 (1985) in autumn, with most records occurring during the last half of August.

Willet
Catoptrophorus semipalmatus

Common in spring, summer, and autumn. Within the Malheur-Harney Lakes Basin, the Willet reaches its greatest abundance on the meadows south and east of Burns. However, the species does occur regularly at some locations on Malheur NWR. Double O, Wright's Pond, north of Buena Vista, and Malheur Field Station all support nesting pairs, and in late June birds begin congregating on favorable mudflats, particularly at Malheur, Harney, and Stinking lakes. At Stinking Lake, their numbers have exceeded three thousand in mid-July. In April and May, Willets are frequently seen perched on wooden posts along the Center Patrol Road. Also at this time, territorial flights are evident as birds dive, displaying striking black and white wings and giving their familiar "pill-will-willet" calls.

The species arrives on the average spring date of April 12 (earliest March 21, 1958), and peaks between April 15 and 30. Most spring transients have left the refuge by May 10. Resident pairs are on territory by late April. Nesting is in progress in May (earliest April 30), and young fledge in late June and early July. Nesting pairs regularly abandon their unfledged young and move to premigratory staging areas, reaching their peak of abundance in mid-July. Adults begin migrating early and have been seen leaving the refuge on June 18. Flights continue from the refuge through August and few remain by September. The latest autumn record was

September 5 (1964). Most are seen migrating southwest toward their wintering areas along the Pacific coast.

Spotted Sandpiper
Actitis macularia

Uncommon in spring, summer, and autumn. Spotted Sandpipers regularly occur on Malheur NWR during migration, but because of their solitary nature seldom will more than ten be seen on a given day. Habitat consists of shorelines along rivers, streams, ponds, and lakes, and in Oregon, during the nesting season, the species is only surpassed in numbers by the Killdeer.

The earliest the Spotted Sandpiper has been seen in spring was April 21 (1979), but the average is May 2. Peak of migration occurs between May 5 and 20, and transients have left by May 30. Most move on through the refuge heading toward their preferred mountainous stream and lake habitats; however, a few pairs remain to nest. Nesting locations have included Benson Landing, Blitzen River (particularly near P Ranch and Page Springs), Double O area, and Knox Pond. Nesting is in progress in late May and June, and young are seen in late June and July. Like phalaropes, male Spotted Sandpipers are responsible for incubation and brood rearing. Autumn migration starts in August and peaks in late August; a large percentage have left by late September. The latest autumn record was on November 25 (1976), when a single bird was observed along the Blitzen River near Page Springs.

Upland Sandpiper
Bartramia longicauda

Accidental. C. Bendire apparently recorded the Upland Sandpiper in Harney Valley (*fide* Gabrielson and Jewett 1940) while stationed at Camp Harney in the 1870s, but I have no details of his observations. Gabrielson and Jewett (1940) reported that the species had been collected at Summit

Prairie, Crook County (August 9, 1919); near Ukiah, Umatilla County (May 16, 1931); and in Bear and Logan valleys, Grant County (May 23-24, 1931). All four of these areas still had Upland Sandpipers in 1987 (J. Scoville, personal communication). Malheur NWR obtained its first records for this prairie-nesting species in 1987. R. Voss observed one bird near Sod House Dam (2 miles southwest of headquarters) on May 2, feeding in an irrigated bromegrass meadow with other shorebirds. His observation was closely followed by the second record. On August 12, Oregon Department of Fish and Wildlife personnel videotaped an Upland Sandpiper near Knox Springs (about 5 miles northeast of Frenchglen), providing the first documented record for the species in the basin. Both of these records fell within the normal spring and autumn migration period for this long-distance migrant.

Long-billed Curlew
Numenius americanus

Common in spring, summer, and autumn. The Malheur-Harney Lakes Basin is an important nesting area for the Long-billed Curlew. In summer, an estimated fifteen hundred birds nest in the basin, with the majority in the meadows east and south of Burns. Pairs do, however, nest on Malheur NWR, particularly at Double O where saltgrass uplands provide favorable sites; Buena Vista and the southern Blitzen Valley also support nesting pairs. Before European settlement, the pristine prairies in the Great Plains were likely the center of curlew abundance. Agricultural development has destroyed much of this habitat, and today areas such as this basin support a large percentage of the remaining curlews.

The Long-billed Curlew arrives on the average date of March 28 (earliest March 20, 1980), and maximum numbers are present between April 10 and 20. Transients have moved on by May 1. Nesting is in progress by early May. The earliest completed clutch was recorded on May 4 (1973). The latest clutch still being incubated was located on June 8 (1971).

Most eggs hatch during the last week of May. Curlews are early autumn migrants, with birds heading for California wintering regions in mid-July. Migration peak occurs between August 5 and 25, and most are gone by September 15. The latest autumn observation occurred on October 15 (1964).

Whimbrel
Numenius phaeopus

Accidental. This coastal migrant has been recorded at least twice on Malheur NWR. A. and E. Parker observed ten Whimbrels, 2 miles west of headquarters in June 1967, and B. Deuel recorded one with a group of Long-billed Curlews, 1 mile northwest of headquarters on May 19, 1969. These represented the first eastern Oregon records.

Marbled Godwit
Limosa fedoa

Uncommon spring and autumn migrant. The Marbled Godwit is not regularly seen on the refuge because the areas in which it generally occurs (east Malheur Lake and Harney Lake) are generally inaccessible. Although there are records for the Blitzen Valley, most Marbled Godwits use Malheur, Harney, and Mud lakes. Gabrielson and Jewett (1940) reported the species as fairly common in October and November on the southern California coast, but noted that it had always been a rarity in Oregon. Perhaps many of these California-bound birds were moving through the refuge, but Gabrielson and Jewett did not visit the areas where godwits are most prevalent.

The earliest spring record was on April 21 (1978, R. Storm) and the average arrival is May 3. Peak of migration is in early May, with the latest spring record June 1 (1965). The species returns from its prairie nesting areas early. The earliest autumn record was June 26 (1980), and the migration peak occurs in mid-July. On July 10, 1973, flocks of 65 and 45 were seen migrating west over headquarters for the largest groups thus recorded. Most flocks number from ten to twenty individuals. Few have been recorded after September, but the late date was October 6 (1972).

Sanderling
Calidris alba

Occasional spring and autumn migrant. The first refuge Sanderling record was obtained on May 15, 1959, when P. DuMont observed four at Harney Lake (Kridler and Marshall 1962). One was collected the following day. Another was seen September 6, 1959, by D. Marshall and P. DuMont at Malheur Lake. Few were recorded in the late 1960s, but Sanderlings became more evident in the late 1970s. As Malheur Lake increased in size and depth in the early 1980s, Sanderling observations increased and the species is now seen frequently in both spring and autumn.

The earliest record was established April 24 (1986, J. Gilligan) and the latest June 8 (1983). No spring population peak has been noted. In autumn, birds are present for an extended period. The earliest record was July 11 (1979), the latest October 2 (1986). Peak of passage occurs in August. Generally, Sanderlings occur singly or in small flocks. The largest recorded group was ten on August 31, 1977. Most recent observations have been on flooded Malheur Lake roads (Sod House Lane and along Highway 205 where it transversed the lake).

Western Sandpiper
Calidris mauri

Common in spring; abundant in autumn. Western Sandpipers are at times the most abundant shorebird on Malheur NWR. An estimated 23,000 were recorded in late September 1979, with the majority on Harney Lake. Only small groups are seen on the refuge in spring as exposed shorelines and mudflats are limited, but as water recedes through the summer months ideal habitat is available for southbound migrants. Adult birds are the first to arrive in autumn, followed in a few weeks by young of the year. It is after young have arrived and joined lingering adults that peak numbers occur on the refuge.

The Western Sandpiper's average spring arrival is April 20, with the earliest record on April 2 (1966). Peak of migration is between April 25 and May 5. Like other shorebirds, Western Sandpipers migrate rapidly through the refuge in spring and large flocks rarely build up. In autumn, the earliest record was on June 21 (1988). Peak numbers are usually present between August 10 and 31, but in some years not until September. Flocks of two thousand individuals, however, have been seen as early as mid-July. Most have left by early October, but the latest record was on November 10 (1968). Greatest autumn concentrations have been on Harney and Stinking lakes, but when these lakes contain deep water, or if Harney Lake contains limited water, few Western Sandpipers are seen there.

Least Sandpiper
Calidris minutilla

Common in spring and autumn; accidental in winter. Unlike Western Sandpipers, which usually appear in large flocks, Least Sandpipers are generally in smaller groups. While feeding, leasts disperse and forage alone, but once on the wing individuals regroup and form tight, twisting flocks characteristic of the other sandpipers. A few leasts can frequently be seen among the immense flocks of westerns, but normally the two species remain segregated. During migration, this smallest of North American shorebirds is found throughout the refuge where it frequents mudflats, shorelines, or algae-covered wet rocks.

Least Sandpipers have arrived in spring as early as April 11 (1977), but the average is 2 weeks later (April 25). Peak of migration is between April 30 and May 5, with the latest record on May 17 (1970). In autumn, the species arrives early from its northern nesting areas (July 2, 1969) and peaks between July 25 and August 25. The latest autumn occurrence was on November 5 (1962). Harney and Stinking lakes have both been important autumn use areas. Winter records include 40 on December 11 and 21 on December 19, 1986 (G. Ivey).

Baird's Sandpiper
Calidris bairdii

Occasional in spring; uncommon in autumn. Like Lesser Yellowlegs, the majority of the world's population of Baird's Sandpipers migrate through the Great Plains states. In Oregon, the species is not a common bird, but numerous records do exist. While it is apparently more common along the coast, there are many autumn records for Malheur NWR. Birds which migrate through the Pacific states consist primarily of young of the year.

On the refuge, most spring records fall between April 20 and 30, but the earliest was April 8 (1982) and the latest May 8 (1971, 1978). In autumn, the earliest record occurred July 28 (1959) and the latest October 14 (1983, 1985). Most records have been between August 20 and 31. Habitat on the refuge consists of shallow water, algae-covered wet rocks, mudflats, and shorelines, with most records from Harney and Stinking lakes, and recently along the washed-out roads in Malheur Lake.

Pectoral Sandpiper
Calidris melanotos

Rare in spring; uncommon to common in autumn. The Pectoral Sandpiper nests from eastern Siberia eastward to western Hudson Bay, while in winter it is found in the southern one-third of South America. Long-distance migrants, pectorals migrate primarily through the Great Plains states, but a substantial number move through the Great Basin. Malheur NWR usually supports a large number of Pectoral Sandpipers in autumn.

The Pectoral Sandpiper's earliest spring arrival was May 4 (1974) and the latest record was May 24 (Gabrielson and Jewett 1940). In spring, a few are sometimes seen feeding in flooded, mowed, and grazed meadows in the Blitzen Valley and Double O. In autumn, the earliest record was on August 28 (1974), the latest November 7 (1987). Over three hundred pectorals have been seen in mid- to late September at Stinking Lake. One scattered group of 350 was present there in September 1975 and another of 250 in late September 1976.

Dunlin
Calidris alpina

Uncommon spring and autumn migrant. The Dunlin is primarily a coastal migrant, but is frequently seen on Malheur NWR, especially in spring. The species nests in the arctic-boreal regions of Canada and Alaska, and usually does not arrive on the Oregon coast until September and October; however, inland migrants appear earlier. Limited shorebird habitat along the inland corridor might account for this discrepancy between coastal and inland arrivals, as inland birds move rapidly south between widely scattered use areas. Subadult Dunlins, like some other shorebird species, remain south of the nesting range through the summer, but to date there are no June records for the refuge.

In the spring, Dunlins have been seen from March 28 (1985) through May 18 (1971). Peak time of passage is between May 1 and 10. Dunlins on Malheur NWR are usually seen in small groups of two to ten; however, 275 were observed on May 3, 1969. The earliest autumn record was July 24 (1973), but most do not appear until August. Peak of autumn migration is in late August, with the last observation September 1 (1962). Records are mainly from Stinking and

Boca lakes, but Dunlins have been seen at scattered locations throughout the refuge.

Red Knot
Calidris canutus

Rare migrant. A Red Knot in partial breeding plumage was collected on May 17, 1970, for the first refuge record (Littlefield and McLaury 1973). The specimen is in the U.S. National Museum. On May 18, 1971, two knots in breeding plumage were seen at Stinking Lake, and on June 6, 1977, two others were observed by T. Pogson and N. Cobb at Harney Lake. The last records occurred in 1983, when a single bird appeared near headquarters from May 15 to 16, and another near Double O on August 21 (M. Archie). These represent the only records on Malheur NWR for this long-distance migrant. Since all records have been recent, I expect additional observations to occur in the near future. An inland migrational corridor appears to be developing in the western Great Basin for species which in the past have been primarily Oregon coastal migrants, including the Red Knot, Semipalmated Plover, Black-bellied Plover, Dunlin, and Ruddy Turnstone.

Long-billed Dowitcher
Limnodromus scolopaceus

Common in spring; abundant in autumn. While on Malheur NWR, Long-billed Dowitchers prefer freshwater ponds, lakes, and sloughs. In spring, the species migrates through rapidly, but as with other shorebirds, autumn migration is much more leisurely. The species is found in small groups throughout the refuge in spring. In autumn major concentration areas occur at Malheur and Stinking lakes, though smaller groups can be seen at other localities. They feed in shallow water and on mudflats by probing in motions reminiscent of a sewing machine.

The earliest spring record was February 22 (1975), with an average arrival date of April 2. Peak numbers are present between May 1 and 15, and the latest record was May 30 (1971). No sooner have spring migrants left than autumn migrants return from their nesting areas in northern Canada and Alaska. The earliest autumn record was June 27 (1987), but dowitchers do not become abundant until mid-July. Peak of autumn migration is between August 10 and 30 when numbers sometimes exceed thirty thousand. Many remain in the area until October, but most have left for southern wintering regions by November (latest refuge record—November 26, 1971).

Among these large concentrations there are probably a few Short-billed Dowitchers (*L. griseus*), but records are limited. E. McLaury saw what was apparently this species on September 27, 1972, on Wright's Pond.

Common Snipe
Gallinago gallinago

Common in spring, summer, and autumn; occasional in winter. As its name implies, the Common Snipe is one of the common nesting shorebirds on Malheur NWR. All moist meadows usually have nesting snipes, but the greatest concentration is at P Ranch and vicinity. Its "winnowing" can be heard from March through July as males perform their courtship displays. This unique sound is produced as birds dive with beating wings, which results in the vibration of the outside tail feathers. After the breeding season, the Blitzen River near Benson Landing has been an attractive site for the species. From one to five hundred snipes have been seen there in August when the receding river exposed muddy shorelines. When Malheur Lake levels are high no large concentrations have been noted. In past years, snipes also concentrated to feed on earthworms in the flood-irrigated lawn at headquarters, where many were mist-netted and banded. This habitat was eliminated with the construction of a new high pressure sprinkling irrigation system in the late 1970s.

The spring influx occurs from March 20 to 30, and pairs are on territory in April. Nesting begins in early May (earliest May 5, 1973), and continues into July (latest July 24, 1973). Nests are difficult to locate as the incubating female remains on the nest until almost stepped upon. An abnormally early brood was seen on May 5, 1983, but generally young are not present until late May. Common Snipe numbers decline in September, but migrants are still present through October. In winter, the species can be found where there is open water. Nearly all the larger springs support a few wintering snipes. Only during two Christmas counts have Common Snipes not been recorded. Greatest numbers were seen in 1962 (9), 1970 (21), 1972 (12), 1976 (23), and 1982 (12). In 1986, 34 were recorded in the vicinity of Malheur and Harney lakes on December 19.

Ruddy Turnstone
Arenaria interpres

Rare spring and autumn migrant. This coastal migrant has increased on Malheur NWR in recent years after being first recorded near Cole Island on May 18, 1974 (F. Ramsey). As Malheur and Harney lakes increased in size and depth, wet rocks adjacent to roadways provided new habitat. Beginning in 1983 and continuing through 1986, the species was seen annually at these newly created feeding areas. In spring, it has been recorded between May 14 and May 20 (both 1986). The largest spring group was two on May 14, 1986. Autumn observations have occurred between August 15 (1983) and September 6 (1986). Five were seen at west Harney Lake on September 2, 1983, for the largest group thus recorded.

Red Phalarope
Phalaropus fulicaria

Accidental. The Red Phalarope's nesting range lies north of the arctic circle, and wintering areas are generally at sea from the Aleutian Islands, Alaska, south to central Chile. Therefore, a Red Phalarope collected by E. Kridler on Malheur NWR was most unusual. The individual was a female and was captured in a mist-net at Stinking Lake on June 25, 1961 (Kridler 1965). This represented the first known summer inland record for Oregon, and was the easternmost report for the state.

Red-necked Phalarope
Phalaropus lobatus

Uncommon in spring and autumn; occasional in summer. This circumpolar, boreal-nesting species is regularly seen at Malheur NWR on the larger ponds and lakes. Although this small phalarope winters primarily at sea, a substantial number use inland migration routes in western North America. A few nonbreeding birds remain in the south, and the species is frequently seen on the refuge during the summer period.

The Red-necked Phalarope is a late spring migrant; average arrival is May 15. The earliest record was obtained on April 17 (1985) and the latest observation was June 5 (1983). A few nonbreeders regularly summer near Double O, primarily on Stinking and Harney lakes. Two to five generally summer, but 14 were seen in June and July 1973, and 25 in 1982. What was considered an early autumn migrant was recorded July 2, 1925 (Gabrielson and Jewett 1940), but this might represent a summering subadult. Most do not arrive until late July, and peak time of passage occurs between August 25 and September 10. The latest autumn record was October 22 (1969).

Wilson's Phalarope
Phalaropus tricolor

Common in spring and summer; abundant in autumn. The Wilson's Phalarope is an inland species nesting in meadows in the western contiguous United States and in the southern provinces of Canada. Here, females are the first to arrive in spring and the first to depart in autumn, leaving parental responsibilities to the males. Once males are incubating, females leave the territory and move to favorable feeding areas. Flocks seen in early July consist almost entirely of females, with males and young not joining until late July and August. Leaving early, most refuge phalaropes presumably migrate south to Mono Lake, California, then south-eastward to wintering regions in Argentina.

The average spring arrival for Wilson's Phalaropes is April 26, with the earliest April 2 (1964). Peak of migration is between May 10 and 20, and northbound migrants have left by May 25. On Malheur NWR, the species nests commonly, with pairs scattered throughout the refuge where suitable habitat is available. Highest densities have occurred at Double O, Wright's Pond, Benson Landing, and from P Ranch to 5-mile Road. Nesting is in progress by mid-May (earliest May 14, 1979), and a few young have fledged by early July. Wilson's Phalaropes begin congregating in July (five thousand on Boca Lake July 27, 1972), and peak in mid-August (ten to fifteen thousand on Stinking Lake). Stinking, Malheur, Harney, and Boca lakes usually have the greatest numbers. After mid-August, the species leaves en masse and numbers are greatly reduced by September 1. The latest autumn record was September 22 (Gabrielson and Jewett 1940).

FAMILY: RECURVIROSTRIDAE

American Avocet
Recurvirostra americana

Common in spring and summer; abundant in autumn. In spring migration, a few American Avocets are seen throughout the refuge, but their principal migration route is through Double O from the southwest. In autumn, though other

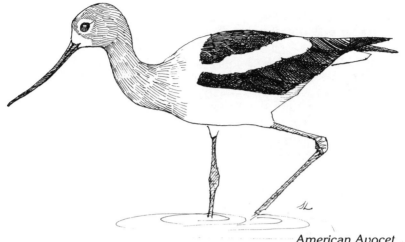

American Avocet

ponds and lakes receive some use, by far the most important use areas are Harney and Stinking lakes, where the birds feed on the masses of shoreflies and other invertebrates which occur along the shorelines and in shallow water. Over fifteen thousand avocets have been seen on Stinking Lake in mid-August.

American Avocets, on the average, arrive March 27, with the earliest record on March 11 (1980). From April 5 to 30 is the peak of spring migration, and most migrants are gone by May 15. Nesting begins in late April (earliest April 25) and continues through June. Young American Avocets near fledging were seen July 2, 1969, but the majority are not ready to fly until mid- to late July. A few flightless young can still be seen in early August. Pairs usually locate their nests in saltgrass or along dikes and roads, and in the past colonies have been located at Double O, Mud Lake, Diamond Swamp, and near Benson Landing. During the last 30 years the refuge population of avocets has declined, and in many areas where the species once nested it no longer does so. The first autumn migrants arrive in early July and peak in August. Their numbers decline in September, but many remain through October. The latest autumn record was November 18 (1970).

Black-necked Stilt
Himantopus mexicanus

Uncommon in spring, summer, and autumn. In the Malheur-Harney Lakes Basin, the Black-necked Stilt reaches the northern limits of its traditional breeding range. In some years the species is seen frequently on the refuge, while in other years it is rarely recorded. In years when little water is available at nesting areas to the south, stilts are more common on Malheur NWR. In 1977, most nesting areas in western Nevada were dry, and the species was abundant on the refuge, and recorded as far north as eastern Washington.

The species arrives late in the spring on Malheur NWR (average April 20). The earliest it has been seen was March 20 (1984), but most nesting pairs do not arrive until May. No spring peak has been noted. Little information is available on the local nesting chronology, as I have examined few nests. Data indicate, however, that nesting begins in early May (earliest May 3), with most eggs hatching in late June. Double O has the greatest nesting densities, but the species has nested along the south shore of Malheur Lake in recent high-water years. Most pairs which nest in the Malheur-Harney Lakes Basin do so south and east of Burns. In autumn, stilts begin leaving in July, and peak numbers occur in early August as fledged young join migrating adults. In recent years, the largest concentration was recorded on Malheur Lake, when two hundred were seen on August 8, 1970. Most have left the refuge by September, but two were still present near Cole Island on October 9, 1971.

FAMILY: LARIDAE

Parasitic Jaeger
Stercorarius parasiticus

Rare in autumn. Beginning in 1979, Parasitic Jaeger observations increased on Malheur NWR, and by the mid-1980s it was considered a rare but regular autumn migrant. The species was first recorded on the refuge in October 1911, when an individual was observed on Malheur Lake (refuge files). Other pre-1979 records were one seen by W. and B. Anderson near the north shore of Harney Lake on August 27, 1971, and a lone bird I saw at Boca Lake on September 15, 1973.

In recent years, the Parasitic Jaeger has been recorded between July 5 (1979) and October 8 (1980), but the majority of records have been from September (particularly between September 8-15). Though the bird generally occurs alone on Malheur and Harney lakes, from fifteen to twenty were present on Harney Lake in September 1985. In this year, jaegers were present from September 8-29, continually harassing Ring-billed Gulls. It remains to be determined if the Parasitic Jaeger has increased as an inland migrant, or if high lake levels made birds more accessible for observation. Based on increased jaeger records in 1979 and 1980, before lake levels increased, I believe the species has increased on the refuge. It is likely an inland migration corridor is developing as for several species of shorebirds. Thus far, most observations have been of immature birds.

Long-tailed Jaeger
Stercorarius longicaudus

Accidental. D. Paullin and M. Smith observed an adult Long-tailed Jaeger during an aerial waterfowl survey on August 19, 1983, as it flew from Derrick Lake to Stinking Lake. The species normally migrates well off the Oregon coast and is rarely seen inland. This represented the refuge's first and only record.

Herring Gull
Larus argentatus

Accidental. There have been four Herring Gull records since the species was first seen on March 26, 1977 (Littlefield

1980). Additional records are one at Knox Pond on February 28, 1982; one near headquarters on March 7, 1984; the decomposed remains of another found at Malheur Lake in mid-August 1984; and one at Harney Lake on December 21, 1987. The Herring Gull is another species which has recently increased on Malheur NWR, and reasons for this increase have yet to be determined.

California Gull
Larus californicus

Abundant in spring; common in summer and autumn; accidental in winter. Fifty years ago both Ring-billed and California gulls were common breeders on Malheur NWR. In the late 1930s and early 1940s, about two thousand California Gull pairs nested on islands in Malheur and Harney lakes. Nesting on the refuge was last recorded in the early 1970s; about one hundred California Gulls nested on an island in a small pond 3 miles northeast of P Ranch in 1971, and a few pairs nested on Malheur Lake in 1973. However, the species still nests in the Malheur-Harney Lakes Basin. About three hundred pairs have nested in an old hay corral 4 miles southeast of Burns since at least 1975, and a colony was recently established on a newly created island in Malheur Lake. The island is approximately 1 mile north of the refuge boundary on private land, and 520 pairs nested there in 1985.

On the average, California Gulls arrive March 9, with the earliest record February 14 (1985). Peak of spring migration is between April 5 and 30, and migrants have left by May 20. In spring, California Gulls often flock to newly flooded, mowed-grazed meadows in the Blitzen Valley. These and other meadows in the Malheur-Harney Lakes Basin are the preferred spring habitat for the species. Nesting begins in April and continues into July, and flightless young have been seen as late as August 1 (1973). There is evidence that some California Gulls initiate autumn migration in June, but generally local birds do not start until July, and peak numbers are present in August. Most have left by mid-September. Migration routes are toward the northwest to the Pacific coast, and apparently these routes are used by most California Gulls in western North America. The latest refuge record was December 3 (1965), and the only winter records were one seen during the 1968 Christmas count and eight on December 19, 1986, at Harney Lake.

Ring-billed Gull
Larus delawarensis

Abundant in spring and autumn; common in summer; rare in winter. Ring-billed Gulls last nested on Malheur NWR in 1973, when a single nest was located in Malheur Lake. Historically, large numbers have never nested on the refuge except in 1938, when S. Jewett estimated five hundred pairs on the lake. Elsewhere in the Malheur-Harney Lakes Basin, large colonies presently exist; about two hundred pairs have nested annually southeast of Burns for many years, and in 1985 and 1986 an estimated five hundred pairs nested on an island in Malheur Lake, 1 mile north of the refuge boundary. The species reaches its greatest abundance in August, and an estimated 25,000 have been seen on Stinking Lake at this time. From the refuge, most ring-bills migrate south or southwest to wintering areas in the California Central Valley, Pacific coast, or Salton Sea. One color-marked individual seen at Stinking Lake in July 1976 was from a colony in Alberta, indicating that at least some birds using the refuge in autumn originate from the southern Canadian provinces.

Ring-billed Gulls arrive early in spring (average February 26), with the earliest record February 9 (1984). Their peak occurs from April 5 to 30, and the majority of northbound migrants are gone by May 30. Migration peak corresponds with irrigation of meadows, where Ring-billed Gulls join with California Gulls to feed on seeds, invertebrates, and small mammals. Nesting, when it occurs, begins in late April on the refuge and continues into June. In autumn migration, the species begins congregating in June and peak of passage occurs between August 1 and 20. Many linger into November, and the latest autumn record was December 10 (1986). Single birds were seen during Christmas counts in 1968, 1976, 1981, and 1983. Additional winter records are for eight at Harney Lake on December 19, 1986, and three at headquarters on both January 24, 1987, and December 19, 1988.

Glaucous-winged Gull
Larus glaucescens

Accidental. In Oregon, the Glaucous-winged Gull is abundant along the coast, but except along the Columbia River it is rare inland. D. Paullin observed a large gull with no black primaries over Harney Lake during an aerial waterfowl survey in November 1988. On December 19, 1988, M. Smith, A. Housley, and I saw an individual of this species associating with Great Blue Herons on Malheur Lake near headquarters. Likely this was the same bird seen earlier at Harney Lake. This is another of the primarily coastal species which have appeared since Malheur and Harney lakes increased in size in the early and mid-1980s, and it is probably only a matter of time before Western (*L. occidentalis*) and Mew (*L. canus*) gulls make their appearance on Malheur NWR.

Franklin's Gull
Larus pipixcan

Common in spring and summer; uncommon in autumn. Much of the Franklin's Gull's history in Oregon has been summarized by Littlefield and Thompson (1981). The species was first recorded on the refuge April 24, 1943 (first state record), when one was observed by C. Sooter, and on June 7, 1948, the first Oregon nest was located in Malheur Lake (Jewett 1949). Franklin's Gulls increased annually, with minor fluctuations, until a nesting peak was attained in 1981 (1,330 nests). For a few years after Malheur Lake increased in size, few nested on the refuge, but some pairs did continue to find suitable sites on private land and at Double O. In 1986, 520 pairs nested in the Malheur-Harney Lakes Basin, including 70 pairs at Knox Pond. By 1987, Knox Pond pairs increased to 1,000, with 725 pairs nesting in 1988.

The species arrives on the average date of April 17, with the earliest spring arrival on March 30 (1986). By May 15, the resident population has arrived and nesting is in progress by June 1. Nesting has been recorded mostly on Malheur Lake, Warbler Pond (1984 and 1985), and Knox Pond (1986-88). Young fledge in July and early August, with autumn migration underway shortly thereafter. Most have left for coastal South American wintering regions by September. The latest autumn record was October 27 (1982). Likely some immatures migrate west to the Pacific coast, but most head eastward to the tall grass prairie of the Great Plains, where the Franklin's Gull is locally known as the "prairie dove." In migration, as on the nesting and wintering grounds, food consists primarily of invertebrates and at the refuge flocks are frequently observed spiralling over meadows feeding on flying insects.

Bonaparte's Gull
Larus philadelphia

Uncommon in spring and autumn; rare in summer. The small Bonaparte's Gull is not common on Malheur NWR, but a few are frequently seen in migration as birds move to and from nesting regions in the spruce-fir forests of Canada and Alaska. There, pairs nest solitarily or in small groups in spruce trees. Throughout the year the species feeds primarily on invertebrates, but a few small fish are occasionally included in their diet. Most Bonaparte's Gulls on the refuge occur on or near Stinking and Harney lakes, where crustaceans probably constitute a large percentage of the food items consumed.

In spring, Bonaparte's Gulls have arrived as early as April 13 (1986), but the average is May 6. Peak of spring passage falls between May 10 and 20, with the latest migrant May 30 (1965). A few nonbreeders spend the summer months on the refuge. Usually no more than three are seen, but ten were at Stinking Lake on both July 2, 1961 (G. McCaskie) and August 19, 1986 (D. Paullin). In September, southbound migrants return. The earliest record occurred August 24 (1978) and the peak is from September 25 through October 10. The latest autumn date was November 22 (1955).

Sabine's Gull
Xema sabini

Accidental. Two Sabine's Gulls were observed feeding on invertebrates at Stinking Lake on September 17, 1975 (Littlefield 1980). This represented the first record for eastern Oregon, and one of the few for inland Oregon. Since then another individual was observed at Buena Vista Pond on September 25, 1987. Normally the species migrates well off the coast, moving between arctic nesting regions and Southern Hemisphere oceanic wintering areas.

Common Tern
Sterna hirundo

Rare in spring and autumn. Several Common Tern records have accumulated since it was first reported September 19, 1975 (Littlefield 1980). Single birds were seen May 11, 1982 (D. Severson); May 28, 1982 (G. Oesterla); October 30, 1984 (C. Littlefield); and October 22, 1985 (G. Ivey). G. Ivey observed eight individuals on Harney Lake October 1, 1986, and fourteen on September 2, 1987, for the largest numbers thus recorded. All reports have been on or near the Malheur-Harney Lakes complex, with the exception of the 1975 bird which was at Warbler Pond. This is another species which has recently made its presence known in southeast Oregon.

Since the first observations occurred before the lakes increased in size, it is doubtful this phenomenon has contributed to the sudden appearance of Common Terns on Malheur NWR.

Forster's Tern
Sterna forsteri

Abundant in spring and summer; uncommon in autumn.
The Forster's Tern is the only medium-sized, white, forked-
tailed tern on Malheur NWR during the summer months.
When Malheur Lake has normal water levels these birds find
suitable nesting habitat on bulrush mats or muskrat houses,
and there the majority of Forster's Terns on the refuge hatch
and rear their broods. However, a few pairs frequently nest at
Wright's and Warbler ponds, as well as Derrick and Boca
lakes. The species feeds on small fish and invertebrates, and
courting males are occasionally seen presenting a small fish
or other morsel to an awaiting female.

The earliest Forster's Terns have been seen in spring is
March 9 (1983), but their average arrival is not until April 23.
Migration peak is between May 5 and 25. Nesting begins for
most pairs during the first week of June and continues into
July. Although I have no definite records, late May nesting is
plausible, particularly in years with mild springs. Autumn
migration is at a peak between August 20 and September 10,
after beginning in early August. Few remain at the end of
September, and the latest record was October 20 (1971).

Caspian Tern
Sterna caspia

Uncommon to common in spring, summer, and autumn.
The Caspian Tern has had an interesting history on Malheur
NWR. The species nested almost every year through 1960,
until drought conditions eliminated nesting islands, and it

was not until 1983 that nesting Caspians returned. In 1983, three nests were located in west Harney Lake on a bulrush mat, but in 1984 pairs increased dramatically in the Malheur-Harney Lakes Basin as 300 to 350 pairs nested on a small island near the north shore of Malheur Lake about 1 mile outside of the refuge boundary. Associated with Ring-billed and California gulls, this colony has been active through 1987, and if islands persist the species will likely continue to nest until severe prolonged drought returns.

The earliest spring record occurred March 30 (1986), and the average arrival is May 2. Birds continue to increase until the nesting period (late May), and no spring peak has been noted. Autumn migration begins in late July, and peak numbers are present between August 1 and September 1. The latest record was October 9 (Gabrielson and Jewett 1940). Caspian Terns are seen throughout the refuge, but most sightings have been from Malheur, Harney, and Mud lakes.

Black Tern
Chlidonias niger

Abundant in spring and summer; uncommon in autumn. While on the refuge, Black Terns generally prefer the smaller ponds and marshes for nesting, but pairs do nest on larger water bodies, particularly Malheur Lake. Usually the species is found in small colonies (ten to thirty pairs) throughout the Blitzen Valley and Double O, but solitary pairs are frequently encountered on Malheur Lake. Colonies have consistently been located on Wright's and Warbler ponds, Dredger Field, Boca Lake, and Krumbo Reservoir, while other colony sites vary from year to year, depending on water depth and available nesting material. After nesting, Malheur Lake increases in importance if it is at normal depths; as many as six thousand have been seen there in the past, but when water levels are too deep few Black Terns occur there. Beginning in mid-summer, adults start losing their dark feathers, and by the time the last leave in autumn their black spring plumage has changed to white.

Black Tern

April 23 (1959) is the early spring arrival date and May 3 is the average, with the peak of passage between May 15 and June 5. One nest was located May 11 (1979), but some pairs do not lay eggs until late June (latest June 25, 1979). Young fledge from late June through July, and migrate shortly thereafter. Peak of autumn migration is between August 10 and 30. Gabrielson and Jewett (1940) reported the latest record October 11, but the latest sighting in recent years was September 24 (1970); however, Black Terns are rarely seen after the first week in September.

ORDER: COLUMBIFORMES
FAMILY: COLUMBIDAE

Band-tailed Pigeon
Columba fasciata

Occasional in spring and summer; rare in autumn. The first refuge record was obtained on October 16, 1945, when

G. Benson collected a Band-tailed Pigeon near Benson Pond. This was the only record until an individual was captured at headquarters on June 18, 1968 (Littlefield and McLaury 1973). Since 1968, the species has increased in southeast Oregon, and several additional refuge records have accumulated. On May 3-4, 1970, one was seen at headquarters, and other single birds have been recorded at headquarters in spring on June 5, 1971; May 31, 1973; June 2, 1973; and April 1, 1984. Other spring records were one on June 17, 1972 (2 miles west of headquarters); one on June 3, 1973 (north of P Ranch); two on June 17, 1973 (P Ranch); one on May 18, 1974 (P Ranch); three on May 22, 1977 (Page Springs by F. Ramsey); one was killed on Highway 205 on May 23, 1979; and one on June 30, 1982 (P Ranch by A. Small and H. Clarke). Other than the 1945 record, only two autumn records have been obtained, both at headquarters; one on October 3, 1973, and another on October 28, 1984 (G. Ivey).

Rock Dove
Columba livia

Occasional in summer. In the early 1940s, twelve to fifteen Rock Doves resided at headquarters, but since then resident birds have disappeared. A few banded Rock Doves appear each summer at scattered localities throughout the refuge, and these individuals represent exhausted or lost birds from annual "pigeon" races. The majority of refuge records are in June, but stragglers can be seen well into August.

There are two naturalized Rock Dove colonies near Malheur NWR. One colony is located on a rimrock about 2 miles southwest of Princeton, and the second is along Catlow Valley rimrocks where the species can particularly be seen in Home Creek Canyon. No birds from these colonies have been noted on the refuge, but in winter "pigeons" roost in an abandoned homesteader shack about 5 miles southwest of Frenchglen near Highway 205.

Mourning Dove
Zenaida macroura

Common in spring, summer, and autumn; accidental in winter. Mourning Doves occur throughout the refuge, with greatest densities along the Center Patrol Road between P Ranch and Benson Pond in spring and autumn. Here, birds feed on the abundant weed seeds at the road's edge, loafing and roosting in the adjoining dense willows. Several hundred have been seen along this stretch in past years, but generally their numbers do not exceed fifty. In autumn, concentrations are on private land east of Malheur NWR where grainfields attract large numbers in late August and September, and it is in this area where most birds spend time before heading south for the winter. Many doves probably migrate southeast to Arizona, but the only return from a refuge bird was one banded on August 22, 1963, and recovered 11 days later near Los Angeles, at Piru, California.

One early Mourning Dove was recorded on February 2 (1979), but the average date is not until April 1. The species is most commonly seen between May 1 and 25. As the nesting season approaches, Mourning Dove numbers decline, but some pairs do remain on the refuge to nest. Nests are generally found in June and July, and most pairs in this region are thought to be double-brooded. However, five half-grown young found at Malheur Field Station on September 9, 1982, indicate a few pairs may produce three broods annually. A variety of nesting sites is used, but local doves seem to prefer sagebrush expanses and rimrocks during the summer months, where they nest on the ground. Migration in autumn begins in late July and peaks between August 25 and September 10; most have left by mid-October, but a few linger into November. The latest autumn record was November 17 (1970). Single birds were seen near Page Springs on December 18, 1976, and December 15, 1979, and two in the southern Blitzen Valley on December 18, 1986.

ORDER: CUCULIFORMES
FAMILY: CUCULIDAE

Yellow-billed Cuckoo
Coccyzus americanus

Accidental in spring and summer. At the turn of the century, Yellow-billed Cuckoos were not uncommon in Oregon. Nesting in brushy willow thickets, cuckoos were regularly seen along the Columbia and Snake rivers (Gabrielson and Jewett 1940), but except for one nesting record near Ontario on August 2, 1876 (Bendire 1877) the species was not recorded in southeast Oregon until 1970. On May 20, 1970, one was observed among willows along the Blitzen River 1 mile north of Krumbo Road, but an attempt to collect the individual was unsuccessful (Littlefield and McLaury 1973). Another was observed at headquarters on June 24, 1971, and one of two was killed there after colliding with a window on June 6, 1972. These represented the first reports for the state since 1944 (Marshall 1969). Other than one pair which likely nested along Pike's Creek in the late 1970s, I know of no additional nesting records for southeast Oregon.

ORDER: STRIGIFORMES
FAMILY: TYTONIDAE

Common Barn-Owl
Tyto alba

Occasional permanent resident. This cosmopolitan species was first added to the refuge list on May 29, 1942, but nesting was not detected until 1970 when a pair fledged three young at headquarters. A nesting attempt in 1971 was unsuccessful, and no additional nests were found until 1978 when a pair which was nesting in the headquarters tower fledged one young. The species has increased in the northern Great Basin and has now been seen on the refuge in all months. However, a major limiting factor in this region is severe cold with deep snow. Between January 11 and 18, 1982, eighteen were found dead in the northern portion of the refuge, and all had died from starvation except for one which had been killed and partially consumed by a Great Horned Owl.

Barn-owl records have been primarily from headquarters, but the species has been seen at scattered localities throughout the refuge. Numerous nesting sites are available, not only around human habitations, but in the extensive rimrocks on and adjacent to the refuge. Rimrock nests have been located near Buena Vista, Rock Quarry Field, Upper Krumbo Pond, and Double O. In winter, autumn, and early spring, individuals are often found among dense, dry emergent stands throughout the refuge. Eight were encountered in bulrush stands at Boca Lake during a prescribed burn on February 24, 1982.

FAMILY: STRIGIDAE

Western Screech-Owl
Otus kennicottii

Rare permanent resident. Limited Western Screech-Owl habitat is located within the refuge boundary, and it is more common in the canyons and juniper slopes adjacent to the southern Blitzen Valley. Bendire (1877) first reported the species when he collected an egg set near Malheur Lake on April 16, 1877. The second record was not until December 13, 1940, when one was found dead in a mink trap on McCoy Creek (Jewett 1941). Other records were the remains of one found in Bridge Creek Canyon on May 6, 1971 (W. Anderson); two calling near Frenchglen Spring on July 30, 1974; one at Page Springs on November 28, 1983; one near headquarters on November 24, 1984; one along Bridge Creek in the winter of 1984 (W. Radke); and one at Page Springs on August 19, 1987 (G. Ivey).

Flammulated Owl
Otus flammeolus

Rare spring and autumn migrant. Flammulated Owls are frequently seen some years, but may not appear again for a decade or more. First recorded on April 30, 1939, and September 20 and 30, 1940, the species was not again seen for 22 years when one was captured and banded at headquarters on May 31, 1962. Individuals were also banded on June 7, 1962, and May 4, 1963. Thirteen years later one was seen on May 9, 1976. The last spring record was May 28-29, 1988 (headquarters). There have been two recent autumn observations, one at Malheur Field Station on September 26, 1982 (it spent the day in a garage), and one at headquarters from September 27 through 29, 1986. In spring, the species has been recorded between April 30 and June 7, and in autumn between September 20 and 30.

The species has been observed primarily at headquarters, but it surely occurs elsewhere on the refuge during invasion years. This insectivorous owl feeds extensively on moths, and unlike other local owl species it is highly migratory. Flammulated Owls move from the region as insect supplies decline, migrating to favorable wintering areas in Mexico south into Central America.

Great Horned Owl
Bubo virginianus

Common permanent resident. There are an estimated forty to sixty pairs of Great Horned Owls on Malheur NWR. Pairs remain together throughout the year, and are regularly found on their nesting territories during the winter period near rimrocks and large willows and cottonwoods. One pair

Great Horned Owl

nests regularly at headquarters, and the species is also present annually at Ramalli Bridge, P Ranch, Page Springs,
Double O, Benson Pond, Unit 9 Pond, near Lava Beds Pond,
and other localities throughout the refuge.

   Great Horned Owls are one of the first birds on the refuge
to nest, with the earliest record February 11 (1971). Peak of
nesting is in late February and March, with young hatching in
late March and April. A few pairs delay nesting until April,

and these probably represent females laying for the first time. Young generally leave the nest in late May and June, but remain with the adults on their territory through the summer. Rarely are young within the adult's territory by October. In winter, the species has been recorded during all but five Christmas counts. Years with highest numbers were 1943 (sixteen), 1967 (eight), 1970 (eight), 1980 (nine), and 1981 (eight).

This largest of the eared owls feeds on a wide variety of organisms. Prey sizes range from mice to young Greater Sandhill Cranes, and they have been known to take adult Canada Geese. At headquarters, this pair prefers medium-sized birds, with American Coots being one of the most popular components of their summer diet.

Snowy Owl
Nyctea scandiaca

Accidental. The only refuge record for this northern species was of a single bird seen near Page Springs on March 22, 1974. However, there are several additional records from the Malheur-Harney Lakes Basin, all within 35 miles of headquarters. Bendire (1877) listed the Snowy Owl as "a rare winter visitor" and observed it on several occasions near Camp Harney (10 miles east of Burns). In the 1917-18 winter, there were numerous reports of this species—it was called the winter of the "white owl." Recently one was recorded 3 miles east of Burns in October 1972, and the last record was a single bird seen near Foster Flat on December 9, 1974.

Northern Pygmy-Owl
Glaucidium gnoma

Accidental. This small owl inhabits the coniferous forest of the Blue Mountains and generally remains north of Burns throughout the year. In autumn and winter, there is some movement into the Stinking Water Mountains, southeast of

Buchanan, but the species seems to avoid the desert lowlands. There are two old records for Malheur NWR; on January 1, 1937, S. Jewett saw a Northern Pygmy-Owl on the refuge, and one was found dead on April 30, 1939.

Burrowing Owl
Athene cunicularia

Uncommon in spring, summer, and autumn; accidental in winter. Among the sagebrush expanses surrounding Malheur NWR, many Burrowing Owl pairs find suitable nesting habitat, and a few pairs regularly nest on the refuge, but numbers have declined in recent years. In 1941, about thirty pairs were present, but now it is doubtful if there are more than five. The species has frequently nested north of Malheur Lake, north and south of Harney Lake, and north of the Double O substation. Elsewhere Burrowing Owls nest sporadically where ground squirrel and badger burrows are available.

The earliest spring occurrence was February 27 (1970, 1983), but in most years Burrowing Owls are not seen until March (average March 27). Pairs are incubating by the end of April or early May, and young emerge from the nesting burrows in June and July. Adults are somewhat elusive until young are well developed. Large broods are a characteristic trait of the species, with six to eight young normal for locally nesting pairs. As this large crop of young approach fledging, both adults are required to do considerable hunting even during daylight hours, and it is at this time that birds become conspicuous. Although young are capable of foraging on their own, they usually remain with the adults into August. In September, these small, long-legged owls start migrating, and by mid-October few are seen. The latest refuge record was on November 28 (1969); however, one was seen near Burns in December 1969. S. Jewett reported the species as extremely abundant in the winter of 1935, but there are no recent winter records for the refuge.

Long-eared Owl
Asio otus

Occasional to uncommon permanent resident. Long-eared Owls are sporadic nesters on Malheur NWR, with several nests being found one year and none the next. Reasons for such erratic nesting behavior are presently unknown, but populations of small mammals—which are its principal prey—probably play an important part. In addition, most refuge Long-eared Owls nest on abandoned Black-billed Magpie nests among dense willow thickets; therefore, magpie numbers perhaps determine the number of available nesting sites and subsequently the number of nesting owls. Whatever the reason, this medium-sized owl cannot be expected as a nesting species every year on Malheur NWR.

Several nests with young were found in the Blitzen Valley in late April 1958, and a nest with four young was among dense willows near Grain Camp Dam on April 27, 1961. In 1962, one nest with two young was located among willows in northwest Boca Lake, and another near Kado Bridge, both on May 30. These represented the last nesting records until 1979 when an extensive survey yielded eight nests and 24 pairs (R. Johnstone). The species nests early (earliest March 11, 1979) and most pairs are on eggs by mid-April, with hatching in late April and early May. Young leave the nest about 10 days before fledging, and have been seen out of the nest as early as April 30 (1980). In winter, the species is occasionally seen in the juniper-covered canyons and rimrocks between Frenchglen and Krumbo Road, and for several years Long-eared Owls wintered among the taller sagebrush near Malheur Field Station. Elsewhere the species is a rare winter visitor. The remains of one was found at headquarters in January during the severe winter of 1982, having been captured and consumed by a Great Horned Owl.

Short-eared Owl
Asio flammeus

Common in spring, summer, and autumn; uncommon in winter. On cloudy days or at dusk, Short-eared Owls can sometimes be seen flying (mothlike) low over meadows and grasslands throughout the refuge. When rodent populations, particularly meadow voles, are low this species is rarely seen, but when rodent numbers are high this ground-nesting owl can become exceedingly common. From July through October, birds often concentrate in shrub expanses, particularly around Harney Lake. Through the remainder of the year favored locations are along the Center Patrol Road from P Ranch to 5-mile Road, Diamond Lane to Unit 9 Pond, Wright's Pond, and Double O.

During the first week of March, northbound migrants appear, and Short-eared Owls are at their peak of abundance between March 25 and April 25. Nesting birds are apparently the first to arrive as nests containing eggs have been found as early as March 14, and nests containing young as early as March 29 (1963). Their spectacular territorial flights can occasionally be seen in March and April, and most pairs are ready to nest in April and May. The latest nest with eggs was located June 4 (1937). Wildrye-shrub-covered uplands surrounded by meadows and marshes are their preferred nesting habitat on the refuge. A shallow depression lined with dried vegetation fragments is all that is necessary for egg deposition. Nests are usually placed below a shrub or next to dense bunchgrass. Clutches are large (up to eight eggs), but rarely produce more than three young. Autumn migration begins in September and peaks between October 25 and November 25. Twenty were observed near Knox Pond on November 15, 1972, for the largest group noted in recent years. Migrants have left the refuge by December 7. In winter, the species has been seen during fifteen Christmas counts, with greatest numbers in 1941 (nine), 1958 (eighteen), and 1975 (eight).

Northern Saw-whet Owl
Aegolius acadicus

Occasional in spring and autumn; rare in winter; accidental in summer. The Northern Saw-whet Owl is sporadic, abundant some years and absent in others. S. Jewett reported on the first refuge record on March 19-21, 1936, and the first autumn record was obtained on October 24, 1940. The species nests in the coniferous forest of the Blue Mountains, where Bendire (1892) reported on an egg set taken near Camp Harney on May 2, 1881. Most records obtained on Malheur NWR are from headquarters, particularly in the coniferous trees there.

In spring, saw-whets have been recorded between March 19 (1936) and May 21 (1970). Most records fall between May 1 and 15. The species has been seen more frequently in autumn. Extreme dates are September 9 and November 30, with the majority of records occurring between October 5 and 25. Seven were banded between October 2 and November 11, 1961; five between September 9 and October 10, 1962; and fourteen between September 12 and October 20, 1963. One which wintered at headquarters in 1971-72 first appeared on December 6 and remained through February 10. The remaining winter records were one at headquarters on January 12, 1977, single birds at Sod House Ranch on December 18, 1979, and December 22, 1980, and one which had been consumed by a Great Horned Owl at headquarters on February 25, 1985. An immature saw-whet collided with a window at headquarters on July 5, 1985. The bird later recovered and was released. This individual had been produced in 1985 and had likely moved from the Blue Mountains shortly after fledging, providing one of two summer refuge records. The second record was obtained on June 25, 1988, when another immature was observed at headquarters.

Common Nighthawk

ORDER: CAPRIMULGIFORMES
FAMILY: CAPRIMULGIDAE

Common Nighthawk
Chordeiles minor

Abundant in late spring, summer, and autumn. The Common Nighthawk is the last species to arrive in spring; migration is leisurely as birds feed their way north from their South American wintering regions. There is some indication that males arrive first, with females not appearing until about 2 weeks later. Once females arrive, males are often heard and seen performing their aerial territorial dives; air rushing through the males' wings produces the characteristic "booming" sound. While on the refuge, Common Nighthawks can regularly be seen perching parallel on cables, tree branches, fence posts, or rail fences. These birds are particularly common near Unit 8 Pond, Malheur Field Station, Saddle Butte, and headquarters.

In spring, Common Nighthawks arrive on the average date of May 24. Very little variation occurs between the earliest (May 20, 1977) and the latest (May 28, 1964) arrival dates. Numbers rapidly increase and by the first week of June nighthawks are abundant; there is usually a second wave of migrants between June 15 and 25. Nesting begins in June and eggs usually hatch in July. One clutch at Malheur Field Station hatched July 10, 1972. Young fledge usually in August and autumn migration begins shortly afterward. Peak of migration takes place between August 15 and 31. A heavy migration was noted at Page Springs on August 25, 1984, as more than one hundred birds passed over in about 30 minutes. Most have departed by the first week in September, but a few, in mild Septembers, linger through the month. The latest autumn record was obtained on October 3, 1971, when three were seen at headquarters.

Common Poorwill
Phalaenoptilus nuttallii

Uncommon in spring, summer, and autumn. Common Poorwills are something of a mystery on the refuge. This is the only refuge species known to hibernate, and it is presently not known if all poorwills leave Malheur NWR in autumn or if some remain among the rimrocks in deep sleep. Cold winter temperatures would probably prevent survival through the winter, but birds are seen more frequently near rimrocks when cool weather arrives in September, and possibly most of these late individuals go into torpor among the rocks on cool evenings before leaving the refuge in late September and early October. T. Darrow found one in a torpid condition in November 1980 near Buena Vista. Poorwills are sometimes heard near Malheur Field Station and in the sagebrush expanses which surround the refuge in summer, and occasionally their reflecting pink eyes can be seen in headlights along the Center Patrol Road, particularly near Buena Vista and between Krumbo and 5-mile roads. Several are usually killed annually by vehicles on Highway 205 between Buena Vista substation and Sod House Lane.

The earliest record of March 14 (1964) is far ahead of their average spring appearance on May 14. The species is most evident in June and July. No nests with eggs have been located in the area, but two birds were found together on Saddle Butte on June 13, 1976 (C. Talbot). Both were among sagebrush and a scrape was nearby, indicating nesting was about to begin. I have no additional information on nesting chronology, though if nesting occurs in June it is likely that the young would fledge in July. Poorwills are frequently seen through August, but numbers decline in early September. During the mild autumn of 1977, the species was seen on September 30 (Buena Vista) and October 3 (near east shore of Malheur Lake) for the latest autumn dates of active birds.

ORDER: APODIFORMES
FAMILY: APODIDAE

Black Swift
Cypseloides niger

Accidental. A dead immature Black Swift was found near Frenchglen Hotel on September 11, 1985. The specimen is now in the Humboldt State University collection, after being prepared by S. Harris. Information received from Dr. Harris indicated the bird had died from starvation. Although the species has been reported from northeast Oregon this represented the first record from the southeast portion of the state.

Vaux's Swift
Chaetura vauxi

Occasional spring and autumn migrant. Vaux's Swift, the smallest of North American swifts, is a common summer resident in the Blue Mountains, particularly near the Strawberry Wilderness Area, southeast of John Day. On Malheur NWR the species is strictly a migrant, occurring in spring between April 26 (1987, M. Houck) and May 24 (1971), and in autumn between September 7 (1982) and September 25 (1986). Peak of spring passage is around mid-May, and in autumn the peak occurs in mid-September. Usually Vaux's Swifts are seen alone or in small loose groups of two to eight individuals; however, C. Cogswell observed twenty to thirty on May 10, 1986, at headquarters for the largest number thus recorded. While on the refuge, the species is often associated with the aerial foraging flocks of Barn Swallows. Most observations have been from headquarters, but individuals do occur throughout the Blitzen Valley. At the present time there are no records from Double O.

White-throated Swift
Aeronautes saxatalis

Accidental. Although White-throated Swifts commonly nest near the Steens Mountain summit and along Catlow Valley rim, few have been seen on Malheur NWR. The only known records are of single birds at Knox Pond on September 4, 1970; P Ranch on June 24, 1973; Malheur Field Station on September 5, 1983; and a flock of ten over Malheur Field Station on May 16, 1988. Swifts which nest on Steens Mountain apparently migrate through the Alvord Valley, as six were observed near Alvord Ranch on May 13, 1970, about 5,000 feet below their favored nesting cliffs. During periods of unfavorable summer weather, the species has also been seen near the Alvord Desert, particularly in Pikes Creek Canyon. The White-throated Swift is considered by many to be the fastest North American bird, and during unseasonably cool and wet periods, little time is required for individuals to escape from the climatically harsh highlands down to the warmer desert lowlands. The swift seen near P Ranch on June 24, 1973, occurred during such a period and it is likely that this bird had moved down from the Catlow rim region to the warmer Blitzen Valley.

FAMILY: TROCHILIDAE

Black-chinned Hummingbird
Archilochus alexandri

Occasional in spring; accidental in autumn. The first refuge record for the Black-chinned Hummingbird was obtained May 23, 1970, at Benson Landing when members of the Portland Audubon Society found three individuals (Littlefield and McLaury 1973). Efforts to collect a specimen proved unsuccessful. Through the 1970s the species was seen five other times, but it was not until the 1980s that it became a regular spring migrant. Presently, Black-chinned Hummingbirds have been seen between May 12 and June 3, with most records falling between May 15 and 20. One pair remained at headquarters from May 21 through June 1, 1979, and another was seen among junipers west of Frenchglen in early June 1975 (J. Riggs), but to date no nest has been located. There are only three autumn records: one on September 2, 1982 (M. Archie); one female on September 12, 1985 (H. Nehls); and one female on August 19, 1987, all at headquarters. Most records have been from headquarters, but the species has also been seen at Page Springs, near Frenchglen, and at P Ranch.

Calliope Hummingbird
Stellula calliope

Occasional in spring; accidental in autumn. Smallest of North American birds, the Calliope Hummingbird is a common nester in the Blue Mountains of eastern Oregon, where it finds suitable habitat in coniferous forest near open meadows or along mountain streams. However, few records exist for

Malheur NWR. The species was not recorded until a female was captured and banded at headquarters on May 16, 1963. Since then calliopes have been seen on several occasions between May 1 and 24, with most occurring from May 8 through 16. There are two autumn records—August 10, 1979, and September 11, 1985— both from headquarters. Records are mostly from headquarters, but the species should be looked for throughout the refuge, particularly near Page Springs, Benson Pond, and P Ranch. Several records have now accumulated in Alvord Valley, and it could be that this valley is an important migration corridor for the Calliope Hummingbirds which nest in the eastern mountainous regions of the state.

Broad-tailed Hummingbird
Selasphorus platycercus

Accidental. Littlefield (1980) saw and heard an adult male Broad-tailed Hummingbird on May 9, 1973, about 30 miles south of headquarters, for the only refuge record. However, the species had previously been reported on neighboring Steens Mountain (Gabrielson and Jewett 1940). Considering this Rocky Mountain species nests in the Santa Rosa Mountains, Nevada (about 90 miles southeast of Malheur NWR) it is surprising other records have not occurred on the refuge.

Rufous Hummingbird
Selasphorus rufus

Uncommon in spring; common in autumn. The Rufous Hummingbird is the most northern member of its family, nesting as far north as southern Alaska and Yukon. On Malheur NWR, it is by far the most commonly encountered hummingbird, particularly in autumn. Formerly, when flowers grew in profusion at headquarters, Rufous Hummingbird females and immatures were attracted to this abundant food source and it was not uncommon to see twenty to thirty individuals on a given August day. Since few flowers are presently planted, the species has declined substantially and few now concentrate around the headquarters gardens and lawns.

The few birds seen in spring have occurred between April 21 (1959) and June 13 (1972). On the average they first appear on May 1, and peak period of abundance is from May 10 to 15. In autumn, Rufous Hummingbirds are in greater numbers, with the earliest record June 27 (1970) and the latest September 22 (1971); July 25 through August 25 is the likely period for observations. By early September the majority have moved on toward their wintering quarters, primarily in central and southern Mexico.

ORDER: CORACIIFORMES
FAMILY: ALCEDINIDAE

Belted Kingfisher
Ceryle alcyon

Uncommon permanent resident. The Belted Kingfisher may be seen throughout the refuge, but its center of abundance is from Buena Vista south to Page Springs. Individuals are regularly encountered along the Blitzen River near Page Springs, East Canal from Bridge Creek south, West Canal from Krumbo Road to Frenchglen Spring, and Benson Pond. Here individuals are seen perched on power-lines or tree branches near clear water, watching for small fish or other aquatic organisms. Generally they are heard long before being seen as they fly up and down streams, giving their familiar rattling calls.

On Malheur NWR, nesting burrows are in eroded canal and river banks, and for several years one pair has nested along the Blitzen River near Page Springs. Nesting begins in May and extends well into July. Although nest sites are usually well protected from avian and mammalian predators, some eggs and young are lost to other predatory species. In July 1974, a gopher snake was discovered in a nesting burrow adjacent to the Blitzen River. The snake had killed all but one young, and the survivor was rescued, raised, and later released by Malheur Field Station students. Once young fledge, individuals disperse to favorable feeding areas throughout the refuge. Kingfishers are regularly observed at headquarters and Double O during spring (April) and autumn (October) migration, and in winter have been recorded during all but one Christmas count in the southern Blitzen Valley. The average count number is four, but has varied from one to thirteen. Highest counts were in 1965 (nine), 1974 (seven), 1975 (thirteen), 1982 (nine), and 1985 (eight).

ORDER: PICIFORMES
FAMILY: PICIDAE

Lewis' Woodpecker
Melanerpes lewis

Uncommon to common spring and autumn migrant. Lewis' Woodpeckers can be seen at scattered localities throughout the refuge in both spring and autumn, but most concentrate among the large trees around headquarters and P Ranch. This flycatching, crow-like species has declined over much of its range but it is still regularly seen on Malheur NWR during migration. Birds moving through this region appear to be using a southwest-northeast corridor. On September 15, 1978, five Lewis' Woodpeckers were watched as they migrated from headquarters in a westerly direction, probably moving to the eastern Cascade foothills before turning south to favorable wintering areas.

The earliest spring record for the species was March 14 (1970), but their average arrival is not until April 26. Migration peak occurs between May 1 and 12, with the latest observation May 20 (1967). In autumn, Lewis' Woodpeckers have arrived as early as August 26 (1985). Peak of migration falls between September 10 and 25, and the latest autumn occurrence was October 7 (1966). In 1966, twelve individuals lingered at headquarters through the first week of October, but generally the species is not recorded after September.

Red-headed Woodpecker
Melanerpes erythrocephalus

Accidental. The Red-headed Woodpecker is an extremely rare bird on the west coast, and Oregon's first record was obtained on Malheur NWR at P Ranch. M. O'Leary found the bird on June 21, 1987, and the observation was accepted by the Oregon Bird Records Committee. However, no details were provided to the refuge and the bird could not be relocated on subsequent days. Roberson (1980) listed one record from California and two from British Columbia through 1979, for the only west coast records. The nearest known nesting area for this attractive woodpecker occurs along the foothill region of Colorado, and in eastern Wyoming and Montana.

Red-naped Sapsucker
Sphyrapicus nuchalis

Uncommon spring and autumn migrant. Although the Red-naped Sapsucker nests commonly in aspens on Steens Mountain and in the Blue Mountains, it is strictly a transient on Malheur NWR. Bendire (1895) reported the species in winter in the Harney Valley in the 1870s, but there are no recent winter records. In fact, this sapsucker migrates further south than most North American woodpeckers.

The average spring arrival date is April 11, with the earliest March 23 (1988) and the latest May 14 (1967). Red-naped Sapsuckers are likely to be seen from April 22 through May 5. In autumn, the earliest record was August 18 (1977) and the latest October 18 (1970). They are most common in autumn from September 15 through 25. When migrating through the refuge individuals are found alone and usually no more than two birds can be seen on a given day; however, on September 25, 1987, six were seen in the Blitzen Valley. The majority of observations have been from headquarters, and some trees there show evidence of "sap wells" which have been drilled by this sap-loving species.

Red-breasted Sapsucker
Sphyrapicus ruber

Accidental in spring and autumn. The Red-breasted Sap-sucker is a new addition to the Malheur NWR bird-list. Since it was first observed by O. Schmidt, R. Smith, and J. Gilligan on September 25, 1982, four other records for this far western species have occurred. One was at headquarters April 7, 1983, and others were there on August 26-27 and September 27, 1985 (T. Crabtree). Another was at Frenchglen on September 22, 1988, accompanied by a Red-breasted Red-naped hybrid. To date these are the only refuge records, but it is likely the species is expanding its range eastward and others can be expected in the future.

Williamson's Sapsucker
Sphyrapicus thyroideus

Accidental in spring; rare in autumn. The Williamson's Sapsucker is the only North American woodpecker which shows a great amount of sexual dimorphism, and from 1857 to 1874 the male and female were described as separate species. Like some other members of its family, surprisingly few records for the Williamson's Sapsucker exist on Malheur NWR as it is a common nesting species in the yellow pine forest north of Burns. It is possible birds migrate westward along the Blue Mountain foothills to the Cascade Range before heading south to favored wintering regions. There are only twelve records for the species on the refuge. The first was

a male collected March 28, 1958 (refuge museum), at headquarters. Since then, this sapsucker has been recorded on
September 3 and 21, 1961 (banded at headquarters); April 8,
1970 (female at headquarters); August 18, 1977 (female at
Benson Pond); October 3, 1982 (male at headquarters); September 23-27, 1986 (female at Frenchglen); and in 1987 a
female was at headquarters on September 25, a male at
Frenchglen Spring on October 26, males at Frenchglen on
September 23 and October 10, and a female at Benson Pond
on November 2.

Downy Woodpecker
Picoides pubescens

Uncommon in spring, autumn, and winter. The Downy
Woodpecker nests in deciduous forest in the Blue Mountains
north of Burns, and has also been seen in summer on Steens
Mountain. It is absent from the refuge in summer, but once
nesting duties have been completed a few individuals move
onto the desert lowlands. Downy Woodpeckers have been
seen on the refuge as early as August 18 (1976); generally
they are not seen until October. They are never seen in large
numbers and most records have been of single individuals,
usually searching for food in willows and alders near P Ranch
and Page Springs. In winter, Downy Woodpeckers have been
recorded during eleven Christmas counts, with four observed
in 1987 for the largest number. Two were at headquarters
February 25-26, 1982, and these were likely northbound
migrants. The latest spring record occurred on May 8, 1976.
No spring (or autumn) migrational peak has been detected as
individuals trickle from the region toward mountainous aspen groves where they find their preferred nesting habitat.

Hairy Woodpecker
Picoides villosus

Uncommon in spring, autumn, and winter. Although the
Hairy Woodpecker has a wide geographical distribution,

nesting from Alaska and Canada south to Panama, it occurs sparingly on Malheur NWR. Since it nests in forested regions, little nesting habitat is available in the deserts and it is usually not until October that this medium-sized woodpecker moves onto the lowlands. On the refuge, the Hairy Woodpecker is seldom seen as individuals occur alone at widely scattered locations. Favorable refuge habitat includes cottonwoods, willows, alders, and junipers, and it is here that the species should be looked for.

An exceptionally early Hairy Woodpecker was at head-quarters August 9, 1986, but generally the species is not seen until October (second earliest October 1, 1977). The autumn peak of abundance occurs in late October and migrants have left the refuge by mid-November. Hairy Woodpeckers have been recorded during thirteen Christmas counts, with three being seen in 1970 and 1978. Spring migration usually starts in April (earliest March 8, 1985), with an average date of April 2. No spring migration peak has been noted, and the latest spring observation was May 20 (1979).

White-headed Woodpecker
Picoides albolarvatus

Accidental. The striking White-headed Woodpecker nests abundantly in the yellow pine zone of the Blue Mountains north of Burns. There it is sedentary, rarely leaving mountainous regions even in the most severe winters. The only refuge record I have was an individual which appeared at refuge headquarters on October 12, 1982, remaining there for about one week (L. Ditto, B. Ehlers). The sedentary nature of this species makes this record unique, even though it nests regularly within 40 miles of the refuge.

Northern Flicker
Colaptes auratus cafer

Common permanent resident. The "red-shafted" form of the Northern Flicker can be found throughout the year anywhere on the refuge. Until recently the "red-shafted" and "yellow-shafted" flickers (*C. a. auratus*) were considered distinct species, with the Great Plains grasslands separating the two. With settlement and subsequent plantings of shade trees and shelter belts and tree encroachment along major river systems, the eastern "yellow-shafted" form moved westward, while the western "red-shafted" form pushed eastward. When the two forms met an extensive hybridization zone developed.

There is a noticeable influx of flickers at the refuge in both spring and autumn. The spring influx usually occurs from March 7 through April 7, with nesting in progress by late April. Nesting occurs where suitable habitat is available, whether it be large trees, buildings, or fence posts. Nesting pairs are consistently found at headquarters, P Ranch, Malheur Field Station, and Buena Vista. Autumn migration begins in mid-September and continues into November, with the major influx between October 10 and November 10. Flickers have been recorded during all Christmas counts, with greatest numbers seen in 1975 (42), 1977 (49), 1979 (80), 1983 (55), and 1984 (51).

There are several refuge records of "yellow-shafted" individuals. First collected in 1935 by G. Benson, they have been seen thirteen times since. In autumn, they have been seen as early as October 13 (1971) and in spring as late as April 19 (1972). There were six records in the winter of 1971-72, probably representing two individuals. There are no summer records.

ORDER: PASSERIFORMES
FAMILY: TYRANNIDAE

Olive-sided Flycatcher
Contopus borealis

Uncommon spring and autumn migrant. Among the large conifers of the Blue Mountains, the Olive-sided Flycatcher can frequently be seen perched near the top of a tall tree performing its familiar "quick-three-beers" call. On Malheur NWR, the species is strictly a migrant, uncommonly appearing in both spring and autumn. During its brief visits to the refuge, this long-distance migrant is usually found at localities which have lofty trees. I have regularly seen birds at headquarters, P Ranch, Frenchglen, Benson Pond, and Sod House Ranch.

Olive-sided Flycatchers generally arrive the second week of May; the earliest spring record was May 1 (1987). Because of the lack of records, it is difficult to determine their migration peak, but May 15 to 20 would be the most likely time to see the species on the refuge. The latest spring migrant was observed June 7 (1985, M. Archie). This medium-sized flycatcher usually reappears in September, but the earliest autumn record was obtained August 18 (1976). Peak of passage falls between September 10 and 15, and the latest was seen September 24 (1977). Recently individuals have been discovered wintering in southern Mexico, and more unusually in southern California, but the majority push onward to southern Central America and northern South America.

Western Wood-Pewee
Contopus sordidulus

Common spring and autumn migrant; rare in summer. The Western Wood-Pewee is the most abundant flycatcher on the refuge in spring and autumn. It can be found throughout the refuge, but greatest densities occur at headquarters,

P Ranch, Benson Pond, Buena Vista, and among Blitzen Valley willow thickets. There is some evidence of breeding at headquarters and Frenchglen and suitable habitat is also available at Benson Pond and P Ranch. The species commonly nests in Steens Mountain aspen clones and in the open woodlands of the Blue Mountains.

The earliest spring record was April 16 (1968), but the average is not until May 10. The species is most common between May 20 and 31, and the latest was a straggler which lingered until June 22 (1963). The earliest autumn migrant was seen August 5 (1962), the latest September 30 (1962). The peak of their abundance is between August 25 and September 10, but if migratory conditions are unfavorable because of weather conditions the species will linger. Such was the case in 1986 when fifteen were at headquarters on September 22. Like the Olive-sided Flycatcher, Western Wood-Pewees are long-distance migrants, wintering in tropical regions from Panama to Peru.

Willow Flycatcher
Empidonax traillii

Common in spring, summer, and autumn. The Willow Flycatcher is presently a common summer resident at the refuge, nesting in the shrubby thickets bordering watercourses throughout the Blitzen Valley. From late May through July their familiar "fitz-bew" call can be heard from wooded streambottoms, canals, channels, and ditches, particularly from Krumbo Road south to Page Springs. The species has increased dramatically on Malheur NWR since the early 1970s as a result of reduced livestock grazing and subsequent improved riparian nesting habitat. On an annual breeding-bird survey from Benson Pond to Page Springs, no Willow Flycatchers were recorded in 1973, but as habitat conditions improved 71 were recorded in 1986.

The average Willow Flycatcher arrival date is May 12, with the earliest recorded April 29 (1969). Nesting begins in June and continues into mid-July. Although Brown-headed Cowbirds regularly parasitize Willow Flycatcher nests in other regions, this does not appear to be a problem on the refuge. To date no parasitized nests have been located, but probably some minor parasitism does occur at localized areas. Autumn migration has been noted in late July, but the peak does not occur until late August. The latest autumn record was September 25 (1962), but most have left for warmer climates by mid-September.

Hammond's Flycatcher
Empidonax hammondii

Rare spring and autumn migrant. There are presently few refuge records for the Hammond's Flycatcher, but its true status has not been determined because of its similarity to the other small flycatchers. It most resembles the Dusky Flycatcher and away from breeding areas it can only be safely identified in the hand. During the nesting period, the Hammond's Flycatcher is found at higher elevations in the coniferous forests of western North America, and I have numerous sightings from the dense evergreen forests adjacent to the Strawberry Wilderness Area, southeast of John Day.

There are two spring and five autumn records: individuals were captured, measured, banded, and released at headquarters. Spring records were birds captured on May 16, 1966, and May 8, 1983; autumn records were obtained August 29, 1965; September 17, 1963; September 27, 1962; and September 28, 1962 (two birds).

Dusky Flycatcher
Empidonax oberholseri

Common spring and autumn migrant; rare in summer. The Dusky Flycatcher nests commonly in the aspen and juniper woodlands on Steens Mountain and in brushy-yellow pine regions of the Blue Mountains. It has been found in summer west of Highway 205 on the juniper-covered slopes between Diamond Lane and Frenchglen. Based on banding data, only the Willow Flycatcher is more abundant on Malheur NWR during spring and autumn. Transients occur throughout the refuge, but it is most numerous at headquarters, Page Springs, Benson Pond, P Ranch, and Frenchglen.

Although the Dusky Flycatcher's status is imperfectly known because of its similarity to sibling species, banding data indicate the following migrational chronology. The earliest spring records occurred April 22 (1962, 1966), and the average arrival is May 3. It is most abundant and widely distributed between May 5 and 20. The latest record was June 12 (1961). Autumn migrants have been recorded between August 14 (1984) and October 22 (1963), and the species reaches an autumn peak between September 5 and 20.

Gray Flycatcher
Empidonax wrightii

Uncommon in spring, summer, and autumn; accidental in winter. Gray Flycatchers are not common on the refuge, but they are regularly encountered in summer on Steens Mountain, Warm Springs Mountains, and the sagebrush expanses to the west and east. Breeding haunts are generally in large sagebrush and in juniper woodlands, but I have also found summer birds in the yellow pine-mountain mahogany associations north of Burns. The species is one of two small flycatchers which can be identified with some certainty in the field. Pale gray coloration, white wing-bars, and its habit of flicking the tail downward like a phoebe are important identifying characteristics.

The earliest spring Gray Flycatcher was recorded April 28 (1969) and the latest transient on May 21 (1963). There is no pronounced peak on the refuge as individuals trickle through the region. Nesting reports on Malheur NWR are few, but one of the earliest historical records for the species is from the

Narrows area, where an adult and two eggs were collected on July 6, 1896 (Gabrielson and Jewett 1940). W. Anderson found territorial birds west of Highway 205 near Krumbo Road in May 1972, a lapse of 76 years between nesting reports. In autumn, records have occurred between August 4 and September 24 (both 1961), but again the species is so sporadic that no peak period of passage has been noted. Most unusual were reports of two birds at separate locations on December 22, 1940, seen by two different parties. I have no additional details on these observations and it would be highly unlikely that these birds would have survived the winter months in southeast Oregon.

Western Flycatcher
Empidonax difficilis

Uncommon spring and autumn migrant. The first southeast Oregon record for this widely distributed western species did not occur until E. Kridler collected an individual at headquarters on May 30, 1961. Since then numerous records have accumulated, mostly from headquarters. Western Flycatchers are more common in western Oregon, but recently there has been a decided increase in eastern Oregon, at least at Malheur NWR. Yellowish underparts (even on the throat) and olive-greenish back help distinguish the Western Flycatcher from other members of its genus.

Observations in spring have fallen between April 23 and June 17 (both 1970). The species is most abundant in mid-May. The earliest autumn migrant was recorded August 12 (1965). Peak of autumn passage occurs from August 25 through September 15, with the latest October 3 (1961). While visitants are in the area, they are regularly seen hunting from the lower branches of trees, particularly in the evergreens which surround the headquarters lawn.

Say's Phoebe
Sayornis saya

Common in spring, summer, and autumn. The Say's Phoebe is an early spring migrant, usually arriving in the midst of winter in late February. At this time its major food is likely seeds, but even as snow falls individuals may be seen perched on a prominent vantage point as if watching for passing insects. This arid land flycatcher has adapted well to human habitation and most refuge pairs now nest under eaves, in abandoned buildings, in porches or, as was the case in 1984 and 1987, upon an outhouse at Page Springs. Some pairs do, however, still occupy traditional rimrock sites, particularly from Diamond Lane south to Page Springs. During the nesting season, Say's Phoebes are consistently seen at headquarters, Malheur Field Station, Sod House Ranch, P Ranch, and Page Springs.

The earliest record was obtained January 18 (1941), and the average is February 23. Resident males are the first to arrive, with females arriving about one week later. Northbound transients peak between March 15 and 25. Nesting begins in mid-April (earliest April 16, 1973), with hatching occurring in early May. The first young have fledged by the end of May, and shortly after a second clutch is laid in early June. Most of these young have fledged by mid-July. Autumn migration begins in August, but no pronounced peak has been noted as birds trickle from the region. The majority have left the refuge by September's end, and the latest record was October 11 (1986).

Western Kingbird
Tyrannus verticalis

Common in spring, summer, and autumn. The Western Kingbird is a conspicuous nester around human habitations where tall trees, power-poles, and buildings provide nesting sites. Settlement has benefitted the species in southeast Oregon as it has in other regions of the United States and southern Canada. In regions which were formerly void of trees, such as in most of the lowland Great Basin deserts, shade trees planted around human habitations have allowed the Western Kingbird to expand its range, and today it is common in southeast Oregon during the summer months.

The average arrival date on the refuge in spring is April 25, with the earliest observation April 5 (1981). Peak of passage occurs from May 5 through 15, and transients have left the area by May 25. In periods of inclement weather, Western Kingbirds will occasionally use communal roost sites. On May 7 and 8, 1983, J. Anderson watched 55 go to roost in a spruce tree at headquarters. These were accompanied by twenty Yellow-rumped Warblers and two Northern Orioles. Nesting is in progress by early June and fledged young have been seen as early as June 30 (1976). Most pairs have raised their families by late July. During the nesting season, pairs have traditionally been located at headquarters, Buena Vista, P Ranch, Malheur Field Station, Page Springs, and Frenchglen. If a nest is situated near human activity, Western Kingbirds can become rather pugnacious, and pairs which have nested at Malheur Field Station have become so aggressive that they have attacked humans which approached their nests too closely. Autumn migration begins in early July, with the peak occurring from August 15 to 25. Most have left the refuge by September, with the latest record September 14 (1985). During migration the species is seen throughout the refuge, perched on power-poles, wires, fence posts, or upon any other upright structure.

Eastern Kingbird
Tyrannus tyrannus

Uncommon in spring, summer, and autumn. The Eastern Kingbird arrives late in spring and departs early in autumn. Nesting territories are along willow-bordered watercourses and ponds; the species is particularly common in the willow thickets along the Blitzen River from 5-mile Road south to its confluence with Bridge Creek. Elsewhere on the refuge, individual pairs are scattered throughout the Blitzen Valley, but few have been seen at Double O. On June 28, 1971, 32 were recorded along the Blitzen River from Rattlesnake Butte to Dunn Dam in the northern Blitzen Valley. Since the late 1970s, Eastern Kingbirds have increased and expanded their range on the refuge. Improved nesting habitat resulting from a decrease in livestock grazing in riparian zones is believed responsible for this expansion and increase.

The earliest spring record was May 4 (1963), but the average arrival is not until May 19. Few migrants occur in the region, and birds seen in migration eventually nest on the refuge. Nesting activity begins shortly after arrival. Eggs are laid in June and young fledge in July. Unlike its near relative, the Western Kingbird, the Eastern Kingbird avoids human habitations on Malheur NWR and prefers to restrict its activities to riparian habitats. Autumn migration is initiated in August, shortly after young fledge, and by September few remain. No pronounced migration waves have been noted as individuals trickle from the refuge on their way to South American wintering areas. The latest autumn record was September 15 (Gabrielson and Jewett 1940).

Scissor-tailed Flycatcher
Tyrannus forficatus

Accidental. There are two refuge records. R. Ross, with students from Linn-Benton Community College, observed one about 3 miles west of headquarters in 1967, but date and details are presently unavailable. The second record occurred on July 4, 1973, when T. Haislip, Jr. and his Malheur Field Station ornithology class watched an individual for about 5 minutes before it flew toward headquarters from Kado Bridge.

Ash-throated Flycatcher
Myiarchus cinerascens

Uncommon in spring, summer, and autumn. Ash-throated Flycatchers are possibly more common than my records indicate as few observers investigate the habitat used by this species in the summer months. Nesting is primarily confined to the juniper slopes adjacent to the southern Blitzen Valley. This flycatcher has been recently seen during the nesting season at Page and Frenchglen springs, and among the junipers west of Highway 205 from Buena Vista to Frenchglen. On July 31, 1979, a large number was observed in an extensive juniper grove near Diamond Craters about 3 miles east of the refuge. Generally, pairs are found alone and this is the only locality where I have found large numbers in southeast Oregon.

Ash-throated Flycatchers are mostly late refuge migrants—the earliest record was April 21 (1984), but the average is not until May 17. Upon arrival they immediately occupy nesting territories; therefore, few migrants have been noted in spring. Nesting is in progress in June and one pair was observed feeding young in a cavity of a post at Frenchglen Spring on July 1, 1974. The species is more evident in autumn and is often seen at headquarters. Numbers peak in August and the majority have left by mid-September. The latest record was October 13 (1975).

FAMILY: ALAUDIDAE

Horned Lark
Eremophila alpestris

Common in spring, autumn, and winter; uncommon in summer. Favored habitats for the Horned Lark include plowed fields, crested wheatgrass seedings, and expanses of low sagebrush. Because few of these habitats occur within the refuge boundaries the species is not abundant; however, in spring and autumn it can become locally common. When the refuge is snow covered Horned Larks have concentrated along roads where snow has melted, exposing seeds. The area between Rattlesnake Butte and Diamond Lane (along the Center Patrol Road) has been an important use area, and after a snowfall an estimated seven hundred were there on April 4, 1975. The species is one of the few which has benefitted from extensive crested wheatgrass seedings, as it prefers bare ground interspersed with scattered bunches of grass. There it finds both feeding and nesting habitat.

There is an influx of Horned Larks between March 10 and April 10, but by the time the nesting season approaches few remain on the refuge. About the only favorable nesting habitat is around Harney and Malheur lakes, and in crested wheatgrass seedings south of Boca Lake and near Krumbo Reservoir. The species begins congregating in September and reaches a peak between October 5 and November 5. Although many remain in the Malheur-Harney Lakes Basin in most years, they are more common in the Alvord Valley. In winter on the refuge, Horned Larks have been recorded during eight southern Blitzen Valley Christmas counts, but little habitat is present within the count circle.

FAMILY: HIRUNDINIDAE

Purple Martin
Progne subis

Accidental in spring. The Purple Martin is more common in western Oregon and there are only three records for the refuge. Willett (1919) observed a single male at Malheur Lake on May 10, 1918. W. Anderson obtained the second record when he watched two males near P Ranch (1.5 miles north) on May 29, 1971. The third record was a male observed about 2 miles south of the Diamond Lane-Highway 205 junction on the very early date of March 15, 1982 (D. Severson).

Tree Swallow
Tachycineta bicolor

Abundant spring and autumn migrant; common at certain localities in summer; accidental in winter. On Malheur NWR, the Tree Swallow is the most abundant member of its family, often occurring by the thousands. On March 12, 1972, an estimated six thousand were near Benson Landing after the first individuals had arrived March 5, and an estimated ten thousand were in the Blitzen Valley April 26, 1975. When emergent stands are present in Malheur Lake, the species can become abundant in both spring and autumn at headquarters. Here, birds feed over land by day, moving into Malheur Lake to roost among the dense stands of hardstem bulrush at night. These sites are frequently up to 3 miles from land, secure from potential predators.

Tree Swallows usually arrive in early March (average March 1), but in mild winters a few individuals appear in February. The earliest spring record was February 6 (1977). Peak of passage is usually in mid-April but occasionally in March. Transients have left by mid-May, but unseasonably cool and wet weather in adjoining montane nesting areas sometimes pushes birds back onto the lowlands after mid-May. About one hundred were seen near P Ranch on June 3, 1976, after a period of cold weather. The species reaches greatest nesting densities in this region in the aspen clones of Steens Mountain, and near water bodies in the Blue Mountains, though a few pairs remain on the refuge to nest, primarily in the southern Blitzen Valley in the vicinity of Frenchglen, P Ranch, and along the Center Patrol Road north of P Ranch. In addition, nesting pairs can be found at headquarters and Malheur Field Station. Nest construction begins in mid-May and a few have completed nesting duties by late June and early July. Autumn migration is somewhat later for this species than for most other swallows, beginning in mid-August and peaking between September 10 and October 1. The latest autumn record was November 27 (1979). There are two winter records; Marshall (1959) collected a male in poor condition on January 9, 1958, at headquarters, and S. Thompson observed an individual at Harney Lake on December 22, 1980.

Violet-green Swallow
Tachycineta thalassina

Common spring and autumn migrant; occasional in summer. Violet-green Swallows are regularly seen in summer throughout southeast Oregon where cliffs and trees provide favorable nesting sites. In July and August the species is frequently seen near Steens Mountain summit as it flies along precipitous escarpments searching for insects which have been windblown upward from the desert below. Among the jagged cliffs it finds suitable nesting habitat, and within the Great Basin mountain ranges seems to prefer crevices to tree-cavity nesting sites.

Violet-green Swallows arrive early (average March 28), with the earliest record February 24 (1982). Peak of spring migration occurs during the last week of April. Occasionally a pair will remain on Malheur NWR to nest, but generally all move on to montane regions. A nest box was used by a pair for a couple of years at the Frenchglen Hotel, but presently this site is occupied by House Wrens. During June, individuals will occasionally be seen with Tree and Barn swallows circling around the P Ranch Tower in late afternoon. Turkey Vultures on the tower remove numerous small feathers while preening, and as feathers float toward the ground they are caught by swallows to be used as nest-lining material. Before their southward departure in autumn, no large concentrations have been noted. Many leave in August and early September and few are seen after mid-September. The latest record was of five dying at headquarters September 30 (1971) during a period of unseasonably cold weather.

Northern Rough-winged Swallow
Stelgidopteryx serripennis

Common in spring and autumn; uncommon in summer. In spring, this species is widely distributed throughout the refuge, but unlike some other members of its family it migrates through this region in small, widely scattered flocks. On a trip from headquarters south to Page Springs, it is rare to see more than fifty on a given day. However, when mixed flocks of swallows congregate in July, Northern Rough-winged Swallows can become abundant. At one of these staging areas, an estimated 750 were seen July 13, 1967. The species does not nest colonially, and solitary pairs are found primarily along the Blitzen River, Silver Creek, West Canal (from Frenchglen to Krumbo Road), and in the vicinity of Page Springs. One of the highest densities recorded in recent years has been along the Blitzen River from Rattlesnake Butte to Dunn Dam. On June 28, 1971, 67 were seen along this stretch, where eroded banks provided ideal sites for their nesting burrows.

The earliest spring arrival was March 6 (1968); the average is April 6. The species is most abundant and widely distributed between April 22 and May 1, but transients have left the refuge by mid-May. For the pairs which remain to nest, nesting begins in May and by late June or early July young have fledged. As southbound migrants arrive, rough-winged swallows reach their greatest numbers. Traditional staging areas are at headquarters and Buena Vista in mid-July. From these areas individuals begin moving south in late July. The majority have left by September; 150 lingered at headquarters through September 15, 1971. The latest autumn record was October 4 (1975).

Bank Swallow
Riparia riparia

Uncommon in spring, summer, and autumn. The Bank Swallow was first recorded from Malheur NWR on May 27,

1875, when Bendire (1877) collected eggs from a large colony on an island in Malheur Lake. Colonies still persisted on islands through 1918 (Willet 1919), and even today a large colony exists in a gravel pit near the south shore. In 1983, an estimated one thousand pairs were using the site. Within the refuge boundary small colonies are occasionally found along the eroded banks of the Blitzen River, particularly from Rattlesnake Butte to Dunn Dam and near P Ranch. Recently, high water in Harney Lake created nesting habitat among the wave-washed sand dunes along the northeast shore, and about one hundred pairs were nesting there in 1985 and several hundred in 1987 and 1988.

The Bank Swallow is the last member of its family to appear in spring, with the earliest arrival April 21 (1966). The average spring arrival is May 9. Nesting activities begin shortly after pairs arrive, and eggs are usually present by the end of May. Communal nesting sites occur in steep banks adjacent to streams and lakes, or in gravel pits, and for pairs nesting on the refuge site localities vary annually. Young fledge in late June or early July. In some years, Bank Swallows congregate in the vicinity of headquarters with other swallow species in July before migrating from the region. Greatest numbers in recent years were one hundred on July 13, 1967, and fifty on July 6, 1969. Generally most have departed by mid-August, but in 1986 and 1987 Bank Swallows reached unprecedented numbers in late August. Beginning in mid-August birds began congregating at the Diamond Lane-Center Patrol Road junction, and by the end of the month an estimated fifteen hundred could be seen lining power-lines and fences adjacent to the Blitzen River. Shortly after August individuals migrated rapidly from the refuge and were last seen in early September (September 8, 1986). The latest record was reported for Harney County by Gabrielson and Jewett (1940) as September 12, but year and location were not given.

Barn Swallow
Hirundo rustica

Common in spring, summer, and autumn. Before settlement few Barn Swallows nested in the Malheur-Harney Lakes Basin. Bendire (1877) considered the species rather rare, and reported only a few pairs breeding around the buildings at Camp Harney in the 1870s. As the human population increased, buildings, bridges, and culverts became widespread throughout the basin. Barn Swallows readily adapted to these structures, and today the species is one of the most common summer residents. Throughout Malheur NWR Barn Swallows nest where such structures occur, particularly at headquarters, Malheur Field Station, and Buena Vista. Upon completion of a new structure, this species will readily pioneer. In 1966, a pair constructed their nest on the side of my tent while I was camped at Benson Pond. After the first clutch was destroyed, the female swallow immediately deposited another. When the second clutch disappeared, the pair abandoned the site and likely moved to a more favorable nesting locality.

The earliest Barn Swallows were recorded February 27 (1967), but the average is not until April 7. The peak of spring migration occurs in late April and resident pairs are on territory by this time. Nesting begins in May; however, E. Kridler examined four nests which contained eggs and one with newly hatched young on April 5, 1962. Two broods are usually produced and one pair was still feeding unfledged young at Malheur Field Station on September 10, 1976. The species is one of the last members of its family to leave in autumn. Migration is protracted, extending from mid-August through October. The last observation was recorded November 18, 1982, when a single bird was seen at headquarters. This extended migration period occasionally results in high mortality after birds become trapped by cold weather. This occurred on September 30, 1971, when an estimated one hundred were found dead or dying at headquarters.

Cliff Swallow
Hirundo pyrrhonota

Abundant in spring, summer, and autumn. This species is the most abundant nesting swallow on the refuge, and numerous colonies presently exist on buildings and other structures and on basaltic rimrocks. The largest colonies on structures have been at Ramalli and 5-mile bridges, headquarters, and Malheur Field Station, while colonies have been found on natural cliff sites near Unit 8 Pond, Buena Vista, Derrick Lake, Hamilton Field, and Page Springs. Generally colony locations remain relatively stable; however, their crowded, gourd-shaped mud nests occasionally become infested with insects and are abandoned; large infestations will kill young, and on rare occasions adults. Although Cliff Swallows are known to produce two broods annually at southern nesting regions, pairs which nest on Malheur NWR are single brooded.

Cliff Swallows are generally a late spring migrant; however, one very early observation was obtained February 28, 1982, when B. and S. Ehlers located a single bird at headquarters. Their average arrival is April 10, and the peak of passage occurs in late April and early May. Most residents are on territory by late April, with nesting in progress by mid-May. Young regularly fledge from mid-June through mid-July, but in years with below average spring temperatures nesting is delayed. Cliff Swallows begin congregating with other swallows in late June and early July, with concentrations most frequently seen at headquarters, Frenchglen, Buena Vista, and on power-lines parallel with Highway 205 from Diamond Lane to 5-mile Road. An estimated five thousand were at headquarters July 13, 1967. Flocks begin leaving in July, and by September few Cliff Swallows remain. The latest record was September 7 (1970, 1971).

Occasionally in spring, cold and wet conditions can result in adult Cliff Swallow mortality. In 1980, birds arrived March 18, but in late May unseasonably cold conditions persisted for several days. Dead Cliff Swallows were found at headquarters over the Memorial Day Weekend, and at one colony at Malheur Field Station 67 dead birds were retrieved. Through the remainder of the nesting season Cliff Swallow numbers were greatly reduced.

FAMILY: CORVIDAE

Gray Jay
Perisoreus canadensis

Accidental. The Gray Jay's normal habitat in Oregon is high-elevation coniferous forest, and rarely do individuals stray into the arid lowlands even in the harshest of winters. Only two records have occurred on Malheur NWR: a single bird at headquarters on August 15, 1960, and another at P Ranch on December 31, 1966. Unlike some of the other corvids, the Gray Jay is not considered an irruptive species, making the two refuge records even more exceptional.

Blue Jay
Cyanocitta cristata

Accidental. There are three records for this eastern species. The first was of a single bird which appeared at headquarters from October 25 through 27, 1975; the second was at the same locality on October 6 and 7, 1977. The third record was of a single bird which was first seen at P Ranch on December 18, 1986, remaining through February 1987. All refuge records have been either of autumn or wintering birds which is consistent with recent observations from neighboring areas in California.

Steller's Jay
Cyanocitta stelleri

Accidental. The species is common in the Blue Mountains north of Burns and rarely do individuals wander from their coniferous forest haunts. However, on occasion Steller's Jays irrupt into atypical lowland regions, often a considerable distance from montane habitat. In the winter of 1960-61, an irruption occurred which brought the species to such remote areas as the Arizona desert (Phillips et al. 1964). It was also in 1961 that one of the three refuge records occurred, as a single bird was captured and banded at headquarters on May 17. A second bird was observed by M. Jess at P Ranch November 7, 1984, and the third was seen in Frenchglen on October 9, 1987 (C. Miller). To date these represent the only refuge records.

Pinyon Jay
Gymnorhinus cyanocephalus

Accidental. Although abundant and widely distributed in the dense juniper and pine forests of central Oregon, the Pinyon Jay is only an accidental visitant to the Malheur-Harney Lakes Basin. The only refuge record was of a single bird which appeared near Krumbo Road-Highway 205 junction on January 11 and remained through January 13, 1945 (G. Benson). There is only one other record for the basin as Bendire (1877) reported a flock of about eighty birds flying southward along Rattlesnake Creek near Camp Harney in October 1875.

Clark's Nutcracker
Nucifraga columbiana

Rare. There are seven refuge records for this montane species. The first occurrence was in March 1956, when a lone bird spent several weeks at Buena Vista. Other refuge records were one on September 15, 1961, near Krumbo Road; fifteen seen on December 26, 1962 (location unknown); one in the southern Blitzen Valley on August 29, 1969; one at headquarters on September 22, 1980; three at headquarters on July 7, 1982; and one in Diamond Valley on November 1, 1984

(M. Jess). The irruptive behavior of Clark's Nutcrackers into arid lowlands has been well documented. Individuals can appear during any month of the year, but reports from the refuge and surrounding localities indicate a slight preponderance of records for August and September.

Black-billed Magpie
Pica pica

Common permanent resident. The Black-billed Magpie is a striking member of the Corvid family, and is one of the conspicuous birds of willow-bordered wetlands and sagebrush uplands throughout the refuge. The species is not as abundant as in former years, as habitat losses from mowing, cutting, grazing, and spraying willows, as well as toxic poisoning with chemicals related to the livestock industry, have resulted in a widespread decline of magpies. Malheur NWR is no exception.

Spring migration begins early and is usually in progress by February, extending into April. One major concentration area regularly occurs between Malheur Field Station and Unit 9 Pond, where 50 to 150 magpies can often be seen in March. Elsewhere the species is frequently seen but not in large numbers. By the time nesting begins in April, Black-billed Magpies are widely scattered throughout the refuge, primarily near willow thickets, but a few pairs do nest in the taller stands of sagebrush. At a few localities the species forms loose nesting colonies, particularly if a favorable food source is nearby. One colony of eight pairs formerly nested in willows about half a mile southeast of Malheur Field Station. These birds continually flew to and from their nests and an open-pit disposal site. Once this site was abandoned and covered, magpies deserted the willows and have never returned to nest. A few young fledge in May and most are on the wing by mid-June. After completion of nesting, family groups wander over the refuge, occasionally joining with other groups to form small flocks. Resident birds begin leaving in September, and transients peak in October. Many remain through the winter and have been recorded during all Christmas counts. Greatest numbers were seen in 1958 (201), 1968 (143), and 1971 (102). In winter, magpies are frequently seen near Rattlesnake Butte and along the Center Patrol Road from Bridge Creek to 5-mile Road.

American Crow
Corvus brachyrhynchos

Common in spring and autumn; uncommon in summer; occasional in winter. Although not as common on Malheur NWR today as they were in the past, American Crows still border on abundant during the summer and autumn months in and around Burns. Nesting commonly occurs along wooded streambottoms on the Silvies River floodplain and among the taller trees within the city limits, while on the refuge the few pairs which do nest confine their activities to willow thickets. Generally no more than five pairs nest annually on the refuge.

The earliest spring record was obtained on February 10 (1971), but the average is not until March 16. The peak of migration occurs in late March, and transients have moved from the area by mid-April. In summer, nesting locations are sporadic, but single pairs have been seen regularly southeast of Buena Vista and south of Malheur Field Station. By July, family groups begin congregating at favorable feeding sites. East Grain Camp has been a favored location as birds are attracted to the grain crops there. Autumn migration begins in September and peaks in October. Two flocks totaling sixty birds were seen October 13, 1975, migrating rapidly south over Buena Vista just before a frontal passage. As these birds were leaving others were feeding nearby, showing no inclination to migrate. Most migrants have left the refuge by mid-November. The species has been recorded during ten Christmas counts, but no more than three individuals have been observed per count except in 1980 when 27 were seen. In 1975, about fifty wintered at East Grain Camp for the largest winter concentration recorded at the refuge.

Common Raven
Corvus corax

Abundant permanent resident. The Common Raven is an abundant bird on Malheur NWR, and abandoned buildings, willows, windmills, and particularly rimrocks provide unlimited nesting sites. The species has increased since the early 1970s, and well over eight hundred individuals can now be found at some roost sites within the Malheur-Harney Lakes Basin. In spring, pairs leave the flocks and move to favorable nesting sites, and those which nest adjacent to wetlands prey heavily on the eggs of other species. Common Ravens are readily seen throughout the refuge as they hunt over meadows, marshes, and uplands in spring and early summer.

The species begins nesting generally in late March or early April, and young fledge in May and June. In late June through July, large flocks can be seen at scattered locations on the refuge. One aggregation was seen July 4, 1974, at Boca Lake which consisted of 110 birds, and flocks of over three hundred have been seen in July in the Double O area. Most have left the refuge by August and September and moved onto the surrounding sagebrush expanses or agricultural developments between Crane and Buchanan. Communal roost sites become active in October and are used consistently through January. Formerly, the majority roosted on islands in Malheur Lake, but as lake levels increased in the early 1980s, islands became inundated and birds moved to sites near Burns and Buchanan. In winter, ravens occur more regularly in the vicinities of Crane, Burns, and Buchanan, and few are seen on the refuge until individual pairs arrive in February.

FAMILY: PARIDAE

Black-capped Chickadee
Parus atricapillus

Occasional in autumn, winter, and spring. There are few Black-capped Chickadee records for Malheur NWR. However, the species is common along the cottonwood-lined streams and rivers which drain the Blue Mountains near John Day, and I have also seen it with some regularity along the foothill streams east and north of Burns. On the refuge, the species has been recorded during five Christmas counts: 1957 (three), 1959 (six), 1963 (one), 1970 (two), and 1977 (one). Additional records include observations on September 30, 1940 (one); February 26, 1941 (two); March 26, 1944 (four); April 15, 1961 (several); and September 12, 1966 (one banded). The sedentary nature of this widely distributed species accounts for its scarcity on Malheur NWR, as individuals are primarily permanent residents in the riparian zones which it normally inhabits.

Mountain Chickadee
Parus gambeli

Uncommon in autumn, winter, and spring. Mountain Chickadees are sporadic visitants to Malheur NWR, appearing one year only to be absent the next. Although a few pairs are summer residents on Steens Mountain, their regional center of abundance lies in the coniferous forest of the Blue Mountains. There they feed among the evergreens and are one of the most frequently encountered species. Mountain Chickadees are seen at scattered localities throughout the refuge, but the majority of records have been from headquarters and the willow-bordered watercourses and juniper woodlands of the southern Blitzen Valley.

The earliest autumn record occurred September 19 (1983), and the species is most common in October. Numbers decrease after mid-November, but on occasions Mountain Chickadees winter. They have been recorded during twelve Christmas counts; there are usually less than five birds per count. However, in 1970, 1977, and 1986, 49, 28, and 23 were seen, respectively. The species was decidedly common on the refuge during the 1970-71 winter, first appearing on September 27 and remaining through May 1. From twenty to fifty individuals could be seen daily among the willow thickets of the southern Blitzen Valley. A spring influx occurs in April and early May, and the latest observation occurred May 10 (1972).

FAMILY: AEGITHALIDAE

Bushtit
Psaltriparus minimus

Occasional winter visitant to lowlands; fairly common permanent resident in juniper woodlands. One of North America's smallest passerines, the highly sociable Bushtit borders on common among the juniper woodlands of southeast Oregon. It is only during the breeding season that birds are seen in pairs; they spend the remainder of the year in flocks of ten to fifty individuals. Pairs often lay a second clutch before the first young have fledged and frequently the first brood helps with the raising of the second. Once the second clutch fledges, family groups join with others, and flocking behavior resumes until spring when pairs again separate to repeat the annual cycle. On Malheur NWR, the species is occasionally seen in winter in the southern Blitzen Valley riparian zones, but most of their activities are confined to the juniper woodlands from Diamond Lane south to Page Springs.

Little information is available on Bushtit nesting chronology on the refuge, but pairs have been seen from mid-April through June. Nesting probably is underway by the first week of May, as single birds have been observed between May 2 and 12 at Page Springs. Highest densities are among the junipers west of Highway 205 between Frenchglen and Krumbo Road. On December 15, 1984, 195 were counted in this area during a survey of junipers west of the highway. The species has been seen during 22 Christmas counts and greatest numbers were in 1974 (55), 1975 (73), 1976 (64), 1983 (55), and 1984 (195).

FAMILY: SITTIDAE

Red-breasted Nuthatch
Sitta canadensis

Occasional to common in spring, summer, and autumn. The Red-breasted Nuthatch is rather erratic on Malheur NWR—numerous some years, absent in others. Numbers are dependent on summer food supplies in the spruce, fir, and pine forests, and if food is limited this species will not hesitate to move onto desert lowlands where individuals can be seen foraging in such atypical habitats as sagebrush and bulrush. Generally though, they are most numerous in areas with large trees, and greatest densities on the refuge occur at headquarters where it is not uncommon to see from five to ten individuals on a given day during invasion years.

In spring, Red-breasted Nuthatches arrive late, with the earliest date on April 23 (1978) and the average May 5. They are occasionally seen in June, and these birds could be either late northbound migrants or early invaders in irruptive years. For example, the species was not seen after June 22 in 1971, while in 1969 it became a common bird after first appearing June 14. Peak periods have occurred in late July, August, and early September. The latest autumn record was October 29 (1961). Presently no winter records exist; however, the species should be looked for during the winter months among the juniper woodlands on or near the refuge.

Pygmy Nuthatch
Sitta pygmaea

Rare in summer and autumn. The Pygmy Nuthatch confines most of its yearly activities to the open yellow pine stands of western North America. It is an uncommon erratic, rarely descending into the desert lowlands. Ten additional records have occurred on the refuge since Marshall (1959) first reported one on September 5, 1955. All observations have been from summer and autumn, with dates ranging from July 23 (1966) to November 22 (1967). All other records have been in August and September, with the exception of one on October 4, 1970. The majority have been seen at headquarters, but they likely occur elsewhere on the refuge where juniper woodlands and larger trees are found.

White-breasted Nuthatch
Sitta carolinensis

Occasional in spring and autumn. The White-breasted Nuthatch inhabits deciduous and coniferous forest in montane regions throughout eastern Oregon. Unlike the Red-breasted Nuthatch, however, it does not invade into the desert lowlands, and records on Malheur NWR are limited. Historically, the species was first reported from Oregon at Camp Harney in November and December 1874 (Brewer 1875), and the first nesting record was obtained June 6, 1876, near the same location (Bendire 1877).

Of the few available records from the refuge, in the spring the White-breasted Nuthatch has been seen between April 2 and May 19 (both 1971). No pronounced migration has been noted, but most observations are from early and mid-May. This largest of North American nuthatches has been seen in autumn between August 19 and September 19, but no migration peak has been detected. Most reports have come from areas which have large trees such as at headquarters, Page

Springs, Buena Vista, and Benson Pond. Generally birds of this species occur alone, but occasionally they associate with chickadees, kinglets, and creepers.

FAMILY: CERTHIIDAE

Brown Creeper
Certhia americana

Uncommon spring and autumn migrant. The Brown Creeper is a bird of the forest, rarely seen away from tree trunks or large branches—even the nest is located behind a slab of bark. Like other bark-probing species, the Brown Creeper has a light-colored throat which is believed to aid the bird in finding food by reflecting light into dark crevices. Characteristically, individuals fly from the upper trunk of a tree down to the base of an adjoining tree, only to spiral up the trunk and repeat the process. While on the refuge, creepers have been mostly seen at headquarters, but they do occasionally occur in the juniper woodlands, and at Benson Pond, P Ranch, and Frenchglen.

The earliest spring arrival was March 5 (1982), but the average is not until April 26. Peak of migration is between April 25 and May 7, and the latest the species has been seen on the refuge was June 6 (1983). In autumn, the earliest arrival was October 1 (1962), and the latest departure was November 13 (1961). The most likely time to see autumn birds is between October 10 and November 2. Like some other montane species, many individuals remain at higher elevations through the winter, while others migrate to warmer climates. Brown Creepers are usually seen annually on Malheur NWR, but there have been a few years when they were completely absent. Surprisingly, there are no winter records.

FAMILY: CINCLIDAE

American Dipper
Cinclus mexicanus

Uncommon winter resident. The American Dipper commonly nests along fast-flowing streams on Steens Mountain and, depending on the severity of the winter, may move to lower elevations for the winter. North America's most aquatic passerine has adapted several features which have made such an existence possible such as an oil gland which is ten times larger than that of its near relatives and nostril flaps which can be closed when the bird is under water. Although it lacks webbed feet, it is capable of great underwater mobility as it uses its wings for propulsion. Dippers are hardy and only move to lowland wintering areas after streams become ice covered. They are regularly seen in winter along Bridge and Mud creeks, and a few individuals often move down the Blitzen River to the vicinity of Page Springs. The earliest date recorded was November 1 (1987, P. Sullivan), and the latest spring date was obtained March 24 (1976). The species has been seen during 32 southern Blitzen Valley Christmas counts, with the greatest number recorded in 1980 (nine).

FAMILY: TROGLODYTIDAE

Rock Wren
Salpinctes obsoletus

Common in spring, summer, and autumn; uncommon in winter. The Rock Wren is an inhabitant of arid rocky slopes, rimrocks, and gravel pits, but at least in this region it seems to avoid the sheer cliffs which are the preferred habitat of the Canyon Wren. It nests beneath rocks, making a platform near the entrance. Generally platforms are made of small flat stones, but at a nest on Steens Mountain located by

W. Keithley an arrowhead had been added. Most refuge nests are among rimrocks and rocky slopes, and one pair has used a gravel pit west of headquarters for several years. Greatest densities are from Buena Vista south to Page Springs, particularly in Mud and Bridge Creek canyons.

Spring migration begins in early April and most transients have left Malheur NWR by mid-May. Peak of migration is in early May, and at this time the species can border on abundant. On May 2, 1971, more than fifty were observed from Krumbo Road south to Frenchglen. Most pairs are on territory by early May, and nesting begins shortly thereafter. Some young have fledged in June, and autumn migration begins in mid-August. Peak of passage is in September, but in autumn migrants trickle from the area and no large concentrations or mass movements have been noted. Most transients have left the refuge by late October, but a few remain through the winter in protected canyons and rimrocks. Rock Wrens have been recorded during 22 Christmas counts in the southern Blitzen Valley, primarily in Mud and Bridge Creek canyons.

Canyon Wren
Catherpes mexicanus

Uncommon permanent resident. Although not as common in summer as the Rock Wren, this species can frequently be seen on cliffs and rimrocks, especially in Diamond Craters (east of the refuge), near Page Springs, and in Mud and Bridge Creek canyons. More secretive than the Rock Wren, it prefers sheer canyons and rimrocks near water. Lack of this habitat within the refuge boundary prevents the species from being common, but in some areas of southeast Oregon it is a characteristic bird. Although the Canyon Wren is confined to cliffs and basaltic rimrocks here, in the southern portion of its breeding range it has adapted to buildings. The only atypical nesting site known from this region was of a pair which built its nest in an abandoned Cliff Swallow gourd at Diamond Craters (J. Hammond).

A minor spring influx has been noted in April, but generally birds trickle into the region. Most are on territory by late April and early May. Nesting sites are usually inaccessible and I have no information on nesting chronology. Usually no Canyon Wrens are seen in autumn migration; however, a pronounced movement was noted September 8 and 9, 1977. Several were seen at headquarters among the coniferous trees, and at Malheur Field Station one spent the day climbing in, under, and over a parked vehicle. An autumn passage of this magnitude has not been recorded either before or since on the refuge. In winter, the species has been recorded during 26 southern Blitzen Valley Christmas counts. Greatest densities in winter are in Mud and Bridge Creek canyons.

Bewick's Wren
Thryomanes bewickii

Accidental but increasing. Bendire (1877) reported the Bewick's Wren as a rather rare species in the vicinity of Camp Harney in the 1870s. It was not until January 8, 1982, that the species was again recorded in the Malheur-Harney Lakes Basin, when M. Archie located a singing individual along the East Canal, north of Page Springs. I found what appeared to be two territorial pairs among dense willows about 1 mile northeast of P Ranch on May 6, 1986. These observations were closely followed by another report of two individuals 1 mile north of Page Springs on October 14, 1986 (G. Ivey); one was in the same area on December 19, 1987 (G. Ivey), and another at P Ranch on June 27, 1988. This species is apparently reestablishing or colonizing in the southeast extremity of Malheur NWR at the present time, and outside the nesting season occupying the dense shrubbery along the East Canal from a half to 1 mile north of Page Springs.

House Wren
Troglodytes aedon

Common in spring and autumn; uncommon in summer. Although the House Wren nests commonly on Steens Mountain and in the Blue Mountains, in summer the species is uncommonly encountered on Malheur NWR. Nesting has occurred at Frenchglen, Page Springs, P Ranch, and headquarters, but elsewhere on the refuge it is extremely rare during the breeding season. House Wrens become more abundant in migration, but their elusive nature and preference for brushy tangles make observations difficult. However, migrants are frequently seen at headquarters and near Page Springs.

In the spring, the House Wren has arrived as early as March 2 (1970) and there are a few records from early April, but generally the species is not seen until the first week of May. Except for pairs which have nested in natural cavities at P Ranch, known nesting sites on the refuge have been mostly confined to nest boxes. One pair successfully nested in a box at headquarters in 1982, but was supplanted by Tree Swallows in 1983. Since then this pair has been able to find suitable sites in crevices on other buildings. The earliest autumn record was August 6 (1984), and the latest November 9 (1975). Based on limited observations, the peak of migration occurs between August 20 and 31, but it can still be regularly seen through September. There are few records after October.

Winter Wren
Troglodytes troglodytes

Uncommon to rare in autumn and spring migration; rare in winter. This small, elusive species is the only family member which has successfully colonized the Old World; the remaining members are confined to the New World. While on Malheur NWR, the Winter Wren confines most activities to dense shrubby thickets, brush heaps, tangled roots, and woodland undergrowth, but a favored locality is the vine-covered rock fences, flower beds, and office deck at headquarters, particularly in autumn.

The Winter Wren has a sporadic status, and its migrational patterns are difficult to interpret. They have arrived in autumn as early as August 9 (1986), but usually their arrival is not until September. Most transients have left the refuge by November 1. A few sometimes winter among the canyon bottoms and in thickets, and have been seen during eleven Christmas counts: 1949 (one), 1964 (four), 1965 (one), 1966 (one), 1978 (two), 1979 (three), 1981 (five), 1982 (one), 1984 (one), 1986 (two), and 1987 (one). Most unusual was a single bird seen June 6, 1966, but generally the majority leave in March. Excluding the June record, the latest spring occurrence was April 28 (1970).

Marsh Wren
Cistothorus palustris

Abundant in spring, summer, and autumn; uncommon in winter. This small vociferous species nests abundantly among dense emergent stands throughout the refuge. Even though hardstem bulrush appears to be preferred, nests are regularly placed in cattails, and in 1983 I found several nests in flooded greasewood north of Double O substation. The Marsh Wren's center of refuge abundance was Malheur Lake before high water inundated the extensive stands of bulrush in the early 1980s. It is still abundant among the emergents in the ponds and marshes of the Blitzen Valley and Double O, but its elusive nature results in the species appearing much less common than it actually is.

In spring, a major influx usually occurs in early March and by April Marsh Wrens are abundant and widely distributed. Nesting begins in May, with the female building the globular structure which will eventually contain her eggs, while the male spends his time building several "dummy" nests.

Fledged young are generally prevalent in late June and July. The refuge population remains relatively stable through early August, but as water levels recede birds begin leaving. The species is still evident through mid-October, but by November all but winter residents have left for southern wintering areas. They have been recorded during most Christmas counts, varying in numbers from one to twenty. In winter, habitat preferences are somewhat different than during the nesting season. Although individuals do occur in emergents around some flowing springs, most are seen in riparian zones. Individuals are frequently seen along the shrub-bordered watercourses near Page Springs, and a few have recently been noted at Stinking Lake Spring, Mud Creek Canyon, along the East Canal from Page Dam to Bridge Creek, and West Canal from Frenchglen Spring to 5-mile Road.

FAMILY: MIMIDAE

Gray Catbird
Dumetella carolinensis

Rare in spring and summer; accidental in autumn. This species reaches the western extremity of its breeding range in eastern Oregon, particularly in the northeastern part of the State. Gray Catbirds apparently nested on Malheur NWR in the 1940s, as Sooter (1943) reported three pairs July 18, 1942. In addition, I have an unsubstantiated report of nesting in Krumbo Canyon in the late 1960s, and a single bird was seen north of P Ranch on June 23, 1971. There are no recent indications of nesting on the refuge; however, I located a territorial pair July 4, 1977, along Foley Slough near Burns.

Since the species was first recorded on the refuge on May 31, 1942 (Sooter 1943), there have been sixteen additional records. Four were banded at headquarters between May 27 and June 13, 1962; four were also banded there from May 28 to June 6, 1963; one was killed after colliding with an office window on May 27, 1970; one was banded at headquarters on June 3, 1971; and single birds were observed at headquarters June 11-13, 1982; May 29, 1983 (T. Crabtree); June 3, 1984; May 23-24, 1985; and June 7, 1988 (J. Gilligan). Nesting habitat is available in the southern Blitzen Valley and the species will likely be found nesting among the brushy tangles near the Blitzen River and in Mud and Bridge Creek canyons. The only autumn record is that of an individual seen at headquarters on October 10, 1988 (S. Freshman).

Northern Mockingbird
Mimus polyglottos

Rare. Several Northern Mockingbird records have occurred since the species was first reported in August 1935 and on November 21, 1935 (Mrs. S. Jewett). J. Scharff observed one July 25, 1940, and this was the last record until December 31, 1965, when one was seen near Page Springs and another near Rockford Lane the same day. Since then single birds have been seen on April 28, 1966; May 14, 1967; May 8, 1971; July 24, 1972; August 17, 1973; June 22, 1982 (J. Snively); August 12, 1984; May 1, 1987; September 24-26, 1987; April 18, 1988; and May 30, 1988. One bird remained at Malheur Field Station from late May through mid-June 1978, and another at the same location from May 20 through June 1986. Both of these individuals consistently sang, but were unsuccessful in attracting mates.

Records have been at scattered localities throughout the refuge and no particular area seems favored except at Malheur Field Station. The species may have nested on Steens Mountain, as S. Jewett collected an immature male August 30, 1936 (Gabrielson and Jewett 1940); however, this individual could have been a postfledged wanderer from nesting areas further south.

Brown Thrasher
Toxostoma rufum

Accidental. This eastern vagrant has been recorded four times on the refuge. J. Scharff collected one (refuge museum) at headquarters on March 7, 1954 (Marshall 1959), for the first record. A second bird was seen by M. Jess on September 6, 1977, in Krumbo Valley. In 1974-75, a Brown Thrasher first appeared at headquarters on October 19, 1974, and remained through the winter, being last seen on April 28, 1975. This was the last record until J. Gilligan observed one at headquarters on June 7, 1988.

Sage Thrasher
Oreoscoptes montanus

Common in spring, summer, and autumn; rare in winter. The Sage Thrasher is a characteristic bird of the sagebrush expanses of southeast Oregon. Although not a common nesting species on Malheur NWR, it is abundant in the shrub-covered uplands surrounding the refuge. It is frequently seen near Harney Lake where nests are located in greasewood, sagebrush, and other shrubs, but generally numbers here do not compare with those found on Steens Mountain and along Foster Flat Road. After young have fledged, adults and young move onto the refuge, and at this time Sage Thrashers can border on abundant. The species attains its greatest densities between Malheur Field Station and Rattlesnake Butte, and it is not uncommon to see thirty to fifty birds along this stretch in late July and August.

The earliest spring arrival occurred January 30 (1981), but the average is not until March 23. Sage Thrashers become common in April. Nesting is usually in progress from early May through June (earliest April 24), and young fledge in late June and July. Migration is well underway in July, with the peak of passage varying from early August to mid-September. The majority have left for southwestern

Sage Thrasher

wintering areas by the first week of October, but one belated straggler was seen on November 9, 1977. There are three winter records: one near Krumbo Reservoir on January 8, 1972; one 5 miles north of P Ranch on December 16, 1972; and one near Harney Lake on December 19, 1986.

FAMILY: MUSCICAPIDAE

Golden-crowned Kinglet
Regulus satrapa

Common in autumn, uncommon in spring; occasional in winter. The Golden-crowned Kinglet is a common summer resident in Oregon's coniferous regions, where it favors dense fir, pine, and spruce forests. After raising their families some birds move onto the lowlands, where in southeast Oregon they occupy juniper woodlands, willow-bordered watercourses, and planted trees around human habitations. Within these habitats, Golden-crowned Kinglets occasionally associate with nuthatches, chickadees, Ruby-crowned Kinglets, and other sociable species, but generally individuals or small flocks occur alone. The species commonly forages among the exotic coniferous trees which have been planted at headquarters, but often in autumn individuals feed extensively upon the lawn, where they glean and surface-probe for insects.

Golden-crowned Kinglets occur more commonly in autumn than at other times of the year. The earliest record was obtained August 27 (1966), and peak of passage falls between September 25 and October 25. It is not uncommon for individuals to spend from several days to several weeks at headquarters before moving on to their wintering areas. Late transients were seen at headquarters November 1 (1984, 1985). Occasionally the species winters among the juniper woodlands and streamside shrubs in the southern Blitzen Valley, being seen during the following Christmas counts: 1941 (three), 1958 (thirteen), 1969 (one), 1975 (two), 1977 (one), 1979 (three), 1981 (two), 1983 (six), 1986 (one), 1987 (34), and 1988 (four). Golden-crowned Kinglets are recorded uncommonly in spring, usually first appearing in late March and peaking in April, with the latest spring transient on May 3 (1967).

Ruby-crowned Kinglet
Regulus calendula

Abundant spring and autumn migrant; occasional in winter. The Ruby-crowned Kinglet migrates abundantly through Malheur NWR, concentrating its activities predominantly in and around shrubby thickets, wooded streambottoms, arid woodlands, and human habitations. Wooded streambottoms and arid woodlands in the southern Blitzen Valley provide winter habitat for the occasional winter visitant. As with so many other species on the refuge, headquarters has been a most important concentration area, and it is not uncommon to see fifteen to twenty individuals there daily at the peak of spring and autumn migration.

Early spring migrants, Ruby-crowned Kinglets on the average arrive March 31, but a very early transient was located at headquarters on February 2, 1979. The species is most numerous between April 10 and 27, and the latest spring record occurred May 20 (1970). The earliest autumn transient was seen September 3 (1962), and from September 24 through October 15 it is most abundant and widely distributed. By late October, most individuals have left, but one was still present on November 13, 1961. The species has been recorded during eighteen Christmas counts, and the largest number counted was fourteen in 1983. In addition, one remained at refuge headquarters through most of December 1986, representing the only December record away from the southern Blitzen Valley.

Blue-gray Gnatcatcher
Polioptila caerulea

Accidental. The Blue-gray Gnatcatcher is a recent addition to Malheur NWR, but as yet it has not become established. It was first seen on June 5, 1975 (H. Eshbough), and a pair established a territory and attempted nesting at Page Springs (Littlefield 1980). S. Herman located the nest in mid-July in a western juniper, but it was dislodged by strong winds shortly thereafter. On May 16, 1985, two were again seen at Page Springs and two pairs appeared in May 1984 a quarter mile north of the Krumbo Road-Highway 205 junction. One of the latter pairs attempted to nest in a Siberian elm, but this nest also was destroyed by high winds in June. Other observations were of single birds at headquarters on May 6, 1985, and at Page Springs on June 3, 1988 (P. Sullivan). There have been unconfirmed reports of Blue-gray Gnatcatchers among the junipers northwest of Frenchglen, and it is possible the species has nested successfully in the arid woodlands adjoining the refuge.

Western Bluebird
Sialia mexicana

Uncommon in spring and autumn; accidental in summer and winter. In the yellow pine zones of the Blue Mountains, the Western Bluebird is uncommonly seen in the open woodlands where it normally raises two broods annually. The species has declined in recent years throughout much of its range, but in the Malheur-Harney Lakes Basin it borders on common during some spring migrations. Abundance in the lowlands depends on montane weather conditions; if inclement weather persists north of Burns, departures are delayed. As northbound migrants continue to arrive their numbers steadily increase, resulting in an abnormal buildup within the basin. Such climatic conditions existed in 1969 and 1971, and in March of these years the species was decidedly common.

The Western Bluebird is an early spring migrant, having arrived as early as January 24 (1979). Normally the species arrives on the average date of February 28. The latest spring migrant was recorded April 11 (1975). The only summer occurrence is that of a male which was seen repeatedly at Frenchglen in May and June 1975. It was not determined if this individual had a mate. Nest boxes and abandoned woodpecker holes occur in Frenchglen, and it is possible that the male was a member of a nesting pair. In autumn, the species has been recorded between September 30 (1971) and November 22 (1973), and their migration peak occurs in late October. The only winter records were single birds observed on December 29, 1967, and December 18, 1988.

Mountain Bluebird
Sialia currucoides

Common in spring and autumn migration; rare in summer; occasional to fairly abundant in winter. The Mountain Bluebird is a summer resident of the open juniper, aspen, and yellow pine woodlands, where it normally selects an abandoned woodpecker hole or natural cavity for a nesting site; occasionally a mail box, nest box, fence post, building, or rocky crevice is used. Leaving higher elevations in autumn and moving downslope into the open country and arid woodlands of southeast Oregon, Mountain Bluebirds frequently appear on Malheur NWR alone or in loose flocks of three to fifteen individuals in October. During migration the species is mostly seen on power-lines and fences along Highway 205, particularly between Buena Vista and Frenchglen, while the juniper woodlands adjoining the southern Blitzen Valley provide the majority of winter habitat.

An increase in Mountain Bluebird numbers generally occurs in late February, as birds from the south arrive. Peak of passage is normally between March 15 and 31, and a few stragglers are occasionally seen into mid-May. A few pairs sporadically nest among the juniper-covered slopes west of Highway 205 between Frenchglen and Krumbo Road, but virtually all move to higher elevations, and rarely will the species be seen on the refuge in the summer months. Autumn migrants return to Malheur NWR in early October (rarely late September), and peak between November 15 and December 1, with transients leaving by December 15. In some winters, Mountain Bluebirds can be fairly abundant. During Christmas counts in the southern Blitzen Valley in 1965, 1971, and 1972, 145, 373, and 232 were seen, respectively. However, in most years only one or two can be found wintering on the refuge.

Townsend's Solitaire
Myadestes townsendi

Uncommon to common in autumn, winter, and spring. On and surrounding Malheur NWR, Townsend's Solitaire numbers are dependent on juniper berry crops which are apparently their sole food source through the winter months. Like Phainopeplas in the southwestern states, individuals establish winter territories around favorable food supplies, which they vigorously defend against other conspecifics. For about 2 weeks in September, solitaires are frequently heard singing as territories are being established, and even during the coldest winter days some solitaire calling can be heard among the arid juniper woodlands. Absent on the refuge during the summer breeding season, the species is frequently heard or seen in the coniferous forest of the Blue Mountains, where it nests upon the ground in road cuts, steep banks, or among tree roots. Once the family has been raised, some solitaires begin moving onto the surrounding arid lowlands, but do not become common until November.

The earliest autumn transient was recorded August 16 (1986), but the peak of passage does not occur until mid-November. The majority of autumn transients have moved on by December 1. The species has been recorded during all Christmas counts, with greatest numbers seen in 1971 (53), 1972 (52), 1979 (131), 1980 (62), 1985 (97), and 1988 (137). A spring influx normally occurs in early March, and peak of abundance falls between March 20 and April 7. The latest solitaires have been seen on the refuge was May 11 (1971).

Veery
Catharus fuscescens

Accidental spring and autumn migrant. The Veery has been recorded at scattered localities throughout eastern Oregon, including five reports from Malheur NWR. E. Kridler first reported the species when he collected an adult male on June

6, 1962. In June 1967, an individual was killed after colliding with a window at headquarters, and H. Nehls observed one at P Ranch on September 9 and 10, 1969. The last spring record was obtained when B. Deuel and I found one at headquarters on June 4, 1970. The only other autumn record was accrued on October 12, 1986, when A. Contreras observed a single bird at headquarters. In addition to refuge records, one was seen near Burns by W. Finley on June 24, 1908 (Gabrielson and Jewett 1940), and to my knowledge this was the first Oregon record for this primarily eastern thrush.

Swainson's Thrush
Catharus ustulatus

Occasional in spring; rare in autumn; accidental in summer. Swainson's Thrushes reach their greatest state densities in western Oregon, but among or near the dense riparian zones of the Great Basin mountain ranges they frequently can be heard and uncommonly seen. The species nests at higher elevations on both Steens and Hart mountains, but its status is imperfectly known in the lower canyons. I have also captured and banded several individuals in the Blue Mountains of Grant County (Logan Valley and Canyon Meadows).

Unlike the Hermit Thrush, the species is more common on Malheur NWR in spring than autumn. The earliest spring record was obtained April 30 (1984), but the average arrival is considerably later (May 26). Most spring records have been during the first week of June. The latest spring transient was noted June 17 (1965). On August 12 and 15, 1984, two adults were captured and banded in the dense riparian growth north of Page Springs Campground, indicating the possibility of breeding. Additional work in this area is needed in July to determine the true breeding status of the species on the refuge. Considering the extent of riparian habitat in this region, it is highly probable that a few pairs nest on the refuge. In autumn, transients have been seen between August 29 (1983) and October 12 (1987). From a limited number of autumn records, the majority appear to move through this region between September 15 and 25.

Hermit Thrush
Catharus guttatus

Uncommon spring and autumn migrant; accidental in summer and winter. The Hermit Thrush is a bird of moist woodlands, where its flute-like call is regularly heard in the early morning and evening hours of summer. Nesting commonly beneath dense coniferous forest in the Blue Mountains, summer residents also occupy north-facing juniper thickets on Steens Mountain and in the Warm Springs Mountains. In migration, Hermit Thrushes are most often seen at headquarters, but wooded streambottoms, shrubby thickets, and planted trees throughout the refuge provide spring and autumn habitat for this widely distributed species.

The earliest spring transient was observed April 7 (1971), and the average is May 7. Hermit Thrushes are most evident between May 20 and 30, and the latest northbound migrant was noted June 20 (1971). An unusual summer occurrence was that of a single bird which was captured and banded at headquarters on July 26, 1965. In autumn, the species has been recorded between September 3 (1961) and October 31 (1975). Their peak of passage occurs from September 20 through October 10. Although the species winters in western Oregon, it leaves the colder regions east of the Cascades, and there is but one winter record for Malheur NWR; an individual seen at Benson Pond on December 18, 1988.

Varied Thrush
Ixoreus naevius

Uncommon spring and autumn migrant; accidental in winter. The Varied Thrush attains its greatest abundance in the coastal coniferous forest of the Pacific Northwest. However, in summer birds do occur in the dense fir and spruce woodlands as far east as northern Idaho and northwest Montana, and I have found individuals as far south as the Strawberry Mountains in late June. While on the refuge, this stocky thrush is most frequently seen at headquarters, but individuals occur elsewhere on the refuge where suitable habitat is available.

The Varied Thrush is an early spring migrant, having appeared as early as February 10 (1984). On the average it arrives on March 6, and the latest spring transient was seen May 18 (1978). Peak of migration occurs in late March, and generally the species has departed by mid-April. The earliest autumn occurrence was September 12 (1987, T. Crabtree); the latest November 10 (1986). Although considered uncommon in both spring and autumn, it occurs more frequently in autumn and in some years borders on common. In 1970, the species was commonly seen at headquarters after October 3, as eight to ten birds could be seen daily feeding in the lawn. Their numbers remained stable through October 25, and one individual was still present on November 9. Generally all have migrated by early November. There are four winter records from the southern Blitzen Valley: single birds on December 16, 1972, December 15, 1979, and December 18, 1986, and two on December 19, 1987.

American Robin
Turdus migratorius

Abundant in spring and autumn; common in summer; rare to abundant in winter. American Robins are a characteristic summer bird of southeast Oregon, where they find favorable nesting sites in open woodlands and streamside thickets, and around human habitations. On Malheur NWR, nesting pairs are most evident around headquarters and in riparian zones of the Blitzen Valley, with lesser numbers nesting in juniper woodlands and at Double O, P Ranch, and Malheur Field Station. At this latitude two broods are usually produced annually and recently fledged young can be seen from late

May through July. Wintering numbers are erratic and dependent on juniper berry crops; some years robins are virtually absent, in others extremely abundant. Occasionally they will be common in early winter, but as food sources become depleted in mid-winter a mass exodus occurs, and by late January few remain.

Migrants appear in late February and usually peak in early April. Flocks are often seen moving through the region (even over sagebrush expanses) in March and April, but by May 1 transients have left for nesting areas further north. Nesting generally begins in May, but a pair was feeding young at Page Springs on May 1, 1972 (W. Anderson). Once the first brood fledges, a second clutch is usually laid in June, and spot-breasted young are regularly seen well into August. Southbound migrants frequently appear in late August, but typically not until September. Peak of the autumn passage is in November, and by December 1 transients have moved from the region. Winter numbers have fluctuated from none during Christmas counts in 1957, 1959, 1960, and 1967, to 1,345 in 1943, 1,540 in 1971, 3,857 in 1972, 3,324 in 1974, and 1,862 in 1983. Most winter use is confined to the juniper slopes and riparian zones from Krumbo Road south to Page Springs, with few records from other refuge localities.

FAMILY: MOTACILLIDAE

Water Pipit
Anthus spinoletta

Common spring and autumn migrant; occasional in winter. In the 1870s, Bendire (1877) first reported the Water Pipit from what was later to become Malheur NWR, when he classified the species as an abundant migrant at Malheur Lake. Presently the pipit is still a common migrant in both spring and autumn where suitable habitat is available. Margins of lakes, ponds, canals, and streams, mudflats, flooded roads, and fallow fields provide favorable feeding sites, but rarely do their numbers exceed fifty at any given locality. In the 1980s, the species was quite common in autumn along exposed portions of the flooded Sod House Lane. Eighty individuals were concentrated there in late September 1986, with a few remaining through mid-October. On the refuge, the species is opportunistic, and areas devoid of vegetation will frequently support a few migrant pipits.

Spring migrants have arrived on February 13 (1969), but on the average pipits do not appear until March 27. They are usually most evident in late April, and the late spring record was obtained May 27 (1971). The earliest returning migrant was seen September 11 (1970). D. Marshall reported about one thousand pipits on September 19, 1957, but generally the peak of passage is not until early October. The majority have continued southward by early November; however, a few occasionally remain through the winter months. In 1961, fifty were recorded during the Christmas count, but most often only one or two are seen sporadically. The most consistent wintering sites are along the margins of the East and West canals (Krumbo Road to Page Springs), and the Blitzen River (where water remains open).

FAMILY: BOMBYCILLIDAE

Bohemian Waxwing
Bombycilla garrulus

Occasional in autumn, winter, and spring. The Bohemian Waxwing is a Holarctic species, nesting in the boreal forest of Eurasia and North America. If food supplies in northern regions become depleted, Bohemians will irrupt southward and occasionally large flocks will occur during flight years as far south as southeast Oregon. In the spring of 1976, several hundred spent about 3 weeks in April southeast of Burns feeding on rose hips, while on Malheur NWR, in 1973, they

invaded the southern Blitzen Valley on March 15, and remained through May 2. About 950 birds were present at the
peak period in late March.

Bohemian Waxwings were not recorded on the refuge until
February 23, 1956. Since then numerous records have accumulated, with the species having been seen between November 9 (1975) and May 2 (1973). Most records have occurred
from mid-December through February. Excluding 1973,
greatest numbers were 250 at Frenchglen on February 23,
1959, 50 at headquarters on December 3, 1975, and 72 at the
same locality on December 21, 1987. Generally the species
occurs in small flocks of five to ten birds.

Cedar Waxwing
Bombycilla cedrorum

Uncommon in spring and autumn; occasional to abundant
in winter. Cedar Waxwings are sporadic on Malheur NWR,
appearing in numbers one year while being scarce the next.
Their annual status is largely dependent on food supplies
elsewhere, and birds which do appear usually remain for only
a short period as few favored berry trees are present on the
refuge. To date, this late-nesting species has not been known
to breed on the refuge, again probably because of the lack of
berry-producing plants. Frequently Cedar Waxwings occur in
late May and early June, when they consume quantities of
petals from several flowering trees at headquarters. Waxwing
flocks have been seen throughout the refuge, but headquarters and the southern Blitzen Valley appear particularly attractive to migrant and wintering birds. An extraordinary 814
individuals were seen in the southern Blitzen Valley in December 1980, but generally flocks of twenty to thirty birds are
more typical.

In spring, Cedar Waxwings have appeared on February 1
(1979), but on the average they do not arrive until April 2.
Usually peak numbers are present in late May. A late spring
transient was noted on June 30, 1971. The earliest autumn

arrival was August 10 (1971), and most transients have left
the refuge by early November. No autumn peak has been
noted. The species occasionally appears in winter, but with
the exception of 1980, flocks are usually small and inconsistent. However, one hundred were seen on January 20, 1977
(one of the few January records), and 653 on December 19,
1988. During migration and winter, the species is more frequent in Burns, where flocks of twenty to forty individuals are
regularly encountered as they fly to and fro among the orna-
mental trees and shrubs in residential areas.

FAMILY: PTILOGONATIDAE

Phainopepla
Phainopepla nitens

Accidental. Marshall (1959) collected an adult male
Phainopepla at Benson Pond on May 18, 1957. The specimen
is deposited at the U.S. National Museum, as it represented
not only the first refuge record but the first Oregon record as
well. This southwestern vagrant normally occupies nesting
habitat from central California to Texas, south through the
deserts to central Mexico. Nearest nesting localities to Malheur NWR are in southern Nevada and the Sacramento Valley of California.

FAMILY: LANIIDAE

Northern Shrike
Lanius excubitor

Uncommon in autumn, winter, and spring. Northern
Shrikes spend the summer months among the coniferous
and deciduous woodlands, shrubby thickets, and taiga regions of Alaska and Canada, and it is not until October that

individuals appear on Malheur NWR. While on the refuge the species generally associates with willow thickets and planted trees, but frequently fence posts and power-lines are used for perching. Unlike wintering Loggerhead Shrikes, which prefer desert shrub habitat, Northern Shrikes spend the majority of their time among willow-bordered meadows at Double O and in the Blitzen Valley, and the planted trees at headquarters. In February and March, individuals are occasionally heard singing at headquarters, just before heading back to their northern breeding grounds.

On the refuge, the species has been recorded from October 7 (1980) through April 16 (1967). There is an influx in November as transients move through the region, but by early December numbers become relatively stable. The species has been recorded during all but the 1943 and 1975 Christmas counts. Count numbers usually range from five to eight, but highest counts were twelve in 1969 and eleven in 1973, 1983, and 1986. Northbound migrants appear in February, and the majority have left the refuge by mid-March, but if inclement weather delays their departure, birds are regularly seen into early April. Such conditions existed in 1975, and Northern Shrikes were seen through April 11.

Loggerhead Shrike
Lanius ludovicianus

Common in spring, summer, and autumn; uncommon in winter. Generally Loggerhead Shrikes on Malheur NWR occupy arid shrublands throughout the year. Unlike their larger cousin, the Northern Shrike, loggerheads are rarely seen on meadows and willow thickets, confining most of their activities to the drier greasewood flats and sagebrush uplands. Greatest summer densities are along the south shore of Harney Lake and in the vicinity of Double O, while in winter they are frequently seen perched on power-lines and fences near sagebrush expanses in the southern Blitzen Valley. One pair nested for several years in a blue spruce at headquarters, and pairs have been seen feeding recently fledged young at Malheur Field Station in August, but for the most part Loggerhead Shrikes are most abundant and widely distributed in the shrub expanses which surround the refuge.

Spring migrants first appear in February, and peak of passage occurs from mid-March to April 1. Most transients have passed through the region by mid-April, and those present in late April usually remain to nest. Nesting is in progress in May, but a nest containing four eggs was located near Stinking Lake on June 13, 1973, and recently fledged young have been seen on August 4 (1976). Once young become independent, individuals begin leaving the refuge and greatest numbers are usually present in late August and early September. Twenty-five were observed between headquarters and Double O on August 27, 1971. By mid-November, only winter residents remain on the refuge. Historically, the Loggerhead Shrike was not reported as wintering in Oregon; however, the species has been recorded during 28 southern Blitzen Valley Christmas counts in numbers ranging from one to six individuals. In addition, birds are regularly seen near Harney Lake through the winter period.

FAMILY: STURNIDAE

European Starling
Sturnus vulgaris

Abundant spring and autumn migrant; common in summer; uncommon to common in winter. The European Starling first appeared on Malheur NWR on December 24, 1943 (first state record) (Jewett 1946), after being first introduced into North America in 1890. In the 1950s and 1960s, the species increased dramatically and at the present time starlings are abundantly seen on the refuge, particularly during migration. Several pairs nest at headquarters, Frenchglen,

P Ranch, and Malheur Field Station, primarily in holes excavated by Northern Flickers. In addition to holes, starlings have been found here nesting in attics, nest boxes, and natural tree cavities, and in fence posts and rimrocks. This species has definitely had a negative influence on other hole- and cavity-nesting species, as starlings on Malheur NWR begin nesting activities about 3 weeks earlier than other birds.

Resident pairs appear in early February, and migrants numbering into the hundreds can usually be seen in spring between March 5 and April 5 (March 30, 1970—five thousand; March 20, 1975—three thousand). Most transients have left by mid-April. Nesting generally begins in April, and most young have fledged by mid-June. On Malheur NWR the majority of nesting pairs do not appear double-brooded as they are in other regions. Shortly after fledging, starlings begin leaving the refuge, and generally observations are limited in July and early August. The species again becomes evident in late August and peak of autumn migration occurs in September and October (September 17-24, 1973—three thousand at headquarters). Winter status is variable; in some years few are seen, while in others the species borders on abundant. On December 17, 1983, 508 were seen near Frenchglen and 91 near headquarters for the largest winter numbers. Only single birds and small flocks are normally seen between December 1 and February 1.

FAMILY: VIREONIDAE

Solitary Vireo
Vireo solitarius

Uncommon in spring and autumn; accidental in summer. Both the Rocky Mountain (*V.s. plumbeus*) and West Coast (*V.s. cassinii*) subspecies of the Solitary Vireo have been seen on the refuge in migration, but the yellowish coastal form is by far the most commonly encountered. Most records have been from headquarters, but at the peak of migration the species is widely distributed on the refuge where suitable tree and shrub habitats are available. I have found nesting birds on Steens Mountain and in the Blue Mountains. A pair on Steens Mountain was nesting in an aspen-juniper association, while pairs in the Blue Mountains have occupied a variety of habitats from monotypic stands of ponderosa pine to quaking aspen.

The earliest recorded arrival for this species was April 18 (1971) (average April 29) and the latest departure occurred June 12 (1983). The peak of spring migration falls between May 13 and 19. The only summer record was that of a single bird at headquarters on June 25, 1965. Likely this was a late spring transient as I have no knowledge of nesting in the arid lowlands from this region. The earliest autumn record was obtained August 21 (1961) and the latest October 24 (1963). Peak of passage occurs between September 15 and October 5.

Hutton's Vireo
Vireo huttoni

Accidental. An inhabitant of the evergreen forest of western Oregon, the Hutton's Vireo has been seen three times on Malheur NWR. F. Ramsey, with members of the Corvallis Audubon Society, first observed the species on May 18, 1975; the second individual was reported by N. Cobb and P. Paquet on May 7, 1976. The third record was on May 17, 1980. All three observations were from headquarters. It is not clear if the Hutton's Vireo is increasing in this region, or if more observers are now visiting the refuge. Since this species closely resembles the abundant Ruby-crowned Kinglet, caution is warranted when identifying this accidental refuge visitant.

Warbling Vireo
Vireo gilvus

Common in spring and autumn; occasional in summer. This is the most commonly encountered and widely distributed member of its family on Malheur NWR. It is frequently seen among the coniferous and deciduous trees at headquarters, and the willow-bordered watercourses, shrubby thickets, and planted trees throughout the refuge. An occasional pair spends the summer on the refuge, but generally most are entirely transients though Warbling Vireos are abundant in summer among aspen clones and wooded streambottoms in the Blue Mountains and on Steens Mountain. In other regions of the west, Warbling Vireo populations are declining because of excessive parasitism by expanding populations of Brown-headed Cowbirds (Garrett and Dunn 1981). I have examined few nests; therefore, what influence parasitism is having on this species in southeast Oregon remains to be determined.

The earliest Warbling Vireo sighting was April 24 (1984) and the average is May 11. Spring migration is at its peak between May 18 and June 2, and the latest spring transient was noted June 17 (1965). The species is occasionally seen in summer among the willows and alders from Page Springs north to Bridge Creek, especially along the East Canal. In autumn, transients have arrived as early as July 24 (1966), but the majority move through between August 25 and September 7. The latest autumn record occurred on September 25 (1987).

Red-eyed Vireo
Vireo olivaceus

Rare in spring, summer, and autumn. Since Kridler and Marshall (1962) reported on an adult male collected on August 31, 1960, at headquarters, the Red-eyed Vireo has been seen 21 times on the refuge through 1988. Most records have been from headquarters, but individuals have also been seen at P Ranch, Benson Pond, and near Page Springs. I know of one record for May, nine for June, three for August, and nine for September. Even though the species nests along the Columbia River and apparently in northeast Oregon, there are no nesting records for the southeast portion of the state. However, a pair was at Benson Pond on June 20, 1975.

Red-eyed Vireos have been seen from May 19 (1973) through June 20 (1975) in spring, with most records occurring during the first week of June. Autumn transients have been recorded between August 15 (1986) and September 21 (1979), with the majority of observations between September 10 and 15.

FAMILY: EMBERIZIDAE

Golden-winged Warbler
Vermivora chrysoptera

Accidental. There is one refuge record for this eastern vagrant. An adult male was photographed by J. Gilligan and observed by many others at headquarters on June 3 and 4, 1983. The nearest known nesting region for the Golden-winged Warbler is northeastern North Dakota, and its major migration route lies east of the Rocky Mountains (A.O.U. Checklist 1983). There are several reports for California, but this was the first documented record for Oregon.

Tennessee Warbler
Vermivora peregrina

Rare in spring and autumn. Kridler (1965) collected a female Tennessee Warbler (USNM #479637) at headquarters on June 12, 1963, and banded an immature on October 15, 1963, for the first and second state records. Since then seventeen additional sightings have occurred at the refuge. The thirteen spring records have ranged from May 5 (1984) to June 12 (1963, 1971), with the majority during the last week of May. The four autumn observations have occurred between August 24 (1966) and September 24 (1981). Single birds were banded at headquarters on August 31, 1965, and September 3, 1966, for the remaining autumn records. The most seen on given days were two on May 14 and 29, 1982. All observations have been from headquarters, except for two at Frenchglen on May 29, 1982, and one at Page Springs on May 5, 1984.

Orange-crowned Warbler
Vermivora celata

Common spring and autumn migrant. The Orange-crowned Warbler is the most nondescript warbler in North America, with neither male nor female displaying any obvious distinguishing characteristics. This is one of the first warblers to appear on the refuge in spring and one of the last to depart in autumn. Planted trees, shrubby thickets, wooded streambottoms, and juniper woodlands all have their complement of Orange-crowned Warblers as they move to and from their nesting areas. A few pairs nest in the Blue Mountains, and Hansen (1956) found them on Steens Mountain from June 23 to August 22 (5,400 to 7,500 feet elevation), but the species has not been recorded on Malheur NWR during the breeding season.

The earliest spring transient was recorded April 13 (1979) and the average arrival is April 26. Between May 3 and 20, Orange-crowned Warblers are most abundant and widely distributed on the refuge. The latest northbound migrant was seen June 3 (1963). Generally it is a late autumn transient, but one bird was observed at headquarters August 9 (1977). Peak of autumn passage falls between September 4 and 22, with the last autumn record October 17 (1962).

Nashville Warbler
Vermivora ruficapilla

Uncommon spring and autumn migrant. For a few days each spring, the Nashville Warbler borders on common among the trees at headquarters, where it is frequently seen feeding at mid- to lower canopy levels. In autumn, the species is less common, but one or two can usually be seen at headquarters, P Ranch, Page Springs, and other localities where wooded stream-courses, planted trees, and willow thickets occur. Nashville Warblers are mostly absent from southeast Oregon during the breeding season, but I located one territorial pair about 10 miles northwest of Seneca in July 1983.

Spring transients have been recorded from April 16 (1961) through June 17 (1975), with most occurrences between May 1 and 15. In autumn, the species has reappeared as early as August 2 (1985, M. Archie), and the majority pass through the refuge between August 25 and September 1. There is evidence that early autumn migrants avoid the dry arid lowlands, moving instead through the cooler moist highlands of Great Basin mountain ranges. S. Herman has captured and banded individuals on Steens Mountain about 10 days earlier than the first lowland migrants appear. After temperatures moderate, Nashville Warblers become regular on the refuge in mid- to late August. This is one of the earliest warblers to leave the refuge; the latest recorded migrant was seen on September 15 (1970).

Northern Parula
Parula americana

Rare spring vagrant; accidental in early summer. The Northern Parula was first recorded on Malheur NWR at Warbler Pond on May 19, 1970 (Littlefield and McLaury 1973). Since then several others have been seen on the refuge. A male was observed at Benson Pond from May 29 through June 1, 1976, and at headquarters the following records have accumulated: one male April 24-29, 1977; one male on June 3, 1984; one female May 29-31, 1985; one female June 4-7, 1985; and one bird on June 1, 1988 (P. Muller). In addition, there has been one summer record, that of a male at headquarters on July 6, 1980 (R. Johnston). The Northern Parula is becoming a regular visitant to the west coast, particularly in California where 204 records had accumulated by 1980 (Roberson 1980).

Yellow Warbler
Dendroica petechia

Abundant in spring, summer, and autumn. The Yellow Warbler is one of three members of the subfamily which nest on Malheur NWR, where it finds suitable habitat among planted trees and hedges (particularly at headquarters), wooded streambottoms, watercourses bordered by willow and alder, and shrubby thickets. Yellow Warblers are abundantly seen from Benson Pond south to P Ranch in the riparian zones adjacent to the Center Patrol Road. With a reduction in livestock grazing and the near elimination of willow cutting and spraying, the species has increased dramatically on portions of the refuge. Along a breeding-bird survey route in the southern Blitzen Valley, two were seen in 1973 compared to 56 in 1986. Elsewhere on their breeding range, Brown-headed Cowbird brood parasitism has been detrimental to local nesting populations, and in regions of the southwest the Yellow Warbler has been virtually extirpated. Most warbler territories on the refuge are on or adjacent to wetlands which have breeding colonies of Red-winged Blackbirds. Blackbirds are known to drive cowbirds away (Terres 1980), and perhaps for this reason few Yellow Warbler nests are host to this parasitic species on Malheur NWR.

The Yellow Warbler has arrived April 16 (1971), but the average is April 26. Peak of spring passage occurs from May 15 to 25, and the majority of transients have moved on by

Yellow Warbler

June 1. Based on banding and recapture data at headquarters, males return annually to the same territory. One male banded in 1972 was recaptured at the same location in 1978, and several others have been recaptured in subsequent years. Nesting is in progress by early June and young fledge generally in July. Autumn migration begins early, with a few transients appearing in late July. Peak movement is between August 15 and September 1. One individual banded as a nestling in July 1984 along Bridge Creek was recaptured in August 1984 at Page Springs (6 miles south) as it was leaving the refuge. The majority have left by September 25, and the latest autumn record occurred October 15 (1987, P. Muller, L. Weiland).

Chestnut-sided Warbler
Dendroica pensylvanica

Rare spring and autumn vagrant. Oregon's first Chestnut-sided Warbler was captured and banded at Malheur NWR headquarters on June 21, 1966 (Zeillemaker 1971). Little-field et al. (1985) reported on an immature seen at headquarters on September 22, 1975; two immatures there on September 10, 1977; one immature at headquarters on September 13, 1977; one adult male at Benson Pond on May 27, 1979 (J. Walcott and E. McVicker); two males at headquarters on June 8, 1980; one male there June 12-13, 1980; and one adult male on June 30, 1981, about 5 miles northeast of Frenchglen. Since these records were published, individuals have been seen at headquarters on September 9, 21, 24-25, and October 12, 1984; May 27 and June 15-16, 1986; June 6, 1987; and June 10 (A. McGie), and September 8, 1988 (M. Smith). In addition, S. Jones observed an individual at Frenchglen on October 2, 1988. Of the twenty records presently available, ten are from spring (range May 27 to June 30), and ten in autumn (range September 9 to October 12).

Cape May Warbler
Dendroica tigrina

Accidental. On June 9, 1967, E. McLaury, with members of the Eugene Natural History Society, observed an adult male Cape May Warbler at Buena Vista, but efforts to relocate the individual later the same day were unsuccessful (Little-field and McLaury 1973). A second record was obtained when an immature female was banded at headquarters on September 9, 1981 (Littlefield et al. 1985). Since these earlier reports, an adult male was at headquarters between May 22 and 23, 1986, and a female between September 13 and 17, 1986. There is an additional record for which I have no details—one on June 3, 1978 (Roberson 1980).

Magnolia Warbler
Dendroica magnolia

Rare. Malheur NWR recorded its first Magnolia Warbler on September 28, 1979, when a single bird was seen at headquarters (Littlefield et al. 1985). Since 1979, five additional records have occurred: one at headquarters September 30, 1981 (D. Cooley, M. Bierly); one at headquarters May 31-June 2, 1985; one at Benson Pond September 24-27, 1987; one at headquarters on May 25-29, 1988; and another at the same location on June 7, 1988 (J. Gilligan). In addition, there are three unconfirmed reports of Magnolia Warblers at headquarters in September 1978 and early September 1979, but details are lacking. This eastern vagrant is becoming regular in the west, and through 1979 there were 325 records for California (Roberson 1980).

Black-throated Blue Warbler
Dendroica caerulescens

Accidental in spring and summer; rare in autumn. Presently there are sixteen refuge records for this eastern species. The first Oregon record was established October 9, 1957, when Marshall (1959) secured a male at headquarters. E. Kridler collected another male on September 27, 1960, and banded a third on October 24, 1961 (Kridler and Marshall 1962). Kridler also observed an adult male May 2-4, 1963, for the first spring record (Kridler 1965). Additional records since these earlier reports include one male photographed on October 8, 1969; one male banded on October 11, 1970 (Littlefield and McLaury 1971); one photographed on October 7, 1978 (P. Summers); one seen October 9-10, 1982; one male on October 12, 1984; one male May 21-22, 1986 (P. Pickering); one male on June 23, 1986; one male at Frenchglen on September 23, 1987 (D. Irons); one female October 12-17, 1987; one at Benson Pond on September 16, 1988 (P. Sullivan); one male October 12-16, 1988; and one male at Frenchglen on September 29, 1988 (S. Jones). There are two records for spring, one for summer, and thirteen for autumn. Except for four late September reports, all autumn records have been in October.

Yellow-rumped Warbler
Dendroica coronata auduboni

Abundant in spring and autumn; rare in winter. The yellow throated "Audubon's" form of the Yellow-rumped Warbler is the most abundant and widely distributed member of the subfamily on Malheur NWR during migration. Planted trees and shrubs, arid woodlands, and riparian zones support the majority, but at the migration peak the species is frequently seen moving through sagebrush expanses far removed from its normal habitat. In the breeding season, this warbler nests abundantly in the montane coniferous forest of the Blue Mountains and among the aspen clones on Great Basin mountain ranges.

This is the earliest warbler to appear in spring; the earliest arrival was March 20 (1980); the average is April 8. Peak period of passage falls between April 20 and May 10, and one belated straggler was still on the refuge June 17 (1975). Autumn birds have occurred between August 5 (1966, 1985) and November 14 (1974), with September 15 to October 15 being the peak period. Two birds were observed on December 30, 1958; one on December 31, 1965; one in December 1979; eight on December 17, 1983; and one on December 19, 1986. These are the only winter records. With the exception of the 1986 record (at headquarters), all winter observations have been in the southern Blitzen Valley.

The white throated form (*D.c. coronata*) is uncommon in spring and autumn. In spring, it has arrived March 24 (1980) and the average is April 20. Even though never common, the subspecies is most evident between May 1 and 20. The latest spring record was May 31 (1975). In autumn, birds have been recorded between September 12 (1971, 1975) and November 15 (1971). Individuals have been seen mostly in early October.

Black-throated Gray Warbler
Dendroica nigrescens

Uncommon spring and autumn migrant; accidental in summer. The Black-throated Gray Warbler is not a common bird on Malheur NWR, and generally only two to three are seen annually. A few pairs remain in the region to nest, usually in juniper woodlands between 4,000 and 6,000 feet elevation. Records on the refuge have been primarily from Page Springs and headquarters, but the species has also been seen near Frenchglen, Benson Pond, and P Ranch. Rarely are these birds seen away from trees and thickets, but W. and M. Radke saw one in the arid shrublands south of Harney Lake on April 25, 1984. In summer, Black-throated Gray Warblers have been seen on Steens Mountain, and a few pairs sometimes nest among the junipers in Page Canyon and the Jackass Mountains.

Records on the refuge have ranged from April 23 (1979) to May 31 (1975). Average arrival date is May 11, and peak of passage is May 5 to 20. One pair feeding young was located on July 8, 1986, about 2 miles north of Frenchglen, and J. Wittenberger saw one on June 20, 1975, at Page Springs. These represent the only summer records. The species is somewhat less common in autumn than spring. The earliest arrival was August 19 (1985) and the latest was seen at headquarters by L. Spring on October 12 (1984). Of the few available autumn records, most have been between September 10 and 20.

Townsend's Warbler
Dendroica townsendi

Uncommon in spring and autumn; accidental in summer. The Townsend's Warbler is a summer bird of the Pacific Northwest coniferous regions, occurring only as a spring and autumn transient in the arid lowlands of southeast Oregon. Migrants are frequently seen moving through juniper woodlands, but while on Malheur NWR major stopover areas are the larger trees which have been planted around human habitations. On the refuge, headquarters is the most important use area, but the species is also regularly seen at Benson Pond, Frenchglen, and P Ranch.

The Townsend's Warbler is a fairly late spring migrant, with the earliest arrival date on April 27 (1981). Their average arrival is May 8. The spring passage peak usually occurs between May 15 and June 1. A late spring straggler was seen July 3, 1971, but generally the majority have left the refuge by June 15. A few pairs have been seen in summer north of Burns (Blue Mountains), but except for the early July record the species is absent from the lowlands. However, in late July southbound migrants appear at higher elevations on Great Basin mountain ranges. One individual was seen on Steens Mountain (6,000 ft.) by V. Bailey on July 30 (Gabrielson and Jewett 1940), but August 9 (1979) is the earliest an autumn transient has been recorded on Malheur NWR. Autumn passage is at a peak between August 23 and September 7. The latest autumn record was obtained October 17 (1987).

Hermit Warbler
Dendroica occidentalis

Accidental. The Hermit Warbler commonly summers west of Malheur NWR in the Cascade Range, and the majority apparently migrate through montane regions of the Pacific and southwest states. S. Herman, with students from Evergreen State College, observed two at headquarters on May

15, 1986, and one was at the same locality between September 17 and 23, 1987. These are the only documented records within the refuge boundary; however, J. Wittenberger watched a single individual about half a mile south of Page Springs Campground on May 15, 1976. There is an undocumented report of an individual seen near P Ranch on June 16, 1983, but details are lacking.

Black-throated Green Warbler
Dendroica virens

Accidental. An adult male Black-throated Green Warbler was observed at Benson Landing on May 17, 1975 (Littlefield 1980), for the first refuge record. I observed a second bird at headquarters June 14, 1986. Although extremely rare in Oregon, this species had been seen 130 times in California through 1979 (Roberson 1980). The nearest probable nesting region for this eastern vagrant is east-central British Columbia and northern Alberta (A.O.U. Checklist 1983).

Blackburnian Warbler
Dendroica fusca

Accidental. On September 15, 1986, I located a female Blackburnian Warbler as it was feeding in a Russian olive tree at headquarters. The individual was seen again by M. Smith and members of the Portland Audubon Society on September 17 and 18. This represented not only the first refuge record, but the first Oregon record as well. This was shortly followed by a second observation, that of a male at Benson Pond on May 29, 1988 (H. Nehls). Through 1979, there had been 166 records for California, of which 153 (92 percent) were of autumn birds (Roberson 1980).

Yellow-throated Warbler
Dendroica dominica

Accidental. This eastern vagrant has been recorded one time on the refuge. On June 9, 1985, one appeared at headquarters and remained through June 11. Many observers saw the bird and photographs were obtained. The nearest known nesting area for the Yellow-throated Warbler is central Oklahoma, southeast Kansas, and central Missouri (A.O.U. Checklist 1983), and this represented the first west coast record away from California, where through 1979 there had been thirty records (Roberson 1980).

Palm Warbler
Dendroica palmarum

Accidental. The Palm Warbler is included on the basis of an undocumented observation near the Narrows on May 19, 1985. There is one record from southwest of Malheur NWR, where S. Jewett secured a specimen (male) in Catlow Valley on September 13, 1913 (Gabrielson and Jewett 1940). The lack of records from the refuge is unexplained, as the Palm Warbler had been reported 1,536 times in California through 1979 (Roberson 1980). Since California records are mostly coastal, the species likely migrates through the coniferous regions of western Oregon, avoiding the arid eastern lowlands.

Bay-breasted Warbler
Dendroica castanea

Accidental. This inhabitant of the spruce woodlands of the northeast United States and Canada has been recorded four times on the refuge. D. DeSante found the first when he located an adult male Bay-breasted Warbler at headquarters on June 7, 1976 (Littlefield 1980), and the second was an

adult male seen by S. Thompson and R. Johnstone at headquarters on June 9-13, 1980 (Littlefield et al. 1985). A third
record was obtained when an adult male was seen by several
observers at headquarters on May 21, 1986, and a fourth
occurred September 16-23, 1988, when one was also seen at
headquarters.

Blackpoll Warbler
Dendroica striata

Accidental in spring; rare in autumn. Presently there are
sixteen records of the Blackpoll Warbler on Malheur NWR;
six in spring and ten in autumn. In spring, birds were seen on
the following dates: an adult male at Benson Pond May
27-29, 1974; two at headquarters on May 19, 1984; one at
headquarters May 15-18, 1985; one male at headquarters on
May 21, 1988; and a female on June 7, 1988. Autumn records include one immature male collected at headquarters
on September 7, 1967 (Littlefield and McLaury 1973); one at
headquarters on September 12, 1972; one-half mile west of
headquarters on September 28, 1983; one at headquarters
on October 13, 1983; and one at headquarters on September
27, 1986. In 1987, individuals were seen September 11-12
(two), September 17-18 (one), October 3 (one), and one was
seen September 3-4, 1988. The Blackpoll Warbler is one of
the more commonly encountered eastern vagrants on the
west coast, particularly in California where 1,405 records had
accumulated through 1979 (Roberson 1980).

Black and White Warbler
Mniotilta varia

Rare in spring; accidental in autumn. There are twenty
records for the Black and White Warbler on Malheur NWR, of
which seventeen are from spring. In spring, the species has
been seen between May 7 (1982) and June 15 (1985), with
eleven records occurring between May 20 and 31. The only

autumn records were a female collected at headquarters on September 17, 1960 (Kridler and Marshall 1962), which represented not only the first refuge record, but also the first Oregon record, and single individuals on September 6 and October 9, 1987. As with other eastern vagrants, Black and White Warbler sightings have been primarily from headquarters; however, individuals have been seen at Cole Island, Benson Landing, and Benson Pond. This species is one of the most frequently encountered vagrants on the west coast and, through 1979, 764 had been recorded in California (Roberson 1980).

Prothonotary Warbler
Protonotaria citrea

Accidental. A brief observation of a Prothonotary Warbler occurred at Malheur NWR headquarters in the early 1980s, but the record has remained unconfirmed as the bird could not be relocated (L. Ditto). The first documented refuge record was obtained on October 11, 1987, when A. and T. Mickel and J. Carlson photographed a male of this species at headquarters. There is one additional record for Oregon, that of an immature male banded at Hart Mountain on August 19, 1976. This cavity-nesting, water-loving species had been seen 33 times in California through 1979, with most records from autumn (Roberson 1980).

American Redstart
Setophaga ruticilla

Occasional spring and autumn migrant. The American Redstart is a late spring migrant on Malheur NWR, with most not appearing until late May. While on the refuge, the species inhabits wooded streambottoms, willow thickets, and planted trees. The majority of observations have been at headquarters, but individuals have also been seen at Frenchglen, Benson Pond, Benson Landing, and in the riparian zones of the southern Blitzen Valley. Two to three redstarts are generally seen in both spring and autumn, but in the autumn of 1986 there were nine records, including four at headquarters on September 18. It is a rare summer resident in the Blue Mountains, and I found a territorial male at Canyon Creek, about 20 miles southeast of John Day, in Grant County, but I know of no nesting records for Harney County.

The earliest the species has been seen in spring is May 2 (1974), but the average is not until May 22. A belated straggler was recorded June 22 (1962). Peak numbers are present between May 25 and June 5. In autumn, the earliest record occurred August 9 (1979) and an extremely late individual was seen November 14 (1970). Most autumn records are between September 1 and 20, and few remain after October 1.

American Redstarts have increased in southeast Oregon since Kridler and Marshall (1962) first reported on a specimen collected on the refuge on September 8, 1960.

Ovenbird
Seiurus aurocapillus

Occasional in spring; accidental in autumn. The Ovenbird is one of the more frequently encountered eastern vagrants on Malheur NWR. It was first recorded on June 4, 1961, when Kridler (1965) secured a female (USNM *478486) at headquarters—the first Oregon record. Since then it has been recorded eighteen times, with the majority in spring. All records are from headquarters, except for one seen at Page Springs on June 8, 1983, and two at Benson Pond on June 5, 1988. The species has been seen in spring between May 19 (1973) and June 13 (1963), with the majority from May 25 to June 5. In autumn, it has only been reported on five occasions; October 1, 1977 (J. Gilligan); August 26, 1981 (C. Cogswell); September 28, 1986; September 22, 1987; and September 3, 1988 (S. Jones).

This ground-nesting species breeds as far west as central Colorado, and through 1979 there had been 320 records from California. Earlier Oregon Ovenbird records were summarized by Littlefield and McLaury (1975).

Northern Waterthrush
Seiurus noveboracensis

Rare in spring and autumn. In migration, the Northern Waterthrush now borders on occasional in southeast Oregon where suitable habitat is available. Wooded wetland bottoms, willow-bordered watercourses, and trees and shrubs around moist lawns provide the majority of refuge habitat, but occasionally an individual is seen in atypical areas (e.g., along the Center Patrol Road). Records have been mostly from headquarters, Buena Vista, Page Springs, and Benson Landing, but ideal habitat is available in the riparian zones of the southern Blitzen Valley, and undoubtedly if intensive field work were conducted in this region the species would be encountered with some regularity.

Kridler (1965) obtained the first refuge specimen when he collected a male at headquarters on May 9, 1961. Spring transients have been reported between May 9 (1961) and June 11 (1967), with most observations in late May. The majority of autumn transients have appeared between September 20 and 28, but I banded an individual at Page Springs on August 26, 1984, which preceded the previous early date by 2 weeks. The latest occurrence was September 30 (1983).

MacGillivray's Warbler
Oporornis tolmiei

Uncommon spring and autumn migrant. This inhabitant of dense shrubbery, weedy patches, and brush piles uncommonly migrates through Malheur NWR, but observations are limited as the species regularly remains concealed in thick vegetation. MacGillivray's Warblers may appear anywhere on the refuge, but most records have been from headquarters,

MacGillivray's Warbler

Page Springs, Buena Vista, and Sod House Ranch. Mac-Gillivray's Warblers commonly nest among the moist brush tangles and willow-bordered watercourses in the Blue Mountains and on Steens Mountain, but no refuge records are available at this season.

The species has arrived on April 15 (1961) (average May 3), and the latest departure was June 15 (1966). The spring passage peak falls between May 10 and 25. Individuals have arrived in autumn on August 7 (1961, 1972, 1979), and remained through October 10 (1971). Most pass through Malheur NWR between August 15 and 25. In autumn, with some effort, the MacGillivray's Warbler can be occasionally glimpsed among the weedy patches south of Sod House Spring and in the willow thickets north of Page Springs. This warbler may eventually be found breeding along the willow-bordered watercourses of the southern Blitzen Valley, as nesting habitat in this portion of the refuge certainly meets the requirements of this elusive species.

Common Yellowthroat
Geothlypis trichas

Common in spring and autumn; abundant in summer. In late May and June, there are few Malheur marshes where the male Common Yellowthroat's "wichity-wichity-wichity" calls cannot be heard. Preferring dense stands of emergents, the elusive yellowthroat is by far the most abundant member of its subfamily on the refuge. During autumn migration, the species borders on abundant in the weedy patches and shrubby thickets at headquarters and in the vicinity of Page Springs Dam. Sixty-three were banded between August 5 and September 15, 1984, as they were migrating from the refuge near Page Springs, and one immature male banded at headquarters on August 28, 1985, was recaptured on February 17, 1986, near Rancho El Limon, Nayarit, Mexico. Fledgling success appears to be high on the refuge, as a large percentage of the autumn population consists of immature birds. Some minor losses, however, occasionally occur from Brown-headed Cowbird parasitism. One female yellowthroat was watched for some time as she fed a recently fledged cowbird near Benson Landing in July 1975.

The Common Yellowthroat has arrived as early as April 13 (1984), but the average spring arrival does not occur until May 1. There does not appear to be a period of peak spring

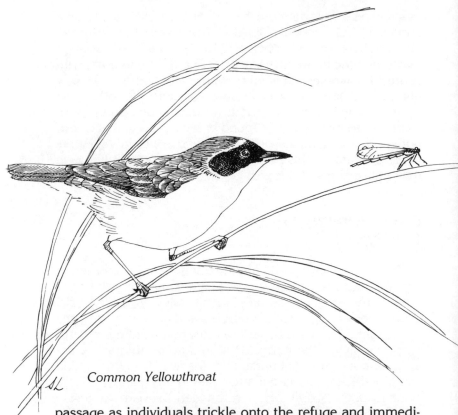

Common Yellowthroat

passage as individuals trickle onto the refuge and immediately establish territories. In late July, migrants begin leaving the refuge and they are more commonly encountered during the last 2 weeks of August than at any other time. Adults leave the refuge earlier than immatures and by September most adults have left for warmer climates. The latest record was October 2 (1981).

Hooded Warbler
Wilsonia citrina

Accidental. On May 20, 1977, J. Wiens observed an adult male Hooded Warbler at headquarters for the second state record and the first for Malheur NWR. Interestingly, in the spring of 1977, the Hooded Warbler was also recorded seven times in southern California (Garrett and Dunn 1981), indicating something of an invasion into the west coast states. The nearest known nesting locality to the refuge for this eastern species is southeast Nebraska (A.O.U. Checklist 1983), and through 1979 there had been seventy records for California and three for Oregon (Roberson 1980). The two other Oregon records are coastal (Washburn State Park, Lane County), occurring on July 20, 1974, and July 10, 1979 (Roberson 1980).

Wilson's Warbler
Wilsonia pusilla

Common spring and autumn migrant. The Wilson's Warbler is one of the commonly encountered migrant warblers on Malheur NWR. Although the species has a wide nesting distribution, I have no breeding records from neighboring montane areas, but surely a few pairs nest in the moist shrubby habitat zones of the Blue Mountains. While on the refuge, Wilson's Warblers may appear anywhere, but the majority are seen among planted trees, willow thickets, and wooded streambottoms, and at times they can be abundant at headquarters: May 19, 1973 (25); August 28, 1974 (25); and May 17, 1975 (40). Other localities where the species is frequently seen include Buena Vista, Page Springs, P Ranch, and adjacent to Warbler and Benson ponds.

The species has been recorded from April 19 (1963, 1968) through June 17 (1975), with the peak of spring migration between May 15 and 31. The average arrival is May 1. In autumn, they have been seen from August 9 (1985) through October 22 (1962), and they are most numerous from August 25 through September 20. In migration, Wilson's Warblers are easily seen as they forage on the outer branches of both deciduous and coniferous trees.

Canada Warbler
Wilsonia canadensis

Accidental. The first record for the Canada Warbler was obtained on September 25, 1982, when J. Gilligan, O. Schmidt, and R. Smith found an individual at headquarters. I captured, banded, and released the bird on September 26. It was recaptured on October 2, but not seen thereafter. This represented the first Oregon record, though there had been 78 records for California through 1979, mostly autumn coastal migrants. The second refuge record was obtained September 2-4, 1988, when a male was observed at headquarters by numerous observers. The nearest known nesting region to the refuge is in northeast British Columbia.

Yellow-breasted Chat
Icteria virens

Uncommon in spring, summer, and autumn. On the refuge, this large tanager-like warbler inhabits dense thickets, brushy tangles, and woodland undergrowth, particularly in the vicinity of Page Dam and along the East Canal. In general, it remains well hidden within the thick foliage, but occasionally individuals can be seen on a conspicuous perch. Throughout May and June, a variety of calls can be heard from the willow and dogwood thickets near Page Dam, and after a time this brightly colored species will often appear. In migration, they are uncommonly seen at scattered localities throughout the refuge. There are numerous records from headquarters where several have been banded over the years, but their center of abundance is in the riparian zones of the southern Blitzen Valley.

The Yellow-breasted Chat's earliest spring appearance was May 7 (1968, 1969, 1972, 1982), and the average is a short time later on May 12. Individuals trickle through the refuge and no pronounced peak has been noted. The latest spring transient was at headquarters June 7 (1976). Pairs are generally on territory by mid-May, and nesting is in progress by

Yellow-breasted Chat

early June. In 1974, five pairs occupied territories near Page Dam, and at least two pairs nested along the East Canal (J. Wittenberger). Several individuals were heard calling along the East Canal in 1986 and north of Page Springs and P Ranch in 1987, indicating the species is increasing in that portion of the refuge. Autumn migrants appear in August, but what I consider an early transient was seen at P Ranch on July 30, 1967. Peak of passage occurs between August 25 and September 10, and their latest date was September 27 (1960).

Summer Tanager
Piranga rubra

Accidental. There are presently four records for this refuge visitant (Littlefield et al. 1985). Oregon's first Summer Tanager record was obtained May 19-21, 1976, at P Ranch when an adult male was seen by J. Wittenberger and numerous others. The second observation was obtained at headquarters May 19-20, 1980, when an adult male was seen on several occasions, and the third record was of a first year male at headquarters on June 9, 1987. The fourth record for Malheur NWR was a male at P Ranch on September 30, 1988 (M. Smith). Other than a male at Hart Mountain on June 14, 1979 (Delevoryas 1980), I know of no additional Oregon records.

Subspecific status of the individuals observed at the refuge was not determined, but considering most vagrants are of the eastern subspecies (*P. r. rubra*), it is likely that they were of this form rather than the southwestern race (*P. r. cooperi*).

Scarlet Tanager
Piranga olivacea

Accidental. A male Scarlet Tanager was seen and photographed at headquarters on May 31, 1979 (Littlefield et al. 1985), representing the first Oregon record. Thirteen days later the second state record was obtained at Hart Mountain (Delevoryas 1980). Other than an adult male recorded in the Trout Creek Mountains on May 18, 1980, and a female at Pike's Creek on May 31, 1987, I know of no other occurrences of this eastern vagrant in the state. Through 1979, there had been 33 records for California, one in British Columbia, and two in Alaska (Roberson 1980).

Western Tanager
Piranga ludoviciana

Common to abundant in spring and autumn migration. Brightly colored Western Tanagers are characteristic transients on Malheur NWR, as they are moving to and from their montane coniferous breeding areas. Throughout the Blue Mountains of eastern Oregon, the species is frequently seen in summer in a variety of evergreen habitats from open yellow pine to dense fir-spruce forests. In the arid lowlands,

Western Tanagers can become abundant in spring, and as many as 77 have been mist-netted in a single day at headquarters, including an adult male which had previously been banded 6 years earlier in Las Vegas, Nevada. Their migration is protracted and in the summer there is a period of only 23 days in late June and early July when the species has not been seen on the refuge. Planted trees around human habitations, streamside trees and thickets, and juniper woodlands are the principal habitats used on the refuge, but at the peak of passage Western Tanagers can even be seen moving through the sagebrush expanses.

The earliest Western Tanager record for Malheur NWR was April 10 (1977), but on the average the species does not arrive until May 2. It reaches its greatest annual abundance between May 20 and June 8, and the latest spring transient was recorded June 23 (1966). The first autumn migrant was recorded July 16 (1966), and from July 25 through August 20 the species is commonly seen on the refuge, particularly at headquarters. By September 15, the majority have moved from the region, but one belated straggler was noted on October 21 (1963).

Rose-breasted Grosbeak
Pheucticus ludovicianus

Rare in spring; accidental in summer and autumn. Since the Rose-breasted Grosbeak was first recorded (May 19-21, 1973) on Malheur NWR (Littlefield 1980), there have been fifteen additional observations—eleven in spring, one in summer, and three in autumn. In spring, this eastern vagrant has been seen between May 18 (1984) and June 15 (1976), with the majority of records from May 25 to June 5. The only summer record was of an adult male at Stinking Lake Spring on July 4, 1976 (S. Herman, K. Shea). Autumn occurrences were all at headquarters: on August 30, 1980; September 22, 1982 (banded); and October 11, 1977 (S. Lindstedt). All Malheur NWR records have been of males, with the exception of a male and female seen together at headquarters on June 15, 1976. The majority of the refuge occurrences have been from headquarters, but the species has also been seen at P Ranch, Stinking Lake Spring, Frenchglen, and Sod House Dam.

Black-headed Grosbeak
Pheucticus melanocephalus

Uncommon in spring and autumn; accidental in summer. The Black-headed Grosbeak is primarily a transient on the refuge and is most commonly seen at headquarters. Elsewhere, it frequents shrubby thickets, wooded streambottoms, and planted trees, and may appear anywhere but never in large numbers. There are very few refuge summer records, but along some of the willow-bordered watercourses of the Blue Mountains it borders on common, and on Steens Mountain this attractive but elusive species has been seen from June 21 to August 29, between 4,600 and 7,800 feet elevation (Hansen 1956).

The Black-headed Grosbeak arrives late in the spring (average May 17). The earliest record was April 20 (1964), the latest June 15 (1963). Spring passage peaks between May 20 and June 1. Nesting was suspected in 1973 after a pair was seen repeatedly in the riparian zones about 1 mile north of P Ranch; in addition, J. Wittenberger saw a male among the willows 1-1/2 miles northwest of P Ranch July 9, 1973. Also several males were singing and appeared territorial between Busse Dam and Unit 9 Pond in late May 1986, but nesting was never confirmed. It is likely that a few pairs remain to nest annually, among the dense willow thickets in the Blitzen Valley, but presently the refuge breeding status of the species is imperfectly known. Autumn migration is generally early, with the earliest occurrence on July 30 (1962). The peak of migration is between August 15 and September 1. One belated straggler remained at headquarters from September 17 through 25, 1986, but previously the latest date was September 7, 1961.

Lazuli Bunting
Passerina amoena

Uncommon spring transient; rare in summer; occasional in autumn. Although there are scattered spring and autumn records from throughout the refuge, the majority concentrate near Page Springs and headquarters. Little Lazuli Bunting breeding habitat occurs on the refuge, but pairs frequently spend the summer months in the lower canyons of Steens Mountain and in the Blue Mountains, being regularly encountered from late May through late July. On Malheur NWR, the species has been seen in summer west of Highway 205 north of Frenchglen, Page Springs, and in Mud Creek Canyon, but breeding has not as yet been confirmed.

The Lazuli Bunting has arrived on April 24 (1966) and the average is May 4. The latest migrant was recorded June 10 (1963). Summer records include a male west of Highway 205 (Highway 205-Krumbo Road junction) on July 6, 1971, and one pair in Mud Creek Canyon on June 20, 1972, and there are several summer observations from near Page Springs. The earliest autumn occurrence was on August 7 (1971), with the passage peak between August 15 and 20. The late date for the species was August 25 (1971) until 1986, when single immatures were located at headquarters and Frenchglen Spring on September 15 and 23, respectively.

Indigo Bunting
Passerina cyanea

Accidental. There are several records for the Indigo Bunting from Oregon. It was 16 years after the first record in the state in 1972 before Malheur NWR obtained its first record. A male appeared at headquarters on May 25, 1988, and remained through at least June 3, allowing numerous observers the opportunity to view him at close range. Although this was the first record within the refuge boundary, S. Summers had previously observed a male Indigo Bunting adjacent to the refuge above Page Springs Campground on May 29, 1983. In addition, there are several records from the eastern canyons of Steens Mountain, where territorial males were seen in the mid- to late 1970s. Observations can be expected to increase on the refuge for this eastern invading species as "California has recently averaged about 55 Indigo Buntings a year. . ." (Roberson 1980).

Painted Bunting
Passerina ciris

Accidental. The normal summer range of the Painted Bunting lies from southeast New Mexico, eastern Kansas, and central Virginia, south to northeast Mexico and central Florida. Thus, the two records for Malheur NWR were most unusual. The first record occurred June 3, 1963, when E. Kridler collected an adult male (USNM #479638) at headquarters (Kridler 1965). The second record was obtained June 11, 1977, when H. Nehls and M. Koninendyke observed an individual also at headquarters. These are the only known records for the Pacific Northwest; however, as of 1979 there were seventeen acceptable records from California (Roberson 1980). The specimen collected by Kridler was of the western form (*P. c. pallidior*).

Green-tailed Towhee
Pipilo chlorurus

Occasional in spring and autumn; rare in summer. In southeast Oregon, Green-tailed Towhees reach their greatest densities in the juniper-sagebrush and aspen-sagebrush associations of the desert mountain ranges, and in the ponderosa pine-sagebrush association of the Blue Mountains, north of Burns. While migrating through the lowlands, transients confine most of their activities to shrubby thickets and tangles. On Malheur NWR, the majority of records are from the southern Blitzen Valley and headquarters, but because of its elusive nature the species is only seen occasionally.

The earliest refuge record was obtained April 21 (1979), but on the average Green-tailed Towhees do not arrive until May 9. No spring peak has been noted as individuals trickle through the region. The latest lowland record was May 15 (1974), but its late spring migrational status is imperfectly known. In summer, the species has been found west of Highway 205 between Krumbo Road and Frenchglen where a few pairs breed. A single bird was seen near Frenchglen Spring in July 29, 1971, but this individual could have been an early autumn transient. The majority move through in late August and early September, and the latest occurrence was on October 11 (1971).

Rufous-sided Towhee
Pipilo erythrophthalmus

Common in spring and autumn; accidental in winter. One of the earliest passerines to arrive in spring and latest to depart in autumn, the Rufous-sided Towhee may appear anywhere on the refuge in shrubby thickets, planted trees and shrubs, willow-bordered watercourses, and sagebrush uplands. It is decidedly common at headquarters and along the Center Patrol Road in late March and September, but in these months the species is also frequently seen throughout the refuge where suitable habitat is available. There is no known nesting record for the refuge, but it is occasionally seen in summer in the lower canyons of the Blue Mountains and Steens Mountain among the streamside willow-alder thickets and tangles.

On the average, the Rufous-sided Towhee arrives on March 4, but it has been seen as early as February 17 (1977). Spring passage peaks between March 15 and April 5, and the majority of transients have left the refuge by mid-May. The earliest southbound migrant was seen August 27 (1966) and the latest December 3 (1983). It is most abundant and widely distributed between September 10 and October 5. Single birds were reported in the southern Blitzen Valley during the

1949 and 1971 Christmas counts, representing the only refuge winter records.

American Tree Sparrow
Spizella arborea

Uncommon in autumn and winter; rare in spring. There are numerous American Tree Sparrow records for the refuge, but at no time or place has it been seen with any regularity. Willow-bordered watercourses are its favored wintering haunts, but occasionally a few individuals can be found

American Tree Sparrow

among sagebrush or greasewood, or along weedy fence lines. The species has recently been seen along the Center Patrol Road from Benson Pond south to 5-mile Road, near Busse Dam, on the East Canal Road east of Knox Pond, and west of Diamond Craters.

This far northern breeding species has arrived on Malheur NWR as early as October 17, 1970 (only October record), but normally it is not seen until December. Flocks are generally small, numbering from two to six individuals, but fifteen were at Kado Bridge on January 4, 1978; twenty at Benson Pond on January 20, 1978; and 34 near Busse Dam on December 17, 1984. There are few records after mid-February; however, the latest occurrence was on March 25 (1970).

Chipping Sparrow
Spizella passerina

Common in spring; uncommon in summer and autumn. In the breeding season, Chipping Sparrows are regularly encountered among the juniper woodlands on Steens Mountain and in the open yellow pine belt of the Blue Mountains, but on Malheur NWR they are mostly absent during the summer months. Occasionally, the species becomes quite common in spring, as Willett (1919) found several hundred in the sagebrush expanses near Malheur Lake on May 14, 1918, but generally flocks are small. Arid woodlands and planted trees attract individuals, and the majority of the Malheur NWR records have been from headquarters and near Page Springs.

The Chipping Sparrow has arrived as early as March 28 (1980), and the average arrival is April 26. The species is most abundant and widely distributed on the refuge between May 1 and 15. The latest spring migrant was noted May 31 (1975). A few pairs remain to nest among the junipers west of Highway 205 from Diamond Lane south to Frenchglen. Pairs probably also nest in Mud and Bridge Creek canyons. Nests have been found as early as May 27, and one nest with four young was located on June 12, 1971 (W. Anderson). The earliest autumn transient was recorded on August 8, the latest October 12 (both 1961). The autumn peak occurs between August 25 and September 10. Generally, individuals and small flocks in autumn trickle from the refuge and no large concentrations occur, but about thirty spent a week feeding on the headquarters lawn in late August 1985.

Brewer's Sparrow
Spizella breweri

Abundant in spring, summer, and autumn. This nondescript species is an inhabitant of the sagebrush expanses and greasewood flats. From late May through June, their singing is a characteristic sound along the south shore of Harney Lake, southeast of Busse Bridge, near Malheur Field Station, and elsewhere on the refuge where desert shrubs provide suitable nesting sites. Similar habitat is used by transients, but Brewer's Sparrows are frequently observed and several have been banded in autumn among the planted trees at refuge headquarters and riparian zones near Page Springs. In some years, the species borders on abundant in late July and August among the shrubs along the Center Patrol Road from Wright's Pond to Rattlesnake Butte.

Spring migrants arrive late and usually the first seen are territorial individuals. An exceptionally early Brewer's Sparrow was reported on April 6, 1974, but the average date is not until May 1. The peak of passage occurs shortly after their arrival: May 10 to 20. Considering the number which remain to nest, late migrants are difficult to detect, and therefore I have no records for late spring transients. Nesting begins in early to mid-May, but the majority of pairs wait until late May and early June. Young fledge in June and July, and shortly after the family has been raised birds begin leaving for their southern wintering areas. Loose flocks have been seen as early as July 15, and the species remains abundant through August. After August, numbers decline rapidly, and the late record was obtained on September 23 (1986).

Vesper Sparrow
Pooecetes gramineus

Common in spring and autumn; accidental in winter. In summer, Vesper Sparrows are regularly encountered among the sagebrush expanses above 4,100 feet elevation which surround the refuge. In the breeding season, the species is strictly a straggler on the refuge, but during migration it is commonly encountered throughout, particularly along the Center Patrol Road and near Page Springs. In autumn, individuals are attracted to weedy roadsides, shrubs, and grasslands. Along the Center Patrol Road in late August and early September, scattered small flocks or lone individuals are regularly seen as they fly ahead of a vehicle with their white outer tail feathers clearly visible. It is at this time that the species reaches its greatest abundance on Malheur NWR.

Vesper Sparrows usually arrive on the refuge on the average date of March 27, but one early record was obtained on February 28 (1975). Peak of spring passage occurs between April 15 and May 1, but it is most abundant after April 25. The latest spring transient was noted on May 17 (1970). The species returns early; autumn migrants have been recorded on July 27 (1971), but peak numbers are not present until early September. Departure is rapid and the latest autumn record was September 23 (1970). On very rare occasions one or two individuals are seen in winter, having been recorded during five Christmas counts: 1941 (one), 1965 (two), 1970 (two), 1971 (one), 1987 (one).

Lark Sparrow
Chondestes grammacus

Common in spring; uncommon in summer and autumn. The Lark Sparrow is another species which moves to higher elevations for most of its nesting activities; however, a few do nest west of Highway 205 from Diamond Road south to Frenchglen, and several pairs are frequently seen during the breeding season a short distance east of the refuge boundary fence along the Steens Mountain Road. These large and attractive sparrows are most numerous near Page Springs and along the Center Patrol Road north of P Ranch during spring migration, but a few individuals can be seen at scattered localities throughout the refuge. In autumn, Lark Sparrows generally trickle from the area and no large flocks have been noted.

The earliest the species has been seen in spring was March 19 (1971), but in most years it arrives much later. The average is April 26. Peak of spring passage occurs between May 5 and 20. The latest spring transient was recorded June 5 (1975). One nest which contained five eggs was located on June 4, 1971, west of Highway 205, and it contained five young on June 12. Once young fledge, individuals begin leaving the area. The earliest southbound transient was noted on July 16, 1976, and the autumn peak occurs between August 5 and 23. The latest autumn record was on September 19 (1986), as an individual fed for a few days among the wet rocks along the flooded Sod House Lane.

Black-throated Sparrow
Amphispiza bilineata

Rare to occasional summer resident. The Black-throated Sparrow has been recorded throughout the lowlands of Harney County, but its center of abundance appears to be on the arid slopes surrounding the Alvord Desert. Most records northwest of Steens Mountain are near Malheur NWR, but there are few reports within the refuge boundaries. Oregon's first record was obtained on June 24 and 25, 1908, when two specimens were taken by W. Finley and H. Bohlman on Wright's Point (10 miles south of Burns). S. Jewett next collected the bird northwest of the refuge (near Stinking Lake) on July 15, 1912 (Gabrielson and Jewett 1940).

The earliest the species has been recorded was May 16 (1984), but nesting generally does not begin until June. The

Black-throated Sparrow

Black-throated Sparrow is a sporadic nester on the refuge, with pairs being evident in some years, but absent in others. Recent records include territorial pairs along the south shore of Harney Lake in 1966 and 1967, and one pair near Double O on June 11, 1981. A few nesting pairs are usually present near Malheur Field Station. A nest with young was located in June 1974 about one-half mile southwest of Malheur Field Station, and one pair fledged a single Brown-headed Cowbird in 1985 on South Coyote Butte (Malheur Field Station). These are the only nests located on the refuge, but pairs and individuals have been seen near Malheur Field Station in most years since 1981. I have no information on autumn migration, as there are no records after July. Family groups apparently leave for their southwestern wintering regions shortly after the young fledge.

Sage Sparrow
Amphispiza belli

Common in spring and autumn; uncommon in summer, accidental in winter. Sage Sparrows are frequently seen among refuge shrubby areas in migration, but few remain to nest. Although a limited number of birds have been seen in the vicinity of Harney and Stinking lakes and near Malheur Field Station in summer, the species reaches its greatest abundance in the surrounding sagebrush expanses, particularly toward Foster Flat and on the lower slopes of Steens Mountain. Probably Sage Sparrows winter more frequently on and in the vicinity of the refuge than records indicate, as little work has been done in the sagebrush zones during the cold and often snowy months.

The Sage Sparrow is one of the first passerine migrants to appear in spring, usually arriving in late February (earliest February 17, 1975). It is most abundant and widely distributed between March 15 and 25, and the majority of transients have left by the end of April. Little information is available on their nesting chronology, but they are known to nest early. Pairs are usually on territory in late March, with nesting in progress by early April, continuing into June and July. Family groups and small flocks begin congregating in late July, and autumn migration is underway by August. Peak of passage is in mid-September, with a late autumn straggler seen on November 20 (1970). There is one winter record, a lone bird near south Harney Lake on December 22, 1980.

Savannah Sparrow
Passerculus sandwichensis

Common in spring, summer, and autumn; accidental in winter. Savannah Sparrows commonly nest in the drier dense grasslands throughout the refuge. Nest sites are usually well concealed among residual grasses, but in years past when the refuge was excessively grazed by cattle, I found several nests which had been constructed beneath dried cow patties. Both Double O and the Blitzen Valley have large numbers of nesting pairs, and the species is one of the few breeding sparrows found in meadow habitat on the refuge. In migration, individuals are frequently observed along the Center Patrol Road, and in recent years small numbers have been seen along Sod House Lane (west of headquarters) in autumn.

The earliest arrival date is March 1 (1986, S. Speich) and the average is March 22. Peak of spring passage occurs between April 5 and 25, with most northbound transients gone by early May. The nesting season is rather prolonged, with the earliest record on May 10 (1979) and the latest with eggs (two) on July 11 (1969). Autumn migration begins in August and peaks between September 10 and October 5. The majority of transients have left the refuge by November, but one belated straggler was seen on November 25 (1976). The only winter record was of a single bird near Frenchglen on December 20, 1975.

Savannah Sparrows are divided into several geographical races. Those nesting on Malheur NWR are the Nevada Savannah Sparrow (*P.s. nevadensis*), while subspecific status of those migrating through the area remains to be determined. Generally the Nevada form arrives late in spring and departs early in autumn (Gabrielson and Jewett 1940); therefore, most individuals seen in March and probably all after September consist of a northern race, likely the Western Savannah Sparrow (*P. s. anthinus*).

Fox Sparrow
Passerella iliaca

Uncommon in spring and autumn; accidental in winter. Nesting Fox Sparrows are frequently found in shrubby thickets on all mountain ranges surrounding the refuge. Pairs are occasionally seen or heard among the willow-bordered watercourses or chokecherry thickets on Steens and Hart mountains (*P. i. fulva*) and in the Blue Mountains (*P. i. schistacea*). However, on the refuge the species is absent during the nesting period, even though extensive riparian habitat is available. In migration, this large sparrow is regularly seen in brushy areas, particularly at headquarters, Page Springs, and P Ranch. Occasionally, individuals associate with the large flocks of White-crowned Sparrows, as was the one seen feeding along Highway 205 (8 miles north of Frenchglen) during a snow storm on April 26, 1976.

The average Fox Sparrow arrival date is April 13, with the earliest spring record March 16 (1969). The peak of migration occurs between April 15 and May 1, and the latest record was May 10 (1967). In autumn, transients have arrived in August, but the majority do not migrate through the refuge until September and October. The earliest arrival was reported by Willett (1919) who recorded an individual near Malheur Lake on August 5 (1918). The latest record occurred November 20 (1970) and the peak generally falls between September 15 and October 5. The species has been recorded during four Christmas counts: 1943 (one), 1965 (one), 1970 (two), and 1980 (two). In addition, one was at headquarters on January 23, 1971.

Song Sparrow
Melospiza melodia

Common to abundant permanent resident. The Song Sparrow is one of the common nesting and wintering passerines on Malheur NWR, occurring primarily in shrubby thickets, wooded streambottoms, and weedy patches. Some 31 Song Sparrow races occur in North America, but during the summer season only one, the Modoc Song Sparrow (*M. m. fisherella*), is found on the refuge. In winter, however, their taxonomic status is unclear, as northern races move onto the arid lowlands; probably the Mountain Song Sparrow (*M. m. montana*) is also present. In addition, several rufous-colored individuals have been seen in migration at headquarters.

An influx of Song Sparrows is generally noted between March 1 and 15, with resident birds mostly on territory by late April. I have no data on transient departure dates, and surprisingly little information on nesting. Territorial singing is frequently heard in late February and March, but nesting apparently does not begin until May. C. Bendire (Brewer 1875) found a nest with eggs on May 29, 1875, near Malheur Lake. Other nesting records include one with eggs along Bridge Creek on May 26, 1966, and one containing four eggs north of P Ranch on May 25, 1984. Both of the latter nests were in roses, adjacent to willows. Undoubtedly some pairs nest earlier than these records indicate. Autumn migrants have been noted at Page Springs in August, and these individuals were likely resident *fisherella*. Transients are most evident between mid-September and mid-October, and these probably include both *fisherella* and *montana*. Migrant birds have left by late November in most years. The species commonly winters and it has been recorded during all Christmas counts (1941-88). Low numbers were recorded in 1962 (five), 1972 (one), and 1973 (five), while greatest numbers were in 1941 (92), 1944 (81), and 1965 (135). Wintering birds generally concentrate in the riparian zones of the southern Blitzen Valley, as limited riparian habitat is found in the northern portion. However, on December 21, 1981, 67 were recorded in weedy fields near headquarters, and on December 19, 1986, eighty were in the same area.

Lincoln's Sparrow
Melospiza lincolnii

Uncommon in spring and autumn; accidental in winter. Typical habitat for the Lincoln's Sparrow on Malheur NWR consists of shrubby thickets, planted shrubs, and weedy patches, where it usually remains rather inconspicuous and hidden, making observations difficult. Around headquarters it occurs with some regularity, but elsewhere on the refuge sightings are sporadic and inconsistent. In the localized grassy and shaggy willow wetlands of the Blue Mountains, the species is often abundant during the breeding season, but I am unaware of any nesting records on Steens Mountain.

The Lincoln's Sparrow has arrived in spring on March 22 (1987), but the average arrival is not until April 24. The species reaches its greatest abundance between May 1 and 15, and the latest spring occurrence was recorded on May 21 (1973). In autumn, the earliest transient was seen August 15 (1978). Peak of passage occurs between September 15 and October 1, and the latest record was obtained on October 23 (1961). There are but two winter records: single birds during the 1944 and 1979 Christmas counts.

White-throated Sparrow
Zonotrichia albicollis

Rare to uncommon in spring and autumn; accidental in winter. The White-throated Sparrow is a frequently encountered vagrant on Malheur NWR, with usually one or more observations annually. On very rare occasions, the species borders on common as was the case in 1960 when fifteen individuals were banded at headquarters between September 11 and October 23. Generally, white-throats are found in shrubby thickets and planted hedges, often associated with the migrant flocks of White-crowned Sparrows which are so common on the refuge.

In spring, records have fallen between April 25 (1960) and May 10 (1972). The earliest autumn record was September 11 and the latest October 23 (both 1960). No peak period of passage has been noted in either spring or autumn. There is one winter record, that of a lone individual banded at headquarters on December 2, 1960.

White-crowned Sparrow
Zonotrichia leucophrys

Abundant spring and autumn migrant; occasional in winter; accidental in summer. The number of White-crowned Sparrows far exceeds all other sparrows in April and September, as migratory flocks are commonly encountered throughout the refuge. Major concentrations frequently occur at headquarters, Malheur Field Station, and along the Center Patrol Road, particularly from Malheur Field Station to Rattlesnake Butte and Benson Pond to P Ranch. The black-lored Mountain race (*Z. l. oriantha*) commonly summers above 7,000 feet on Steens Mountain and also in the higher elevations of the Blue Mountains; however, the majority of refuge migrants are of the northern-nesting white-lored Gambel's race (*Z. l. gambelii*). One which was banded at headquarters on September 9, 1962, was recovered at San Diego, California, on October 13, 1963.

On the average, White-crowned Sparrows arrive on March 23 (earliest February 18, 1975). Numerous flocks occur between April 7 and 18, and the latest spring record was May 23. The only summer record was that of a lone bird at headquarters on June 23, 1976. Autumn migration falls between August 15 (1978) and November 13 (1973), and the species is most abundant from September 18 through October 10. Occasionally they are seen in mild winters, but generally they move from the refuge during the colder months. Most winter records are from headquarters, but one individual wintered at

Malheur Field Station in 1976-77. Greatest wintering numbers were noted on December 18, 1979 (eighteen) and December 19, 1986 (24).

Golden-crowned Sparrow
Zonotrichia atricapilla

Uncommon spring and autumn migrant. This northwestern montane-breeding species reaches its greatest abundance west of the Cascade Range, but a few individuals are seen annually on Malheur NWR. Here, as with other sparrow species, they often associate with the immense flocks of White-crowned Sparrows, especially at headquarters. Habitat preference appears to be identical to that of the White-crowned Sparrow—shrubby thickets, weedy patches, planted shrubs. Generally only one or two individuals are seen in a particular area; however, six were banded at headquarters on both September 23 and October 2, 1961. The greatest number ever recorded on the refuge was twenty seen on April 24, 1940, and the most banded in one season was 59 from September 6 through October 28, 1961.

In the spring, Golden-crowned Sparrows have arrived on March 19 (1972), but generally their arrival is much later (average May 2). Spring migration is usually short-lived, with the latest record May 19 (1971). Peak of passage is between May 5 and 12. Autumn migration is more prolonged, with the earliest on September 6 (1961) and the latest November 27 (1969). Peak numbers are present between September 20 and October 5.

Harris' Sparrow
Zonotrichia querula

Rare in autumn, winter, and spring. The Harris' Sparrow was first recorded and photographed on the refuge October 30-31, 1955 (Marshall 1959). Additional early records included an immature banded and another observed between

October 22 and 30, 1960, followed closely by three immatures being mist-netted at one time on November 6, 1960.
Two were banded and one was secured as a specimen (Kridler
and Marshall 1962). E. Kridler also observed an adult on
October 26, 1961. All of these early records were obtained at
or near headquarters.

Recent records include: one immature November 7
through December 2, 1971; an adult April 29 through May 1,
1972; five wintering birds in 1974-75; one November 28,
1976, through January 12, 1977; one on October 16, 1982
(M. Archie); one on October 27, 1985 (M. Archie); and one
November 17 through December 19, 1986 (G. Ivey). All of the
above observations were from headquarters, and the other
records were one near Frenchglen on December 18, 1985,
and one at Benson Pond on May 15, 1988.

This largest of the North American sparrows nests in the
taiga regions from Hudson Bay northwestward to the Mack-
enzie Valley; the birds that occur on the refuge are probably
from the western portion of their northern Canada nesting
range.

Dark-eyed Junco
Junco hyemalis oreganus

Common in spring and autumn; uncommon in winter. The
Oregon form of the Dark-eyed Junco is a characteristic bird
on the refuge in spring and autumn, as birds are moving to
and from their montane nesting areas. Commonly found in
summer on both Steens Mountain and the Blue Mountains,
the subspecies has not been recorded in the southeast Oregon arid lowlands from June 1 through August 31. On the
refuge, small migrant flocks are frequently seen around
human habitations (Malheur Field Station, headquarters),
streamside trees, shrubby thickets, and arid woodlands,
while wintering birds are mostly found among juniper woodlands and willow-bordered watercourses.

The spring influx of Oregon Juncos generally begins in late February and the subspecies reaches its peak of abundance between March 10 and April 10. They are commonly encountered after mid-April, but the majority have left the refuge by May 1. One belated straggler, however, was still present on May 30, 1962. In early September (earliest September 1, 1962), individuals begin moving from the montane regions into the arid lowlands. They are most abundant and widely distributed between October 5 and 25, but numbers decline after October. A few remain through the winter, mostly in the southern Blitzen Valley where they have been recorded during all Christmas counts. Greatest numbers were in 1941 (352), 1944 (180), 1959 (139), 1970 (122), 1972 (132), 1976 (180), 1978 (147), and 1979 (132).

The nominant "Slate-colored" Junco (*J. h. hyemalis*) has been seen fourteen times on the refuge. First recorded on October 10, 1960, the subspecies has been seen from October 10 (1960) to May 15 (1970). Presently there are two October, three December, four January, one February, one March, two April, and one May record. All observations have been of single birds, except for two seen on both January 2, 1971, and December 21, 1977.

There is one refuge record for the "Gray-headed" Junco (*J. h. caniceps*). On May 22, 1976, C. Talbot and I watched an individual for about 20 minutes at Benson Landing (Littlefield 1981). This represented the first state record for this Rocky Mountain form.

Lapland Longspur
Calcarius lapponicus

Accidental. C. Bendire obtained a specimen north of the refuge near Camp Harney on December 14, 1874 (Brewer 1875), and observed others later (Bendire 1877). It was over 100 years later that the species was again seen in the Malheur-Harney Lakes Basin. On January 9, 1982, I found four Lapland Longspurs among a flock of Horned Larks about 2 miles southwest of headquarters along the Center Patrol Road. There they remained for about 4 days, feeding on Russian thistle seeds which were protruding above snow at the road's edge.

Snow Bunting
Plectrophenax nivalis

Rare winter visitant. This far northern nesting species was rarely seen on Malheur NWR until 1984. Since then more Snow Bunting records have accumulated than had been reported from all previous years. The majority of recent records has been in the vicinity of Malheur Lake, where individuals concentrated along the rocky roadsides and near the receding shorelines; the species has been particularly evident along Highway 205 and near headquarters.

The first refuge record was obtained in January 1936, when J. Scharff observed about thirty Snow Buntings along the north shore of Malheur Lake. There were no additional records until December 11, 1969, when a lone bird was seen near Krumbo Reservoir. Other pre-1984 records include three west of headquarters on November 23, 1970; one at Knox Pond on December 20, 1975; and one near Double O on November 7, 1978. Since 1984, the species has been seen annually on dates ranging from October 29 (1987) through April 7 (1984). Most recent records have been in December and March, generally of single birds, but on December 17, 1985, a flock of sixty was seen near headquarters.

Bobolink
Dolichonyx oryzivorus

Uncommon to locally common in spring, summer, and autumn. Malheur NWR is the center of Bobolink abundance in Oregon, where the species finds suitable habitat among the meadows at isolated localities throughout the Blitzen Valley. Greatest numbers are found near P Ranch; however, I have frequently seen territorial individuals from 3 to 6 miles northwest of P Ranch, 5 miles northeast of P Ranch, 2 miles southwest of headquarters, 1 mile north of headquarters, 2 miles southeast of Buena Vista, and in Diamond Swamp. There are no records for Double O. Recent surveys indicate that generally there are from 200 to 250 males on the refuge during the breeding season.

The Bobolink usually arrives in May, but observations are often limited as the species generally occupies areas away from public travel. The earliest arrival date was April 30 (1977), but in most years it is not seen until mid-May. The majority of the males have arrived by late May, with females arriving shortly afterwards. Nesting occurs in June, and fledged young are present in July. The species is likely to be seen in late August and early September, feeding in flocks along weedy fence rows and in grassy fields. Thirty-five were observed among Boca Lake forbs on September 6, 1973, and twenty to thirty have frequently been seen near Wright's Pond in late August and early September. In autumn, males have lost their black and white breeding plumage and share the yellowish attire of females and fledglings. The majority have migrated toward their South American wintering areas by September 10. The latest autumn record was September 18 (Gabrielson and Jewett 1940).

Western Meadowlark
Sturnella neglecta

Common in spring, summer, and autumn; rare in winter. The Western Meadowlark is a characteristic bird of the southeast Oregon grasslands. Preferred habitat on Malheur NWR includes grass-shrub uplands, dry meadows, and grass-shrub expanses, particularly in the northern portion of the Blitzen Valley. Pairs are frequently seen near Malheur Field Station, along the Center Patrol Road from headquarters to Unit 9 Pond, and in the Double O area near Derrick and Stinking lakes. Western Meadowlarks trickle onto the refuge in spring and no flocks have been noted; in autumn small widely scattered flocks of five to fifteen birds are occasionally encountered. This species has increased on the refuge in recent years, as habitat has been improved by both prescribed burning and a reduction in the number of cattle.

The earliest spring arrival date was February 6 (1984) and the average arrival is February 27. Peak of passage occurs between March 10 and 25, and most northbound transients have left by late April. Some pairs are nesting by late April (earliest April 23), and a few are still tending young in July (latest July 6). It is unknown if the species is double-brooded in this region. Autumn migrants have been noted in early August, with peak numbers from August 20 through September 20. The latest record was December 2 (1983) and many linger into October and November. Winter records include single birds on December 30, 1969; December 23, 1970; January 28, 1972; January 9, 1974; December 24, 1972; January 9, 1982; December 17, 1983; and January 7, 1988; and one wintered at Malheur Field Station in 1985-86.

Red-winged Blackbird
Agelaius phoeniceus

Abundant in spring, summer, and autumn; uncommon in winter. One of the most abundant species on Malheur NWR, the Red-winged Blackbird is also one of the earliest spring migrants. Males establish their territories shortly after arrival, but females do not appear until 2 to 3 weeks later. Except for the arid shrub zones, juniper slopes, and dense emergent stands, red-wings are found throughout the refuge during the breeding season. Taller meadow grasses appear to be their favored nesting habitat in southeast Oregon. Arriving earlier than Yellow-headed Blackbirds, some male red-wings establish their territories within emergents. Upon the arrival of the larger yellow-heads, red-wings are driven back to the meadows or willow thickets, where they spend the remainder of the breeding season. Occasionally nests are attached to different species of grasses. If growth rates and heights of these grasses are dissimilar, the nests will eventually tilt to a point where the eggs roll from the bowl. Several nests of this kind have been found on the refuge in past years.

The spring influx occurs in mid-February, and many males are on territory by late February. However, nesting is not in progress until late April (earliest April 23), as females wait for new vegetative growth to reach sufficient height (about 10 inches) for nest construction. After young have fledged in mid-July Red-winged Blackbirds begin congregating near favorable feeding areas, generally grainfields, mowed meadows, and alfalfa fields. These flocks remain through September, but decrease in October as southbound migrants leave the refuge. There are several winter records, mostly of single birds or small flocks. Exceptions are a flock of 150 seen during the 1960 Christmas count; a flock of about one hundred which wintered near a Malheur Field Station bird feeder in the winters of 1976-77 and 1977-78; and flocks of 1,125 and 995 on December 18, 1979, and December 22, 1980, respectively (about 3 miles west of headquarters).

Yellow-headed Blackbird
Xanthocephalus xanthocephalus

Abundant in spring, summer, and autumn; rare in winter. The Yellow-headed Blackbird inhabits productive cattail and bulrush marshes throughout the refuge, but avoids those which contain few aquatic invertebrates. A noticeable increase has occurred on Malheur NWR since the mid-1970s, and where formerly there were few nesting colonies in the Blitzen Valley (with the exception of Wright's Pond) they now occur locally throughout. Wright's and Warbler ponds and Malheur Lake have been traditional nesting sites; however, in periods of high water, Malheur Lake has little Yellow-headed Blackbird use, as habitat becomes limited. The species begins congregating in mid-July and by mid-August both mixed and pure flocks of several hundred can be seen at favorable feeding sites, particularly in or near refuge grainfields.

On the average, Yellow-headed Blackbirds arrive on March 27, with the earliest date on March 9 (1979, 1981). The major influx occurs about mid-April, but occasionally it is earlier; in 1971, the species became abundant early as more than three thousand were at headquarters on March 31. The majority of pairs are on their communal territories by mid-May, with nesting in progress by late May (earliest May 9). Young, hardly able to fly, appear in late June, and in July adults and young begin congregating. Some adult males initiate their southward migration in July, but generally the majority leave the refuge in September. By October most have left, but a few are occasionally seen into November. Rarely Yellow-headed Blackbirds can be found in winter. An individual was seen at headquarters in 1974-75 and a single bird was seen near Harney Lake on December 19, 1986.

Brewer's Blackbird
Euphagus cyanocephalus

Abundant in spring, summer, and autumn; uncommon in winter. On Malheur NWR, the Brewer's Blackbird prefers drier sites than do the other two blackbird species, nesting commonly in arid shrublands and around human habitations. Most nests are placed low in shrubs and hedges; however, while I was camped at Benson Pond in 1966, five pairs nested on the ground within 40 feet of my tent. This area has since been checked annually and no additional ground-nesting Brewer's Blackbirds have been located. All other nests which I have examined on the refuge have been in shrubs or hedgerows. It is possible these Benson Pond birds were associating with human activity to deter predators, but this is certainly speculative. While on the refuge, the species appears to be the primary host to the parasitic Brown-headed Cowbird, and few nests have been found which did not contain one to three cowbird eggs.

The spring influx occurs around March 15 (earliest February 3, 1972; average March 10) and by March 20 Brewer's Blackbirds can be abundant. Pairs begin nesting in early May, with young being found as early as May 18 (1972). The majority of young fledge in June, but some pairs are still feeding nestlings well into July. Once young fledge, family groups join with other blackbirds in August near favorable feeding sites. The species is most abundant in September before leaving for their southwestern wintering regions, and by November 10 only winter residents remain. Brewer's Blackbirds are usually uncommon in winter; however, where favorable feeding areas are present they can border on common. In 1961 and 1970, 84 and 83 were seen, respectively, during the southern Blitzen Valley Christmas count. Outside the refuge, several hundred regularly winter near Princeton and on private ranches west of headquarters.

Great-tailed Grackle
Quiscalus mexicanus

Rare in spring. The Great-tailed Grackle was first recorded in Oregon on May 16, 1980, when an adult male was seen by numerous observers at Malheur Field Station (Littlefield 1983). Several additional records have since accumulated. Apparently several males were present in 1980, as individuals were at Page Springs, headquarters, and Malheur Field Station. Another was at Malheur Field Station on April 8 and 9, 1981, and at Page Springs on June 19, 1981 (D. Taylor), with additional observations at Malheur Field Station May 9-31, 1985, headquarters May 24 through June 1985, and two at Buena Vista on May 30, 1986.

The Great-tailed Grackle has been expanding its range northward since the turn of the century. By 1953 it had reached Oklahoma, 1964 Kansas, and 1972 Missouri. In the west, California's first record was in 1964, Nevada 1973, and Utah 1979.

Common Grackle
Quiscalus quiscula

Accidental. There are two records for the refuge. On May 28, 1977, S. and P. Summers observed a male Common Grackle at headquarters. The individual was watched for about 5 minutes within 30 feet. Both observers were familiar with the species. This was the first Malheur NWR record and perhaps the first for Oregon (Summers 1977). The second record was from Page Springs on May 21, 1988.

Northern Oriole
Icterus galbula bullockii

Common in spring and summer; uncommon in autumn. The male Bullock's form of the Northern Oriole has to be one of the most attractive birds in the arid lowlands of southeast Oregon. Historically, the species was restricted to localized juniper parklands and wooded streambottoms, but upon European settlement and subsequent tree plantings around human habitations, this brightly plumaged bird is now well established throughout the region. The majority of pairs on Malheur NWR occupy territories in this newly created habitat. Two to three pairs have nested at headquarters, with other pairs at Buena Vista, Benson Pond, the abandoned Witzel Ranch, Double O substation, Frenchglen Spring, P Ranch (since 1976), Malheur Field Station (in 1987), and Frenchglen. The only natural nesting sites of which I am aware are those of two pairs which regularly nest among the junipers near Page Springs.

The earliest spring arrival date was April 10 (1979) and the average is May 6. Males usually arrive a few days earlier than females. Peak of passage is in mid-May, and the majority of pairs are present by May 20. Nesting is in progress by the first week in June. One completed nest was located at Page Springs on June 5, 1971, and young were seen leaving a nest on June 29, 1961. However, most young fledge in July and begin migrating from the refuge in late July. By the end of August few Northern Orioles remain, and the latest records were September 8 (1971) and September 11 (1970).

The eastern Baltimore form (*I. g. galbula*) has been recorded three times on the refuge. Kridler and Marshall (1962) reported on an adult male singing among sagebrush on June 1, 1960. The bird was collected and is now in the U. S. National Museum. J. Gilligan obtained the second record, when he and others observed an adult male at headquarters on May 30, 1985. The third record was that of another male which remained at headquarters from July 31 through August 13, 1987 (G. Ivey).

Brown-headed Cowbird
Molothrus ater

Common in spring and summer; uncommon in autumn. The Brown-headed Cowbird has increased dramatically since European settlement. C. Bendire did not find the species in the Malheur-Harney Lakes Basin in the 1870s, and it is not known when it first appeared. Cowbirds were present, however, by 1918 as Willett (1919) reported the species from Malheur Lake. Cowbirds have been known to parasitize 250 kinds of birds, resulting in detrimental effects on several. On Malheur NWR, the Yellow Warbler, Common Yellowthroat, Red-winged and Brewer's blackbirds, and Black-throated, Savannah, and Song sparrows have all been victims of this widespread species. Headquarters, Malheur Field Station, and the southern Blitzen Valley have the greatest densities, but singles, pairs, and small flocks are frequently encountered throughout the refuge.

The Brown-headed Cowbird arrives late in spring, usually not until late April or early May. Earliest arrival was April 4 (1982) and the average is April 26. The species is most common from mid- to late May. Relieved of parental duties, adults begin congregating in early July and have begun moving southward by mid-July. Young remain into August and early September, mixing with other blackbirds at favorable feeding sites. None has been detected after early September, but a few may remain somewhat later among the immense flocks of autumn blackbirds.

FAMILY: FRINGILLIDAE

Rosy Finch
Leucosticte arctoa

Accidental in autumn and winter. C. Bendire found Rosy Finches common in the vicinity of Camp Harney during the winter, and collected several specimens in the 1870s (Brewer 1875). His observations, and those of others later, indicate the species prefers rocky slopes which are vegetated with scattered grasses or junipers and sagebrush. The lack of such habitat on Malheur NWR perhaps accounts for so few reports. Presently there are only three records; two on November 9, 1977 (Malheur Field Station); eight on December 17, 1977 (half a mile north of the abandoned Witzel Ranch); and ten on November 10, 1985 (about 7 miles north of Frenchglen).

Both the Black Rosy Finch (*L.a. atrata*) and Gray-crowned Rosy Finch (*L.a. tephrocotis*) are found in summer near the summit of Steens Mountain, but only the Gray-crowned has been seen on the refuge. Both forms probably move downslope into the Alvord Basin in autumn, as records are more frequent from that region than on the western slope of Steens Mountain.

Pine Grosbeak
Pinicola enucleator

Rare in autumn and winter. The Pine Grosbeak confines most of its activities to the coniferous-montane regions of the Pacific Northwest, rarely moving onto the arid lowlands of southeastern Oregon. There are but five records for Malheur NWR, but the species should be looked for during winter in wooded areas, particularly in the southern Blitzen Valley. Nineteen were at headquarters from September 1 to 30, 1960 (the largest number recorded). Other records were eleven in the southern Blitzen Valley on December 30, 1969; three females near P Ranch on March 11, 1970; one male at headquarters on November 13, 1981; and three to four between December 15, 1984, and January 22, 1985, along the East Canal north of Page Springs.

Purple Finch
Carpodacus purpureus

Rare spring and autumn vagrant. The Purple Finch is a common bird of western Oregon, but is rarely seen in the southeastern portion of the state. On Malheur NWR, the first record was obtained on November 3, 1961, when Kridler (1965) collected a male (USNM *478849). Twelve years later the second record occurred when one male and two females were seen on May 19, 1973. These birds remained several days and the male was banded on May 20. Since then, the species has been recorded on June 7, 1982 (female, J. Gatchet); September 25 through October 12, 1984 (five); September 20 through 25, 1986 (female, J. Gilligan and others); and October 16, 1988 (female, S. Summers). All observations have been from headquarters.

Cassin's Finch
Carpodacus cassinii

Rare in spring, autumn, and winter. The Cassin's Finch is usually a common breeding bird throughout the mountain ranges of eastern Oregon. Among the aspen clones of Steens Mountain and in the coniferous zones of the Blue Mountains, the species can border on abundant some years, but can be virtually absent during succeeding years. On Malheur NWR, few records for this montane species exist and these are mostly from the southern Blitzen Valley where finches associate principally with the juniper-covered slopes north of Frenchglen and near Page Springs. Cassin's Finches have been seen on the refuge most often during the last week of May and in October. They are usually seen alone, but one flock of forty was observed 10 miles north of Frenchglen on October 26, 1975, and forty were feeding on weed seeds near Krumbo Road and Highway 205 on December 21, 1977.

The scarcity of refuge records results from individuals remaining at higher elevations through the winter months. In autumn, the species moves downslope into the ponderosa pine and juniper-covered foothills, but few continue onto the arid lowlands unless their food sources have been depleted.

House Finch
Carpodacus mexicanus

Common in spring, summer, and autumn; rare in winter. House Finches inhabit the lowland valleys of southeast Oregon, where they find suitable nesting habitat among juniper woodlands and the planted trees in both urban and rural areas. P Ranch, Frenchglen, Benson Pond, Buena Vista, Witzel Ranch, and the junipers at Page Springs frequently support breeding pairs. The species is rarely seen in the large flocks which occur elsewhere within their range, with four or five the normal number here. However, fourteen were seen together at headquarters on January 29, 1987, and sixty wintered at Sod House Ranch in 1988-89. In winter, House Finches usually disappear from the refuge, but they can be common around bird-feeding stations in Burns and Hines at this time of year.

In the spring, the average arrival is April 14, with the earliest on March 10 (1965). After their arrival, birds trickle onto the refuge and no pronounced migration has been noted. Pairs are usually on territory by mid-May, with nesting in progress by late May. In autumn, they leave the way they arrived in spring; individuals are present one day but gone the next. Generally most leave Malheur NWR in October; however, the species has been recorded during eight Christmas counts. In some winters the species borders on abundant; in 1966, 275 were seen for the greatest winter number. Other Christmas count numbers include: 1959 (twenty), 1965 (nine), 1969 (48), 1970 (36), 1971 (38), 1977 (39), and 1985 (nine). For some unknown reason, wintering House Finches disappeared from the refuge in the late 1970s, not returning until the mid-1980s.

Red Crossbill
Loxia curvirostra

Rare. On the refuge, the Red Crossbill occurs sporadically, with no predictability. Usually the species is abundant in the Blue Mountains, but there have been years when it was virtually absent. Such disappearances likely relate to conifer seed deficiencies, and it is during these lean periods that crossbills invade the lowland deserts throughout the west. Interestingly, when food supplies are abundant these birds are capable of nesting during any month of the year.

There are only six records for Malheur NWR. Small flocks were seen at headquarters from July 3 to 11, 1958, and an adult male (banded) was at headquarters on October 22, 1960, as were two in Diamond Valley on June 28, 1972. A male was found dead at headquarters on June 1, 1977, one was at headquarters on June 7, 1981 (J. Gatchet), and the last record was obtained on October 22, 1984, when a male was seen at headquarters.

Common Redpoll
Carduelis flammea

Rare in winter. This circumpolar arctic and subarctic nesting species is rarely seen on Malheur NWR, but there are several records from the Malheur-Harney Lakes Basin. Most

Common Redpolls remain north of the refuge through the winter, being more prevalent in northeast Oregon. There are three records for the refuge. L. McQueen observed two on December 5, 1977, near Benson Pond; S. Thompson and G. Wing saw four in the same area on December 21, 1977; and a flock of thirty spent about 2 weeks in late November 1985 at headquarters.

In addition to the refuge records, thirty spent much of January 1975 along weedy fence rows about 10 miles east of headquarters. They were first seen on January 14, 3 miles southwest of Princeton, and remained through January 26. Bendire (1877) also collected several near Camp Harney in the 1870s.

Pine Siskin
Carduelis pinus

Uncommon in spring and autumn; accidental in winter. The Pine Siskin is a regular migrant and visitant to Malheur NWR, with records from all months except January, February, and July. In the Blue Mountains, the species nests abundantly and it has been seen on Steens Mountain in June and July. Siskins are most frequently seen around headquarters, but other localities where the species has been recorded with some regularity include P Ranch, Frenchglen, and Page Springs. Lawns, weedy patches, planted trees, and willow thickets are their preferred habitat while on the refuge.

In spring, the average arrival is May 7 and the earliest record was obtained on March 28 (1966). Peak of passage occurs between May 15 and June 1, and the latest spring record was June 15 (1963). Pine Siskins have been observed in autumn as early as August 20 (1984), but most do not appear until October. Their peak occurs between October 15 and 31. The latest autumn transient was seen November 9 (1962). The only winter record was of three individuals seen feeding beneath sagebrush at Page Springs on December 17, 1977.

Lesser Goldfinch
Carduelis psaltria

Uncommon in spring, summer, and autumn. Away from the southern extremity of the Blitzen Valley, the Lesser Goldfinch is a rare species on Malheur NWR. At Page Springs, it can border on abundant one year and be only occasionally seen the next. Greatest numbers were present in 1976 when thirty to fifty were frequently seen in May (J. Wittenberger), and in 1984 when 53 were banded between August 5 and September 9 from an estimated two hundred which frequented the willow thickets near Page Dam. Away from Page Springs, the species has been seen at Benson Pond, Frenchglen, P Ranch, and headquarters (one record).

The Lesser Goldfinch has been observed from May 8 (1971) through September 9 (1984), with most records between May 18 and 22, and August 15 and 25. D. Kerley observed a pair in Page Canyon on July 13, 1975, and other pairs have been seen in June near Page Springs Campground, indicating a few pairs breed in that area. The species prefers broad-leafed trees and the lack of this habitat elsewhere on the refuge probably accounts for its scarcity.

American Goldfinch
Carduelis tristis

Uncommon to common in spring, summer, and autumn; occasional in winter. The American Goldfinch has been recorded on the refuge in every month of the year, but is most commonly encountered in May. Wooded streambottoms, planted trees, and willow thickets are the preferred habitats. Goldfinches are often seen at headquarters feeding with Pine Siskins on the lawn in spring and autumn, while in late summer individuals frequent Canada thistle patches along the Center Patrol Road. I have not found any nests on the refuge, but one pair was seen feeding recently fledged young at headquarters in August 1988. A few pairs are also seen annually during the summer months in the southern Blitzen Valley, and some breeding likely occurs there as well. Thistles and other composite seeds are the major food sources for both adult and young, and nesting is usually delayed until these seeds become available. Therefore, pairs are frequently seen through June and into early July.

The average spring arrival is April 21 and the peak of passage occurs between May 10 and 20. The latest spring record was June 14 (1972). In summer, individuals have been seen at Page Springs and near P Ranch in late June and July. Autumn transients appear in August, but the species is most abundant and widely distributed between October 15 and 31. Most migrants have left the refuge by mid-November, but a few American Goldfinches remain through the winter. The species has been recorded during six Christmas counts: 1940 (eleven), 1941 (forty), 1973 (five), 1983 (one), 1984 (eight), and 1985 (three). There are several additional winter records from outside the Christmas count period and area.

Evening Grosbeak
Coccothraustes vespertinus

Uncommon in spring; occasional in autumn and winter. In eastern Oregon, the Evening Grosbeak is primarily an inhabitant of the montane coniferous forest regions. However, in the colder months, particularly in years when food supplies are limited, this large fringillid moves onto the arid lowlands. While on the refuge, the species is mostly seen in areas of planted trees, wooded watercourses, juniper woodlands, and willow thickets. In spring, their arrival usually corresponds to the emergence of elm and box-elder seeds, and cottonwood catkins. At this time, the Evening Grosbeak is most prevalent around headquarters and Frenchglen and near P Ranch, but at other times it can be found throughout the refuge where trees are present.

The species usually arrives in May; however, the earliest spring occurrence was April 4 (1971). They remain well into

June, with the latest record on June 19 (1964). Peak of abundance is between May 15 and 30. The earliest autumn occurrence was September 15 (1971) and their peak of passage is between October 15 and 30. The majority leave the refuge in November, but a few frequently remain through much of the winter. They have been recorded during twelve Christmas counts, with the greatest numbers recorded in 1972 (56), 1973 (65), and 1988 (51). Food supplies generally become depleted by late February, and birds which have lingered through most of the winter leave the refuge.

FAMILY: PASSERIDAE

House Sparrow
Passer domesticus

Local permanent resident. When and how the House Sparrow arrived in the Malheur-Harney Lakes Basin has never been documented. It was not reported by Willett (1919) in 1918; however, Jewett (1936) reported it as well established at P Ranch by 1934. In addition, 52 were at headquarters on December 19, 1939. Sometime within this 16-year period House Sparrows had arrived, and by 1939 were widely distributed around human settlements. How they arrived remains a question. Establishment in other western states centered around railroads. House Sparrows are well known for their ability to become locked into boxcars, and their arrival in this region corresponds rather closely with the arrival of the railroad. By 1916, the railroad had been completed into Crane and by 1924 was extended into Burns. Considering the species was well established on the refuge in 1934 (shortly after the arrival of the railroad), it is highly likely House Sparrows arrived into southeastern Oregon by the same method as they did in other regions of the west.

Presently the House Sparrow is found on the refuge only in localized areas. It regularly occurs at headquarters, Frenchglen, and Malheur Field Station, but in recent years has disappeared from P Ranch and Buena Vista. Nest construction is in progress by March, with egg laying in April. Generally, more than one brood is produced annually. In winter, the species regularly concentrates around homesteads where food is available, particularly in the vicinity of feed-lots. Therefore, House Sparrows reach their greatest abundance off the refuge but 106 were present at Malheur Field Station on December 17, 1983.

Literature Cited

American Ornithologists' Union. 1886. Checklist of North American Birds. First ed. New York, Amer. Ornithol. Union.

American Ornithologists' Union. 1983. Checklist of North American Birds. Sixth ed. Lawrence, Kansas, Amer. Ornithol. Union.

Bellrose, F.C. 1976. Ducks, geese, and swans of North America. Stackpole Press, Harrisburg, Pa.

Bendire, C.E. 1877. Notes on some of the birds found in southeastern Oregon, particularly in the vicinity of Camp Harney, from November 1874 to January 1877. Proc. Boston Soc. Nat. Hist. 19:109–149.

Bendire, C.E. 1892. Life histories of North American birds. U.S. Nat. Mus. Spec. Bull. 1, Washington D.C.

Bendire, C.E. 1895. Life histories of North American birds. U.S. Nat. Mus. Spec. Bull. 3, Washington D.C.

Brewer, T.M. 1875. Notes on seventy-nine species of the birds observed in the neighborhood of Camp Harney, Oregon, compiled from the correspondence of Capt. Charles Bendire, 1st Cavalry USA. Bost. Soc. Nat. Hist. Proc. 18:153–168.

Coues, E. 1874. Birds of the Northwest. U.S. Geol. Surv. Misc. Publ. 3, Washington, D.C.

Delevoryas, P.R. 1980. Scarlet and Summer Tanager captures, Hart Mountain. Oregon Birds 6:118–122.

Finley, W.L. 1912. Report of field agents. Report of William L. Finley, field agent for the Pacific Coast States. Bird-lore 14:415–418.

Foster, C.L. 1985. Habitat definition of nesting birds in the Double-O Unit, Malheur National Wildlife Refuge. M.S. Thesis, Humboldt State Univ., Arcata, California.

Gabrielson, I., and S.G. Jewett. 1940. Birds of Oregon. Oregon State College, Corvallis.

Garrett, K., and J. Dunn. 1981. Birds of southern California. Los Angeles Aud. Soc. Los Angeles, California.

Hansen, C.G. 1956. An ecological survey of the vertebrate animals on Steens Mountain, Harney County, Oregon. Ph.D. thesis, Oregon State College, Corvallis, Oregon.

Houghton, S.G. 1976. A trace of desert waters: The Great Basin story. A.H. Clark Co., Glendale, Calif.

Jarvis, R.L. 1966. Occurrence of European or Aleutian Green-winged Teal in western North America with a recent record. Murrelet 47:15-18.

Jewett, S.G. 1936. Bird notes from Harney County, Oregon, during May 1934. Murrelet 17:41-47.

Jewett, S.G. 1941. MacFarlane Screech Owl in Harney County, Oregon. Condor 43:156.

Jewett, S.G. 1946. The Starling in Oregon. Condor 48:245.

Jewett, S.G. 1949. The Franklin's Gull in Oregon. Condor 51:189-190.

Kridler, E. 1965. Records, obtained while banding, of birds unusual in southeastern Oregon. Auk 82:496-497.

Kridler, E., and D.B. Marshall. 1962. Additional bird records from southeastern Oregon. Condor 64:162-164.

Littlefield, C.D. 1980. New bird records from Malheur National Wildlife Refuge, Oregon. Western Birds 11:181-185.

Littlefield, C.D. 1981. First Oregon record of the Gray-headed Junco. Western Birds 12:53.

Littlefield, C.D. 1983. Oregon's first records of the Great-tailed Grackle. Western Birds 4:201-202.

Littlefield, C.D., and E.L. McLaury. 1971. Black-throated Blue Warbler records for Oregon. California Birds 2:93.

Littlefield, C.D., and E.L. McLaury. 1973. Unusual bird records from southeastern Oregon. Auk 90:680-682.

Littlefield, C.D., and E.L. McLaury. 1975. Ovenbird records for Oregon. Western Birds 6:114.

Littlefield, C.D., and S.P. Thompson. 1981. History and status of the Franklin's Gull on Malheur National Wildlife Refuge, Oregon. Great Basin Nat. 41:440-444.

Littlefield, C.D., J.E. Cornely, and S.P. Thompson. 1985. Recent bird records from Malheur National Wildlife Refuge, Oregon. Murrelet 66:25-28.

Littlefield, C.D., S.P. Thompson, and B.D. Ehlers. 1984. History and present status of Swainson Hawks in Southeast Oregon. Raptor Research 18:1–5.

Marshall, D.B. 1959. New bird records for southeastern Oregon. Condor 61:53–56.

Marshall, D.B. 1969. Endangered plants and animals of Oregon. III. Birds. Spec. Rept. 278. Agric. Exp. Sta., Oregon State Univ., Corvallis, Oregon.

Marshall, D.B., and H.F. Duebbert. 1965. Nesting of the Ring-necked Duck in Oregon in 1963 and 1964. Murrelet 46:43.

Nuechterlein, G.L. 1981. Courtship behavior and reproduction isolation between Western Grebe color morphs. Auk 98:335–349.

Phillips, A., J. Marshall, and G. Monson. 1964. The birds of Arizona. The Univ. of Arizona Press, Tucson, Arizona.

Prill, A.G. 1922. Birds of Harney Valley and Malheur Lake Region, Oregon. Oologist 39:129–131.

Rice, W.R. 1982. Acoustical location of prey by the Marsh Hawk: adaptation to concealed prey. Auk 99:403–413.

Roberson, D. 1980. Rare birds on the West Coast. Woodcock Publ., Pacific Grove, California.

Scharff, J.C. 1944. The Louisiana Heron in Oregon. Condor 46:124.

Sooter, C.A. 1942. Surf Scoter in eastern Oregon. Murrelet 23:16.

Sooter, C.A. 1943. Catbirds nesting on the Malheur Refuge in southeastern Oregon. Condor 45:234.

Summers, S.D. 1977. A Common Grackle record for Oregon. Western Birds 8:156.

Terres, J.K. 1980. The Audubon Society encyclopedia of North American birds. Alfred A. Knopf, New York.

Thompson, S.P., and D.G. Paullin. 1985. First nesting record of the Cattle Egret in Oregon. Murrelet 66:28–29.

Thompson, S.P., C.D. Littlefield, and R.A. Ryder. 1980. Historical review and status of colonial nesting birds on Malheur National Wildlife Refuge, Oregon. Proc. Colonial Water Bird Group 3:156–164.

Thompson, S.P., R.S. Johnstone, and C.D. Littlefield. 1984. Nesting history of Golden Eagles in Malheur-Harney Lakes Basin, southeastern Oregon. Raptor Research 16:116–122.

Willett, G. 1919. Bird notes from southeastern Oregon and northeastern California. Condor 21:194–208.

Zeillemaker, C.F. 1971. Chestnut-sided Warbler in Oregon. Murrelet 52:27.

Appendix

List of Common Names and Scientific Names of Plants, Mammals, Fish, and Reptiles

Plants

alder, thin-leafed	*Alnus incana*
arrowgrass	*Triglochin maritima*
aspen quaking	*Populus tremuloides*
balsam-root, yellow	*Balsamorhiza sagittata*
barley	
foxtail	*Hordeum jubatum*
meadow	*H. brachyantherum*
bladderwort	*Utricularia vulgaris*
bluegrass	
Kentucky	*Poa pratensis*
Sandberg's	*P. sandbergii*
box-elder	*Acer negundo*
budsage	*Artemisia spinescens*
bulrush	
alkali	*Scirpus maritimus*
hardstem	*S. acutus*
burreed, broad-fruited	*Sparganium eurycarpum*
cattail	
common	*Typha latifolia*
narrow-leafed	*T. angustifolia*
cheatgrass	*Bromus tectorum*
cinquefoil, slender	*Potentilla gracilis*
composites	*Compositae*
cottonwood	*Populus* sp.
black	*P. trichocarpa*

currants	
golden	*Ribes aureum*
squaw-	*R. cereum*
dock, curly	*Rumex crispus*
dogwood, red-osier	*Cornus stolonifera*
Douglas-fir	*Pseudotsuga menziesii*
elderberry, blue	*Sambucus cerulea*
fescue, Idaho	*Festuca idahoensis*
fir, white	*Abies concolor*
foxtail, little meadow	*Alopecurus aequalis*
goldenrod	*Solidago* sp.
grass, blue-eyed	*Sisyrinchium angustifolium*
greasewood	*Sarcobatus vermiculatus*
hemlock, water	*Cicuta douglasi*
hopsage, spiny	*Atriplex spinosa*
horsebrush	*Tetradymia* spp.
Indian paintbrush	*Castilleja* spp.
junegrass, prairie	*Koeleria cristata*
juniper, western	*Juniperus occidentalis*
larch, western	*Larix occidentalis*
larkspur	*Delphinium* spp.
mallow, globe	*Sphaeralcea* spp.
mares-tail	*Hippuris* sp.
milfoil, water	*Myriophyllum exalbescens*
monkey flower	
dwarf	*Mimulus nanus*
yellow	*M. guttatus*
mountain-mahogany	*Cercocarpus ledifolius*
muskgrass	*Chara* spp.
mustard	*Crucifera*
needlegrass, Thurber's	*Stipa thurberiana*
olive, Russian	*Eleagnus angustifolia*
parsnip, cow	*Heracleum lanatum*
pea, golden	*Thermopsis montana*
penstemons	*Penstemon* spp.
phacelia, narrow-leafed	*Phacelia linearis*
pine	
lodgepole	*Pinus contorta*
ponderosa	*P. ponderosa*

pondweed
  horned — *Zannichellia palustris*
  Richardson's — *Potamogeton richardsonii*
  sago — *P. pectinatus*
primrose, tansy-leaf evening — *Oenothera tanacetifolia*
rabbitbrush, green — *Chrysothamnus viscidiflorus*
redtop — *Agrostis alba*
reed, common — *Phragmites communis*
ricegrass, Indian — *Oryzopsis hymenoides*
rose, Wood's — *Rosa woodsii*
rush, Baltic — *Juncus balticus*
sagebrush
  big — *Artemisia tridentata*
  black — *A. arbuscula*
  silver — *A. cana*
saltbush — *Atriplex confertifolia*
saltgrass, desert — *Distichlis stricta*
sedge
  awned — *Carex atherodes*
  beaked — *C. rostrata*
  Nebraska — *C. nebraskensis*
  slender-beaked — *C. athrostachya*
senecio
  serrated — *Senecio serra*
  great swamp — *S. hydrophilus*
sidalcea, Oregon — *Sidalcea oregana*
silver weed — *Potentilla anserina*
sloughgrass — *Beckmannia syzigachne*
smartweeds — *Polygonum* spp.
speedwell, American — *Veronica americana*
spikerush — *Eleocharis* spp.
spruce, blue — *Picea pungens*
squirreltail — *Sitanion hystrix*
thistle
  Canada — *Cirsium arvense*
  Russian — *Salsola kali*
timothy — *Phleum pratense*
wada (seablite) — *Suaeda* spp.
wapato (broad-leafed arrowhead) — *Sagittaria latifolia*

water-buttercup
   white   *Ranunculus aquatilis*
   yellow   *R. flabellaris*
watercress   *Rorippa nasturtium-aquaticum*
wheatgrass
   bluebunch   *Agropyron spicatum*
   crested   *A. cristatum*
wildrye
   creeping   *Elymus triticoides*
   Great Basin   *E. cinereus*
willow   *Salix* spp.
yellowbell   *Fritillaria pudica*

Mammals, Fish, and Reptiles

badger   *Taxidea taxus*
carp   *Cyprinus carpio*
coyote   *Canis latrans*
garter snakes   *Thamnophis* spp.
gopher snake   *Pituophis melanoleucus*
meadow vole   *Microtus montanus*
mink   *Mustela vison*
muskrat   *Ondatra zibethica*

Index

Avocet, American, 132

Bittern
 American, 52
 Least, 53
Blackbird
 Brewer's, 267
 Red-winged, 265
 Yellow-headed, 266
Bluebird
 Mountain, 206
 Western, 205
Bobolink, 263
Bufflehead, 86
Bunting
 Indigo, 245
 Lazuli, 245
 Painted, 246
 Snow, 263
Bushtit, 190

Canvasback, 78
Catbird, Gray, 199
Chat, Yellow-breasted, 240
Chickadee
 Black-capped, 189
 Mountain, 189
Chukar, 105
Coot, American, 112

Cormorant, Double-crested, 50
Cowbird, Brown-headed, 270
Crane
 Greater Sandhill, 108
 Lesser Sandhill, 109
Creeper, Brown, 193
Crossbill, Red, 274
Crow, American, 187
Cuckoo, Yellow-billed, 146
Curlew, Long-billed, 122

Dipper, American, 194
Dove
 Mourning, 145
 Rock, 144
Dowitcher, Long-billed, 128
Duck
 American Black, 71
 Wood, 69
 Ring-necked, 81
 Ruddy, 89
Dunlin, 127

Eagle
 Bald, 92
 Golden, 100
Egret
 Cattle, 57
 Great, 55
 Snowy, 56

289

Falcon
    Peregrine, 103
    Prairie, 103
Finch
    Cassin's, 272
    House, 273
    Purple, 272
    Rosy, 271
Flicker, Northern, 167
Flycatcher
    Ash-throated, 176
    Dusky, 170
    Gray, 171
    Hammond's, 170
    Olive-sided, 168
    Scissor-tailed, 175
    Western, 172
    Willow, 169

Gadwall, 76
Gnatcatcher, Blue-gray, 204
Godwit, Marbled, 123
Goldeneye
    Barrow's, 85
    Common, 84
Golden-plover, Lesser, 117
Goldfinch
    American, 276
    Lesser, 276
Goose
    Cackling, 68
    Emperor, 66
    Greater White-fronted, 63
    Lesser Canada, 68
    Pacific White-fronted, 64
    Ross', 65
    Snow, 64
    Tule, 64
    Western Canada, 67
Goshawk, Northern, 96

Grackle
    Common, 269
    Great-tailed, 268
Grebe
    Clark's, 48
    Eared, 45
    Horned, 45
    Pied-billed, 44
    Red-necked, 47
    Western, 47
Grosbeak
    Black-headed, 244
    Evening, 277
    Pine, 271
    Rose-breasted, 243
Grouse
    Ruffed, 106
    Sage, 106
Gull
    Bonaparte's, 139
    California, 136
    Franklin's, 138
    Glaucus-winged, 138
    Herring, 135
    Ring-billed, 137
    Sabine's, 140

Harrier, Northern, 93
Hawk
    Broad-winged, 97
    Cooper's, 95
    Ferruginous, 99
    Red-shouldered, 97
    Red-tailed, 98
    Rough-legged, 100
    Sharp-shinned, 95
    Swainson's, 97
Heron
    Black-crowned Night-, 58
    Great Blue, 53
    Green-backed, 58
    Tricolored, 57

Hummingbird
  Black-chinned, 159
  Broad-tailed, 160
  Calliope, 159
  Rufous, 160

Ibis, White-faced, 60

Jaeger
  Long-tailed, 135
  Parasitic, 134
Jay
  Blue, 184
  Gray, 184
  Pinyon, 185
  Steller's, 184
Junco
  Dark-eyed, 261
  "Gray-headed," 262
  "Slate-colored," 262

Kestrel, American, 101
Killdeer, 116
Kingbird
  Eastern, 174
  Western, 173
Kingfisher, Belted, 161
Kinglet
  Golden-crowned, 202
  Ruby-crowned, 203
Kite, Black-shouldered, 91

Lark, Horned, 176
Longspur, Lapland, 262
Loon
  Common, 43
  Pacific, 43

Magpie, Black-billed, 186
Mallard, 71
Martin, Purple, 177

Meadowlark, Western, 264
Merganser
  Common, 87
  Hooded, 87
  Red-breasted, 88
Merlin, 102
Mockingbird, Northern, 200
Moorhen, Common, 112

Nighthawk, Common, 155
Night-heron, Black-crowned,
  58
Nutcracker, Clark's, 185
Nuthatch
  Pygmy, 192
  Red-breasted, 191
  White-breasted, 192

Oldsquaw, 83
Oriole, Northern, 269
Osprey, 91
Ovenbird, 234
Owl
  Burrowing, 151
  Common Barn-, 146
  Flammulated, 148
  Great Horned, 148
  Long-eared, 152
  Northern Pygmy-, 150
  Northern Saw-whet, 154
  Short-eared, 153
  Snowy, 150
  Western Screech-, 147

Partridge, Gray, 104
Parula, Northern, 222
Pelican, American White, 49
Phainopepla, 214
Phalarope
  Red, 130

Red-necked, 131
  Wilson's, 131
Pheasant, Ring-necked, 105
Phoebe, Say's, 173
Pigeon, Band-tailed, 143
Pintail, Northern, 72
Pipit, Water, 211
Plover
  Black-bellied, 117
  Lesser Golden-, 117
  Semipalmated, 114
  Snowy, 115
Poorwill, Common, 156

Quail
  California, 107
  Mountain, 108

Rail
  Black, 110
  Virginia, 110
Raven, Common, 188
Redhead, 80
Red Knot, 128
Redpoll, Common, 274
Redstart, American, 233
Robin, American, 210

Sanderling, 124
Sandpiper
  Baird's, 126
  Least, 125
  Pectoral, 126
  Solitary, 119
  Spotted, 121
  Upland, 121
  Western, 124
Sapsucker
  Red-breasted, 164
  Red-naped, 163
  Williamson's, 164

Scaup
  Greater, 82
  Lesser, 82
Scoter
  Surf, 83
  White-winged, 83
Shoveler, Northern, 75
Shrike
  Loggerhead, 215
  Northern, 214
Siskin, Pine, 275
Snipe, Common, 129
Solitaire, Townsend's, 207
Sora, 111
Sparrow
  American Tree, 248
  Black-throated, 252
  Brewer's, 250
  Chipping, 249
  Fox, 256
  Golden-crowned, 260
  Harris', 260
  House, 278
  Lark, 251
  Lincoln's, 258
  Sage, 254
  Savannah, 255
  Song, 256
  Vesper, 251
  White-crowned, 259
  White-throated, 258
Starling, European, 216
Stilt, Black-necked, 134
Swallow
  Bank, 180
  Barn, 182
  Cliff, 183
  Northern Rough-winged, 180
  Tree, 178
  Violet-green, 179

Swan
  Trumpeter, 62
  Tundra, 61
Swift
  Black, 157
  Vaux's, 157
  White-throated, 158

Tanager
  Scarlet, 242
  Summer, 241
  Western, 242
Teal
  Blue-winged, 73
  Cinnamon, 74
  Eurasian Green-winged, 70
  Green-winged, 70
Tern
  Black, 142
  Caspian, 141
  Common, 140
  Forster's, 141
Thrasher
  Brown, 201
  Sage, 201
Thrush
  Hermit, 209
  Swainson's, 208
  Varied, 209
Towhee
  Green-tailed, 246
  Rufous-sided, 247
Turnstone, Ruddy, 130

Veery, 207
Vireo
  Hutton's, 218
  Red-eyed, 219
  Rocky Mountain Solitary,
    217
  Solitary, 217

Warbling, 219
West Coast Solitary, 217
Vulture, Turkey, 90

Warbler
  Bay-breasted, 231
  Black and White, 232
  Blackburnian, 230
  Blackpoll, 232
  Black-throated Blue, 226
  Black-throated Gray, 228
  Black-throated Green, 230
  Canada, 240
  Cape May, 225
  Chestnut-sided, 225
  Golden-winged, 220
  Hermit, 229
  Hooded, 238
  MacGillivray's, 235
  Magnolia, 226
  Nashville, 222
  Orange-crowned, 221
  Palm, 231
  Prothonotary, 233
  Tennessee, 220
  Townsend's, 229
  Wilson's, 239
  Yellow, 223
  Yellow-rumped, 227
  Yellow-throated, 231
Waterthrush, Northern, 235
Waxwing
  Bohemian, 212
  Cedar, 213
Whimbrel, 123
Wigeon
  American, 77
  Eurasian, 77
Willet, 120
Woodpecker
  Downy, 165

Hairy, 165
Lewis', 162
Red-headed, 163   *Blue Mtns.*
White-headed, 166
Wood-Pewee, Western, 168
Wren
    Bewick's, 196
    Canyon, 195
    House, 197

✶Marsh, 198
Rock, 194
Winter, 197

Yellowlegs
    Greater, 118
    Lesser, 119
✗ Yellowthroat, Common, 237